Social Desirability and Environmental Valuation

Hohenheimer Volkswirtschaftliche Schriften

Band 66

PETER LANG
Frankfurt am Main · Berlin · Bern · Bruxelles · New York · Oxford · Wien

Tobias Börger

Social Desirability and Environmental Valuation

PETER LANG
Frankfurt am Main · Berlin · Bern · Bruxelles · New York · Oxford · Wien

Bibliographic Information published by the Deutsche Nationalbibliothek
The Deutsche Nationalbibliothek lists this publication in the Deutsche Nationalbibliografie; detailed bibliographic data is available in the internet at http://dnb.d-nb.de.

Zugl.: Hohenheim, Univ., Diss., 2011

D 100
ISSN 0721-3085
ISBN 978-3-631-63258-1

www.peterlang.de

Acknowledgments

During the process of designing and implementing the research plan of the present study and subsequently writing this dissertation, many people supported my efforts by providing advice, support, and encouragement. First and foremost I would like to thank my first supervisor Prof. Dr. Michael Ahlheim. Both as leader of the research project I worked in in China and as academic supervisor he supported and always challenged my work to a great extent. I am especially grateful for the numerous intensive discussions on the topic and the research design, be it in China or Germany. I would also like to thank Prof. Dr. Alfonso Sousa-Poza who acted as second supervisor.

This work also profited a lot from discussions and intellectual exchange with my colleagues. It was Prof. Dr. Oliver Frör who, especially in the early stages of my work, guided my introduction into this field of research and shared his research experience with me. Furthermore, Antonia Heinke and Nopasom Sinphurmsukskul were always ready to discuss new ideas and approaches. Petra Gelléri provided helpful comments on the psychological question inventories employed in this study. I am grateful as well to all assistants and interviewers in Jinghong, the town in Southwest China where the empirical part of this study was conducted. Of indispensable help was Mr. Zheng Lianding, who acted as assistant throughout the duration of the project, did translation work, facilitated contact to local authorities, managed the group of interviewers and was always ready to give advice.

Finally, I am grateful for the support of my parents, which made it possible to move back and forth between Germany and China in such a flexible way.

Stuttgart, January 2012

Table of contents

I. List of figures

II. List of tables

III. Abbreviations

ABCM	Attribute-based choice modeling
CBA	Cost-benefit analysis
CE	Choice experiments
CEG	Citizen expert group
Coeff.	Coefficient
CVM	Contingent valuation method
DC	Dichotomous choice (elicitation format)
BIDR	Balanced Inventory of Desirable Responding
BMBF	German Federal Ministry of Education and Research
EDR	Environmentally desirable responding
EDRS	Environmentally desirable response scale
GBP	Great Britain Pound
GDP	Gross domestic product
GIS	Geographical information system
IM	Impression management
LILAC	Sino-German research cooperation "Living Landscapes – China"
LUCC	Land-use cover change model
MEP	Ministry of Environmental Protection (of the PRC)
MMPI	Minnesota Multiphasic Personality Inventory
MOST	Ministry of Science and Technology (of the PRC)
NEP	New environmental paradigm
NGO	Non-governmental organization
NOAA	(United States) National Oceanic and Atmospheric Association
NRWNNR	Naban River Watershed National Nature Reserve
OE	Open-ended (elicitation format)
OLS	Ordinary least squares
PC	Payment card (elicitation format)
PRC	People's Republic of China
PVM	Participatory valuation method
RMB	Renminbi (Chinese currency)
RUM	Random utility model
SD	Social desirability

SDR	Socially desirable responding
Std. error	Standard error
SED	Self-deception
SEU	Subjective expected utility
TEV	Total economic value
WTA	Willingness to accept
WTP	Willingness to pay

Chapter 1

Introduction

1.1. Motivation and objective of the study

The economic valuation of environmental goods is an important tool of rational public policy in the environmental sector. Over the last decades, this topic has been fervently debated because on the one hand output of such valuation exercises is needed by policy makers, but on the other hand a variety of methodological shortcomings have not yet been remedied. Political decision makers are in need of estimates of the value of environmental goods in order to contrast them to the overall costs of policy measures resulting in the provision of such goods. For example, the prevention of water pollution by closing down factories emitting chemical waste into lakes or rivers or fencing off a forest area against timber production in order to preserve habitat for certain plant and animal species are directly associated with economic costs. Affected companies have to reduce or even completely shut down production, and workers might have to be laid off and compensated, usually from the public budget. In addition to that, government uses public funds to initiate and administer projects of this kind which induce an improvement of environmental quality. So, from a more general point of view, public projects which lead to the provision or preservation of environmental resources are costly. Firstly, such projects are often associated with forgone economic gains due to reduced or more costly production as a result of more stringent environmental standards and regulations. Secondly, direct costs arise for the public budget because such projects have to be administered and compliance to new regulations has to be monitored and enforced when necessary. At the same time, such projects create benefits accruing to society. As the foundation for all human life, the state of the natural environment is one of the major factors affecting the well-being of individuals and societies. The natural environment is the basis for the production of food and other agricultural goods, for fishing and the extraction of inorganic natural resources. At the same time, people directly enjoy breathing clean air or swimming in a natural lake. Others go hiking to enjoy the view of a mountainous landscape, yet others feel happy about the mere knowledge of the existence of certain plant and animal species or ecosystems although they never in their lifetime visit these areas. These examples illustrate that the natural environment benefits society through a variety of different channels. All the above aspects of natural resources are labeled environmental goods, and this study is concerned with the valuation of such goods.

Public projects in the environmental sector aim at the preservation or further creation of such environmental goods. Yet, in order to assure the most efficient use of public funds, government should only implement those public projects the benefits of which exceed the costs. Similarly, if government has the choice between several projects, it should initiate that project with the most favorable benefit to cost ratio first. This is the fundamental idea of cost-benefit analysis (CBA) of public projects, which should be done prior to their implementation. But while the quantification of the costs of such projects is relatively straightforward, the valuation of the benefits is unequally more burdensome. The major difficulty about valuing such benefits is that there is no market where environmental goods are bought and sold. Environmental goods generally fall into the category of nonmarket goods. This fact stems from the public good nature of environmental resources, i.e. that nobody can be excluded from their consumption and that this consumption is often also non-rival. For the case of ordinary private goods, the market price serves as an indicator of the value of that good, i.e. the utility that its consumption generates for a certain individual or household. The price that the household is willing to pay in order to purchase that good is equal to the monetary value of the minimum utility that it derives from it. If the price is higher than the utility of consuming that good, the household – assumed it is a rational decision-maker – will not purchase it because the utility gain from consuming the good will not completely compensate for the loss in utility resulting from spending money for the purchase. Consequently, from the fact that one can observe households actually purchasing certain goods at observable market prices, one can derive the change in utility that the consumption of this good leads to. However, for the case of environmental goods such markets do not exist and therefore no market transactions or market prices can be observed. As a consequence, other means of assessing the changes in utility that these goods induce have to be found; otherwise it would not be possible to conduct a CBA of a public project involving the provision of nonmarket goods, or environmental goods in particular. This is the point where the much debated economic valuation of environmental goods enters the stage.

Among a variety of methods for the valuation of nonmarket goods the contingent valuation method (CVM) is the most prominent and most frequently employed technique. The overall objective of the CVM is the assessment of the utility changes of households resulting from a public project that leads to the provision of an environmental good and the subsequent aggregation of these changes to calculate the social value of that good. It was mentioned above that for the case of ordinary market goods, the price that a household is willing to pay in order to purchase that good is equal to the monetary value of the minimum utility that it derives from its consumption. The CVM takes up this idea and constructs a hypothetical market situation where an environmental good can be bought in order to assess households' utility changes resulting from consuming that good. Therefore, the CVM is a survey-based technique, according to which a sample of households representative for the total population affected by a certain environmental project is confronted with that hypothetical market. In such survey interviews, which can be conducted in-person, by telephone, mail or on the internet, a hypothetical public project inducing a change in the level of provision of an environmental good is presented to the responding households. Subsequently these households are asked how much money they are willing to pay in order to have this project realized. If the change in the level of provision of the environmental good is positive, households are either asked their willingness to pay (WTP) to receive the benefits accruing from that provision, or their willingness to accept compensation (WTA) for forgoing the additional benefits resulting from that good. The idea behind the statement of WTP is that a household is willing to pay at most that amount of money for the environmental good that makes it exactly as well off as before the good was provided. Analogously, if an environmental good is not provided, the WTA is that amount of money that would generate exactly as much utility as the provision of that good would have. Defined this way, such statements of WTP or WTA can be interpreted as a household's Hicksian Compensating Variation (CV). They are measures of the utility changes that a certain household experiences from the consumption of an environmental good.

For the CVM to elicit meaningful statements of either WTP or WTA it is necessary that the hypothetical market situation in the interview resembles a real market situation as closely as possible. This is largely because unlike in an actual market transaction, in a CVM interview the respondents do not have to make real economic commitments, i.e. they do not have to actually make a payment. This is why the CVM is classified as a so-called stated preference approach. Individuals do not reveal their preferences for certain environmental goods by actual behavior but merely by a statement of how much they are willing to pay for the consumption of that good or willing to accept compensation in order to forgo the consumption of it. Stated preference techniques and the CVM in particular provide data which cannot be generated otherwise due to the nonmarket nature of environmental goods, but also face severe methodological problems. To begin with, people are usually not familiar with the task of stating a WTP for an environmental good. Normally, before buying a private good, consumers gather information, compare it to similar goods and actively evaluate the prospective change in utility that will result from consuming that good. This is not the case for public goods and especially environmental goods. These are normally centrally provided by government, so people do not have to make decisions whether or not and how much of such a good they want to consume. In a CVM interview, however, they are confronted with just this situation. They have to decide how much of their income they are willing to give up in order to consume the quantity of the environmental good specified in the hypothetical project description. In addition to that, in a CVM interview respondents cannot actively gather more information in case they need it. Instead the responding household merely takes a passive role and has to base its WTP statement on the information that the interviewer provides.

The discussion of these flaws leads to another – perhaps the most important – methodological problem of stated-preference methods, and CVM in particular: response bias. This procedural shortcoming stems from two underlying characteristics of this method. Firstly, no real market transactions are carried out, and secondly, the WTP has to be stated in some kind of social interaction. That means, unlike in a real market transaction, the focus of this action is not on the exchange of money for a consumption good but rather on the statement of an intention, which is – at least for the duration of the interview – without immediate material consequence. When respondents only have to state verbally what they would do under certain circumstances, the costs of deviating from a truthful response are very low. Even with untruthfully responding to a WTP question in a contingent valuation interview can a respondent expect to be provided with the level of the environmental good that is specified in the hypothetical scenario. Such a deviation from truthful reporting is especially likely when the respondent perceives the hypothetical nature of her response and thus concludes that her statement does not have any consequences for the outcome of the survey anyway. Although there is a branch of CVM research that deals with increasing the consequentiality of the WTP statement as perceived by a respondent, this condition is not necessarily fulfilled. In contrast to this, the deviation from acting according to one's true preferences in a real market situation would result in buying a good which the household does not really want in the first place. That means it would definitely be consequential. So, it becomes clear that stated preference methods such as the CVM allow for both deliberate and accidental misreporting of preferences as a result of the hypothetical nature of the question.

Reasons for such misreporting can be the pursuit of other objectives that arise from strategic motives or from situational factors of the interview procedure. An example for a strategic motive to misreport in a valuation survey is to state a WTP that is higher than one's true valuation in order to influence the result of the survey. If the respondent knows (or at least expects) that the implementation of the proposed environmental project is contingent on the sum of all WTP statements elicited in the survey to exceed a certain amount, such as the costs of the project, there is incentive to falsely state a higher WTP. Another type of misreporting is the deliberate statement of zero in order to express protest against the environmental project or the valuation method itself. Situational motives for deviating from stating one's true WTP are rooted in the social interaction of the interview process. It is evident that the immediacy of the social interaction varies with the mode of administration of the survey. The in-person interview certainly constitutes the most immediate form of social interaction between interviewer and respondent, but even in mail or internet-based surveys does the respondent feel that there is some addressee that is going to evaluate the WTP responses. When situational factors enter the set of motives for the statement of a certain WTP, its original factors, i.e. the true preferences of a household for an environmental good, might take a backseat. This is what is referred to as response bias: factors other than the actual question stimulus "How much are you willing to pay to get that specific good?" determine the final response. One conceivable situational factor is a respondent's desire to be in accordance with prevalent social norms when stating the WTP. This phenomenon is called socially desirable responding (SDR) and constitutes the focus of this study. According to the concept of SDR, certain respondents to a survey are rather concerned with seeking social approval from the interviewer or some other person that perceives her answers than with responding truthfully to the survey questions. Such respondents are very dependent on the expected evaluation of their answers by another person or institution. The motivation of such respondents is rather the urge to immediately satisfy their need for social approval by stating a WTP which they think is socially desirable than to report their true WTP.

The likelihood of the occurrence of SDR with regard to WTP questions in contingent valuation surveys is rather high for three reasons. Firstly, CVM surveys constitute what sociologists call surveys dealing with 'reported behavior'. In situations where a certain pattern of behavior of an individual can for some reason not be directly observed by the researcher, that individual can simply be asked how she would behave in that situation. Such a technique constitutes a time- and resource-saving shortcut to analyzing individual behavior. This exactly describes stated preference surveys such as the CVM, because a household's preferences for an environmental good cannot be inferred by its purchases of that good due to the lack of a respective market place. Instead, the household is asked to verbally state its preference for that good. Sociology finds responses to this type of survey to be very prone to be influenced by SDR. The response to the WTP question in a contingent valuation survey is also a self-report of intended behavior in a certain situation. Biasing the response to this question in order to appear in a better way in front of the interviewer is not associated with an actual change in behavior, so it is easily done and thus very likely to happen. Secondly, in times of increasing environmental concern, today's societies are characterized by more and more pronounced social norms regarding environmental protection. In many areas of life, social norms associated with the protection and conservation of environmental resources influence individual behavior. Consequently, environmentally friendly behavior and attitudes are regarded as good and thus as desirable by an ever increasing number of people. The WTP question in a CVM interview asks for a household's contribution to some public project leading to an improvement of environmental quality. Therefore, it is very likely that the respondent perceives strong social norms that call for an 'environmentally friendly' response. It can thus be expected, that a certain fraction of respondents rather state a WTP that they think is socially desirable than what equals their true valuation for the proposed environmental good. Altogether, the hypothetical nature of the WTP question in contingent valuation surveys of environmental goods and the existence of clear-cut social norms in this field make an occurrence of SDR very likely. Finally, the socio-cultural positioning of the survey reported on in this study immediately suggests investigating the influence of SDR. The empirical part of this study deals with a practical contingent valuation survey in a small town in Southwest China. It is expected that the cultural and political background of the People's Republic of China (PRC) may serve very well to investigate the SDR phenomenon. Reasons for this are the Eastern, Confucian culture and the socialist and authoritarian political system in the PRC. On the one hand, Chinese culture emphasizes the notion of face, i.e. some form of prestige that an individual must preserve in front of others. This stresses the importance of situational factors in a survey interview at the expense of the truthful reporting of preferences. On the other hand, the current political system of the PRC has not been offering its citizens much room for actively stating individual preferences regarding public projects. Therefore, it is very likely that many respondents rather feel urged to support public opinion towards such projects instead of truthfully revealing their own preferences. Since this is a form of socially desirable responding, the investigation of this phenomenon within the framework of a contingent valuation survey in China appears highly advisable.

So far, there are plenty of studies that hint at the fact that SDR affects the results of contingent valuation surveys. These studies mostly find that the perceptibility of WTP statements by individuals other than the respondent increases the amounts of such statements (e.g. Alpizar et al. 2008a, Leggett et al. 2003, List et al. 2004). Such studies compare mean WTP estimates elicited by different survey modes. A usual finding is that in-person surveys yield higher WTP estimates than mail surveys or situations where WTP responses can be written down and be slipped into a sealed ballot box. Obviously, the fact that the WTP response can be perceived by the interviewer might bias it upwards. So, apparently social pressure influences survey responses. In addition to that, another set of studies make out that characteristics of the appearance of the interviewer systematically influence the statements of WTP (e.g. Bateman and Mawby 2004, Loureiro and Lotade 2005). It can be shown that for instance the formality of the interviewer's dress or the relationship of the good to be valued and the obvious origin of the interviewer significantly increases WTP statements. This phenomenon goes by the name of interviewer effects and apparently constitutes a major situational factor that may lead to the misreporting of WTP statements. All of these studies presume that a specific characteristic of the interviewer is likely to activate a social norm in the respondent, so that the latter feels compelled to act in compliance with this norm. This in turn constitutes socially desirable responding. In many of the above studies, SDR is mentioned as a biasing factor of WTP statements and the reported mode and interviewer effects, respectively, are interpreted as empirical evidence for this. However, these results are rather selective and a consistent analysis of the effect of SDR in contingent valuation surveys is still lacking. At most, these findings hint at the influence of SDR but do not constitute direct proof of its existence. Instead, they rather demonstrate that both the level of anonymity perceived by the respondent and the existence of social norms (conveyed through certain features of the appearance of the interviewer) have a significant impact on the statement of WTP for environmental goods. To be quite exact, these types of empirical work do not constitute sufficient evidence of the biasing influence of SDR in CVM surveys.

While most of these CVM studies presume that SDR is potentially biasing the WTP statements, surprisingly little direct research regarding this phenomenon can be found in the relevant literature. Although socio-psychological research has developed means to assess an individual's tendency to respond to survey questions in a socially desirable manner, merely one study attempts to directly measure this phenomenon and relate it to WTP statements (Laughland et al. 1994). Yet, this study has a rather one-dimensional perspective on the concept of SDR and fails to account for the variety of factors that might be at its root. This is where the present study wants to fill a gap in CVM research: the idea of SDR as a multi-component concept and the attempts to directly assess the tendency to respond in a socially desirable manner have to be combined in order to test the influence of this response bias on WTP statements. To this end, the present study pursues two main objectives. Firstly, a behavioral model will be developed that allows for the inclusion of different factors of socially desirable responding. As the above findings suggest, this phenomenon does not merely have one source but might rather be triggered by a set of factors. Based on the theory of rational choice, this study will present a behavioral model that can be used to predict the exact set of constraints within which the validity of CVM survey data is impaired. As a second objective, tools for the empirical assessment of these factors, i.e. of the different components of SDR as specified by the theoretical model, will be developed, tested and applied in a practical survey. This includes both the modification of existing question inventories and the creation of new questions. Before employing these questions in a contingent valuation survey, it has to be scrutinized whether they produce reliable and valid assessments of the theoretical components of SDR. It can be expected that respondents differ to the degree that they are influenced by what they perceive as socially desirable. Additionally, different respondents might also have different ideas of what is socially desirable. So, these assessment tools aim at the identification of those different types of respondents. By assessing a respondent's tendency to respond in a socially desirable way to the WTP question in a contingent valuation interview, the theoretical predictions regarding the composition of factors of SDR can be tested empirically. Therefore, the overall aim of this study is to scrutinize the importance of SDR as a biasing factor in contingent valuation surveys in a comprehensive way.

A note regarding the interdisciplinary nature of this research plan is appropriate at this point. Obviously, SDR is not merely a problem of survey-based environmental valuation and the CVM but of survey research in general. Consequently, research in this field has mostly been pushed on with by sociologists (mostly regarding survey methodology) and psychologists (concerning the definition of the behavioral concept of SDR). Therefore, the mere economic perspective on contingent valuation has to be broadened by integrating theoretical concepts and practical approaches from both sociological and psychological research. This is a secondary objective of this study. Integration in this respect does not mean that it is intended to write a socio-psychological study. Instead, theoretical concepts originating from outside the field of economics shall both be scrutinized from the point of view of economic theory and eventually be employed to explain response behavior in a CVM survey. Since all three disciplines mentioned above strive for an explanation of human behavior, it will be both possible and necessary to interrelate similar concepts at different points in the course of the study. In addition to that, methods originating in experimental research of psychology and behavioral economics will be applied. By employing an experimental approach, certain situational characteristics of the interview can deliberately be modified. In doing so, the effect of these modifications on response behavior and on WTP statements in particular can be isolated. This allows for a more flexible investigation of the impact of situational factors on WTP responses, which is expected to be closely linked to incentives for SDR. Altogether, it is believed that by applying this interdisciplinary approach the situational and interactional nature of the CVM interview can be better taken into account, and consequently more reliable and valid valuations of environmental goods can be produced by this method.

1.2. Outline of the study

Following this introductory chapter, chapter 2 presents the concept and methods of environmental valuation with a particular focus on the contingent valuation method. After introducing the basic mindset of and providing rationales for environmental valuation, the concept of total economic value is discussed and the welfare economic background of the valuation of environmental resources is reviewed. This is the basis upon which different valuation methods are introduced. One of these methods – the CVM – is characterized in more detail because it is the method of choice for the empirical analysis reported on in this study. Issues such as questionnaire design, administration modes and question formats as well as the scientific exposition of certain procedural biases are introduced. This includes a discussion of several current problems, criticism and developments of the method, which are important for the research program of this study. The chapter ends with a review of econometric approaches to estimate the social value of environmental amenities based on contingent valuation data.

Subsequently, chapter 3 provides a profound discussion of the concept of socially desirable responding both from the socio-psychological and sociological point of view. The first part of this chapter deals with the definition of the concept of SDR and adequate tools for its measurement. This issue is tackled from two perspectives. On the one hand, the psychological research in this field is introduced. In the last six decades psychologists working on SDR have mainly been focusing on the personality psychological definition of this concept and on the development of question inventories which are able to assess the degree to which an individual's survey responses are biased by it. The different components of the phenomenon identified by the researchers can be separated according to the questions of who is the addressee of socially desirable response behavior and how a socially desirable picture of the self is conveyed to the interviewer. Sociological research on the other hand has rather concentrated on the question of the dimensionality of the SDR concept. While psychological research focuses on determining the nature of the components, sociologists rather ask how these components are related and how strong their influence is on other variables assessed in a survey. A subsequent discussion of the role of social norms for SDR provides the rationale for an analysis of this response bias in the field of contingent valuation. It will be demonstrated that social norms define what kind of survey responses are socially desirable and which are not. It will become clear that especially regarding environmental protection in today's society strong behavioral norms are at work. Consequently, SDR can be expected to be a serious problem when applying the CVM. In the last part of this chapter, the idea of SDR as a multi-component concept is taken up again. Based on the theory of rational choice a behavioral response model will be developed which is able to integrate different factors into one concept referred to as incentives for socially desirable responding. Both the selection of factors and the specific form of their relationship is determined by means of that model. The analysis of the influence of the variable "incentives for SDR" resulting from this rational choice model on responses in contingent valuation surveys will form the central issue of the subsequent two chapters.

In chapter 4, the behavioral model of SDR developed in the precedent chapter is integrated into the CVM context. Therefore, as a first step, the relevance of SDR for contingent valuation surveys is discussed and existing empirical research on this issue is reviewed. The two main reasons why CVM research should investigate the influence of SDR are the facts that such surveys deal with so-called reported behavior and that their topics, i.e. environmental conservation and protection, are associated with increasingly strong social norms. As it turns out, the existing research on social desirability in the field of CVM is merely confined to the detection of mode effects, i.e. the finding that such forms of survey administration featuring the use of interviewers yield higher mean WTP estimates than self-administered surveys. This difference is usually attributed to SDR. However, as is argued in that section, such indirect results do not constitute sufficient evidence for the existence of SDR in contingent valuation surveys and that instead direct tests for this bias should be applied. This idea serves as justification for applying direct methods to assess incentives for SDR developed by psychologists and sociologists and test the influence of these incentives on WTP statements. If SDR is a factor affecting the behavior of individuals it is quite likely that it also affects the statement of WTP in a contingent valuation survey, i.e. that the SDR variable has a direct impact on stated WTP. In this case the incentives for SDR as specified by the behavioral model in chapter 3 can be identified as significant determinants both of the amount of stated WTP as well as of the decision whether to state a positive WTP amount at all. These are the main research hypotheses to be derived from the theoretical discussion of that SDR-WTP relationship.

The empirical analysis of those theoretical models and the test of the research hypotheses are reported in chapter 5. The framework for that analysis is a practical contingent valuation survey conducted by a subproject of a Sino-German research cooperation in Southwest China. Therefore, the chapter starts with a description of the research area, its main environmental problem and the objectives of the research cooperation in general. Massive expansion of the cultivation of rubber trees in that region have led to tremendous changes in land-use patterns and associated environmental problems such as deforestation, loss of biodiversity, and soil erosion. Within this cooperation, the subproject ECON A conducts a contingent valuation survey to quantify the social value of an alternative future land-use scenario featuring partial roll-back of rubber cultivation and subsequent reforestation.

The analysis of the influence of SDR on WTP statements in the framework of that survey consists of two main parts. Firstly, appropriate question inventories have to be found that reliably measure the components of SDR identified in the theoretical part of this study. To this end, the applicability of existing question inventories is scrutinized and modifications are undertaken where necessary. This process is accompanied by extensive documentation of the reliability and validity of the modified questions. Secondly, the hypotheses derived in chapter 4 are tested empirically. Different types of regression models are employed that relate the variables generated from the question inventories assessing the SDR components with WTP statements. After displaying the results in detail, this chapter ends with a discussion referring back to the hypotheses of the precedent chapter. Chapter 6 provides some concluding remarks and an outlook of future research in this field.

Chapter 2

The economic valuation of environmental goods

2.1. Measuring environmental values

The natural environment is the basis for all human life on earth because it provides the foundations for its existence, such as air to breath, food, temperate climate which constitutes the atmosphere, and many more direct and indirect benefits. Through a variety of different channels the natural environment favors human life. So, in terms of economic theory, the natural environment clearly generates utility for individuals both directly by providing accurate space for their existence, and indirectly by allowing for the production of consumption and investment goods, such as food and inorganic natural resources. Those indirect and direct benefits of the natural environment can be referred to as environmental goods. The decisive difference between such goods and ordinary market goods such as furniture, food, or labor is the public good nature of environmental goods. When environmental goods are produced, i.e. when they exist in the form of an intact ecosystem, clean air, or a beautiful landscape, typically nobody can be prevented from enjoying the benefits provided by these goods. According to Samuelson (1954), this so-called non-excludability is one defining characteristic of a public good. The other characteristic of a public good, non-rivalry in consumption, is also given for many environmental goods. Benefits of a reforestation program or a program to reduce air-pollution for example can be enjoyed by everybody without diminishing the benefits for any other member of society (Samuelson 1954). Even though a pure public good that completely exhibits the two above characteristics is a merely theoretical concept, most environmental goods have clear public goods characteristics. Therefore, property rights for such goods cannot be clearly defined and as a result, markets where such goods are bought and sold do not exist. Consequently, environmental goods can be classified as nonmarket goods, so there are no market prices that would be the result of a market equilibrium, either. When the value of these obvious benefits, which environmental goods provide people and society with, cannot be quantified by means of market prices, other techniques have to be devised. Yet, before discussing ways to value environmental goods, some reasons for their valuation, i.e. uses of the valuation estimates, are introduced.

Traditionally, the valuation of environmental goods serves the three following purposes – as quantitative input for cost-benefit analyses (CBA) of public projects, for the calculation of so-called green GDP and for environmental damage assessment (cf. Ahlheim 2003, Stephan and Ahlheim 1996). The first field of application of environmental valuation is cost-benefit analysis. Public projects in the environmental sector such as the protection or restoration of natural resources in particular, can be interpreted as a public good because the benefits accruing from such projects can be enjoyed by the whole society. In order to provide these public environmental goods, government has to allocate funds to the implementation of the above mentioned environmental projects. Of course, those projects with the highest benefit to cost ratios should be financed and implemented first. Analogously, projects the costs of which exceed their benefits should not be carried out at all. By comparing overall costs to overall benefits of a public project CBA is a means to assure the efficient allocation of public funds into government projects. While the costs of such a project can be calculated in a very straightforward manner, the assessment of their benefits especially in the environmental sector is incomparably more burdensome. The reason for this is the public good nature of environmental goods and the fact that no market prices exist that could be used as value indicators. The costs of for example a reforestation program include categories such as planting new trees and income losses of farmers resulting from forgone agricultural or industrial use of the reforested land. The benefits on the other hand would comprise aspects as different as positive effects on microclimate, the conservation of plant and animal species and the preservation of landscape beauty and recreation possibilities for visitors of the reforested area. Since such benefits are public goods which are not traded in markets and thus do not have market prices, other techniques for their valuation have to be found. This is where environmental valuation enters the stage and provides valuations of environmental goods as input for cost-benefit analyses of public projects in the environmental sector.

The second use of environmental valuation data is for the calculation of green gross domestic product (GDP). Economic development in the form of production growth is usually associated with deterioration of environmental quality and exploitation of natural resources. Therefore, only reporting the strictly economic performance of a society as expressed in the classical form of GDP as an account of all goods and services produced in one economy in a certain period of time neglects the changes in the natural capital stock. Only if these changes are assessed and accounted for in the overall (green) GDP does this represent a complete description of the state and development of an economy. Therefore, valuations of the changes of the level of provision of environmental goods should be included in this calculation.

The third field of application is environmental damage assessment, which is relevant in the USA in particular. Environmental accidents such as oil spills or other accidental pollution including chemical or nuclear materials often do not only cause damage to private property alone but also to public goods such as the natural environment, certain ecosystems or habitat of animal species. Since this constitutes damage done to society as a whole, it is necessary to assess its extent in order to hold the parties responsible for such an accident accountable. Yet, again the problem is the public good nature of environmental goods and the fact that their value cannot simply be derived from market prices. Environmental valuation provides a quantification of the social value lost due to environmental accidents that harm natural resources, which can then be used – at least in the USA – as basis for litigation. After introducing what environmental valuation is needed for, the discussion can now turn its focus on the question of what types of value can actually be assessed.

2.1.1. Total economic value (TEV)

When valuing environmental goods the point of reference is always human society, i.e. the natural environment and all its features are evaluated from the point of view of human-beings. Therefore, the values of environmental goods are assessed based on the benefits that human-beings derive from these goods, be it in the direct manner of consuming those goods or in the rather indirect way of enjoying the mere existence of an environmental amenity. This mindset neglects the idea that natural resources may have intrinsic value, i.e. value which is independent of the valuation of human-beings and is derived from the mere existence of such resources. This alternative concept of value is often brought up by ecologists. However, since the anthropocentric worldview is deeply rooted in economic theory, it will form the basis for the following analysis.

The natural environment can benefit humans in several different ways, which are subsumed under the notion of total economic value (TEV) (Nunes 2002, Randall 1991). Thus, the question to be answered in this section is how and in which components do the functions of environmental goods enter the utility functions of humans. On the first level the TEV concept distinguishes between use and non-use values (cf. table 2.1). Use values are benefits for humans that accrue from the direct or indirect use of natural resources. Therefore, direct and indirect use values fall into this category. Direct use values refer to the active use of natural resources, such as recreation benefits from visiting a natural park or simply breathing clean air. Indirect use values describe functions of natural resources and ecosystems which are favoring human existence or allow for the production of consumption goods. Mostly these are different types of ecosystem services such as water storage capacities of wetlands or climate regulating and carbon absorbing functions of forests.

Table 2.1: Classification of values of an environmental good according to the concept of TEV; modified from Nunes (2002, p. 4).

Total economic value	Use values	Direct use value	e.g. recreation benefits of a forest
		Indirect use value	e.g. ecosystem functions
	Nonuse values	Bequest value	e.g. habitat protection for future generations
		Existence value	e.g. the existence of whales
		Option value	e.g. future medical use of a plant species
		Quasi-option value	e.g. the still unknown and unlikely use

Within the category of non-use values, which are sometimes also referred to as passive use values, different types of values can be distinguished, as well. The concept of bequest value describes the idea that certain amenities have a value because they can be bequeathed to future generations (Krutilla 1967). Although such amenities are not valued by people as a result of their use today, they gain value because of the opportunity of future generations to use them. Moreover, it is possible that certain natural resources or amenities have a value to people simply because they exist. These may be certain animal species or ecosystems which a person might never in her life visit, watch or enjoy, i.e. use in any way. Nonetheless that person would feel worse in case that species or ecosystem ceased to exist. This concept is known as existence value (Krutilla 1967). Since by far not all ecosystem functions and potential relationships between different forms of natural resources have been investigated let alone understood by science today, at present seemingly useless natural resources may have value in the future. This idea is captured by the concept of option value (Weisbrod 1964). Simply because there is a positive probability that certain resources might have value for humans in the future renders them valuable – and therefore worth protecting – today. Note that there is still a positive option value of a resource that can be but is actually never used at all. Sometimes the notion of option value is further distinguished from quasi-option value. This value category describes the idea that a certain environmental amenity might become useful in the future but that the probability of such a development to actually take place is unknown at the moment (Arrow and Fisher 1974). In other words, quasi-option value is a form of option value connected with a certain degree of uncertainty of future states. Consequently, this notion captures the value of future information made available through the preservation of a resource when the alternative would be an irreversible change, such as industrial development of a forest area.

Another difference between use and non-use values is that the latter have more pronounced public good characteristics. While market prices do not exist for public goods, use values accrue from direct consumption – or at least are more closely associated with the consumption of market goods – and therefore tend to have a more private good nature (Nunes 2002). As a consequence, the contribution of non-use values to the concept of TEV is often overlooked when costs and benefits of public projects in the environmental sector are assessed. Similarly, different categories of practical valuation methods focus on either only use values or total economic value. Therefore, the difference between use and non-use will play a role when different valuation techniques, which are able to measure all or merely a subset of these different forms of value, will be discussed. However, before introducing the most common methods of practical environmental valuation, the welfare theoretic background of all these techniques shall be presented.

2.1.2. Environmental values in neoclassical welfare theory

This section provides an overview of the welfare theoretic foundations of the valuation of environmental goods. The illustration is mainly based on Ahlheim (2003) and Stephan and Ahlheim (1996). In order to derive these foundations, it is necessary to take a closer look at the ways that changes in the provision of environmental goods affect social welfare in order to quantify such effects. Social welfare W is typically defined as a function of individual utility levels U_h of all members of society and can be written as

$$W = w(U_1, U_2, \dots, U_H)\,, \frac{\partial w}{\partial U_h} \geq 0 \;\; (h = 1,2,\dots,H) \qquad (2.1)$$

This implies that the first step of the calculation of a change in social welfare ΔW as a result of environmental projects is the assessment of the individual utility changes ΔU_h. This task, the quantification of the impact of a change in environmental quality on the individual utility level U_h, is referred to as identification problem. As a second step, the assessed individual utility changes have to be aggregated to on indicator of the effect on social welfare. This exercise is usually called aggregation problem. Hereafter, the identification problem will be dealt with first. Subsequently, some remarks regarding the aggregation problem are added.

Assume a society with $h = 1,2,\dots,H$ households with each of them consuming a bundle of N different market goods denoted by the vector $x_h = [x_{h1}, x_{h2}, \dots, x_{hN}]$. Additionally, each household disposes of exogenously endowed income I_h. On top of the consumption of the vector of market goods x_h, the households are assumed to be provided with a range of L public goods $z = [z_1, z_2, \dots, z_L]$, such as national defense, a public health care system, or governmental projects in the environmental sector. Note that the levels of the z_L, which can be different public goods or different characteristics of the same good, are not indexed with h, because the level of provision is the same for all households. This stems from the public nature of the environmental good, in particular the assumption of non-excludability. Since nobody can be prevented from consuming that good, all households have to consume the same amount – exactly what is provided.

In the framework of this illustration, the analysis is limited to one environmental good z. The level of provision of an environmental good (alternatively referred to as the *change* in the level of provision of that good) is determined by government policy. Therefore, two states can be defined: state 0 with the environmental good provided at level z^0 before and state 1 with the environmental good provided at level z^1 after a certain governmental project in the environmental sector is implemented. Analogously, the superscripts 0 and 1 with respect to market goods, prices, and household income denote the levels of these variables before and after the environmental project, respectively. Changes in the provision of the environmental goods typically influence social welfare through multiple channels. A change of z induced by some government policy measure affects the well-being of certain or all members of society directly. Programs to reduce air-pollution or the risk of a nuclear fall-out for example have a direct impact on individual well-being, i.e. individual utility. In addition to that, changes in environmental quality influence individual consumption behavior, which in turn lead to changes in prices $p = [p_1, p_2, \dots, p_N]$ for the N market goods consumed by a respective household h. Typically, such government projects have to be financed from tax revenues, so more governmental activity in the environmental sector is associated with higher tax rates, which in turn also affect household income I_h. These different channels of influence on individual well-being can be modeled by means of the direct utility function of a household. Assume that preferences of household h are described by the direct utility function $U_h = u_h(x_h, z)$. U_h is strictly increasing in both x_h and z, i.e. $\partial u_h / \partial x_h > 0$ and $\partial u_h / \partial z > 0$ because an increase in the consumption of these goods leads to a higher level of utility. That means all arguments are in fact considered as goods rather than bads. The change in individual utility induced by a change of the level of provision of the environmental good from z^0 to z^1 can be expressed by means of the direct utility function U_h of household h as

$$\Delta^{01} U_h = U_h^1 - U_h^0 = u_h(x_h^1, z^1) - u_h(x_h^0, z^0) \ , \ (h = 1,2, \ldots, H) \tag{2.2}$$

The argument x_h in the utility function represents the vector of all private consumption goods of household h. The indices 0 and 1 refer to the states before and after the provision of the environmental good (or the change of the level of provision, respectively). So, the difference in equation 2.2 refers to the change in utility between the state before and after the environmental project is implemented.

Maximizing the utility of household h with respect to its budget constraint $I_h = p \cdot x_h$ yields the indirect utility function v_h. The utility difference displayed in 2.2 can thus also be expressed in terms of the indirect utility function as

$$\begin{aligned} \Delta^{01} U_h &= u_h[x_h(p^1, z^1, I_h^1), z^1] - u_h[x_h(p^0, z^0, I_h^0), z^0] \\ &\equiv v_h(p^1, z^1, I_h^1) - v_h(p^0, z^0, I_h^0) \quad , \qquad (h = 1,2, \ldots, H) \end{aligned} \tag{2.3}$$

When it comes to the empirical assessment of this utility difference, both expressions turn out not to be useful because neither the direct nor the indirect utility function can be empirically observed. Therefore, although it is possible to calculate the utility measures derived below also from the indirect utility function (cf. Johansson 1993), a third form of expressing a preference ordering, the expenditure function e_h, is employed instead. Since it is strictly monotonic in the utility difference ΔU but denotes expenditure in monetary terms, it is referred to as 'money-metric utility function'. $e_h(p, z, U_h)$ indicates the expenditure that household h has to make in order to enjoy utility level U_h with given prices p and given level of the environmental good z. In order to express the utility change in terms of expenditure the levels of p and z have to be fixed at an arbitrary level. Plausibly, these levels can be the initial level 0 or the level after the environmental change in state 1. Consequently, two different ways of displaying the utility change are possible, namely the equivalent variation (EV)

$$EV_h^{01} = e_h(p^0, z^0, U_h^1) - e_h(p^0, z^0, U_h^0) = e_h(p^0, z^0, U_h^1) - I_h^0 \tag{2.4}$$

and the compensating variation (CV)

$$CV_h^{01} = e_h(p^1, z^1, U_h^1) - e_h(p^1, z^1, U_h^0) = I_h^1 - e_h(p^1, z^1, U_h^0) \tag{2.5}$$

These concepts hark back to John Hicks (cf. Hicks 1939, 1942) and are thus also referred to as Hicksian welfare measures. Since it is assumed that there is no private saving, the expenditure levels in the two states 0 and 1 are equivalent to the income levels in these states I_h^0 and I_h^1, which is expressed by the second equal signs in 2.4 and 2.5. Now it is necessary to take a closer look at the interpretation of the two Hicksian welfare measures. The basis for the equivalent variation is the initial levels of prices and of the environmental good p^0 and z^0. So, in case of a utility increasing change of the environmental good, this measure indicates the amount of money the household would have to be given to increase its utility to the same extent as the environmental good would have. This is equal to the minimum amount the household is willing to accept (WTA) to forego the improvement and therefore the utility change measured in monetary terms. Analogously, when the provision of the environmental good is reduced, the difference in 2.4 is negative because $U_h^1 < U_h^0$ and the EV represents the monetary amount that could be taken away from the household and still leave it just as well off as if the reduction really occurred. In other words, this amount measures the decrease in utility in monetary terms. It is the amount the household is willing to pay at most to prevent that reduction of the provision of the environmental good. In both cases, the situation of the environmental change is considered ex ante, i.e. with reference to the situation before it actually takes place. This makes clear the name of the EV as a measure *equivalent* to the utility change that actually does not happen. The compensating variation on the other hand takes an ex post perspective on the utility change by employing the levels of p and z in state 1 as reference. Looking at a utility improving environmental change, the difference in 2.5 is positive. In this case the CV represents the maximum amount of money that could be taken away from the household and still leave it just as well off as before the expansion of the provision of the environmental good. This amount is equal to the maximum WTP of this household to make the positive environmental change happen. If it pays more to secure the environmental change, it would end up on a lower utility level, which is why the CV indicates the maximum WTP for such a change. On the other hand, when a utility decreasing environmental change is considered, the CV is equal to the minimum amount of money that the household would have to be given to lift it back up onto the initial utility level. Applying the same logic, this amount indicates the household's minimal WTA compensation for the negative environmental change.

At this point it should be scrutinized whether the two Hicksian welfare measures just derived are reliable indicators of the direction of a specific utility change. What is referred to as indicator criterion of a welfare measure is its ability to unambiguously indicate a utility increase or decrease. This characteristic is given for both the CV and the EV because it holds that

$$CV_h^{01} \substack{<\\=\\>} 0 \;\Leftrightarrow\; U_h^1 \substack{<\\=\\>} U_h^0 \quad \text{and} \quad EV_h^{01} \substack{<\\=\\>} 0 \;\Leftrightarrow\; U_h^1 \substack{<\\=\\>} U_h^0 \;. \tag{2.6}$$

That means that for utility improvements between states 0 and 1 both the CV and the EV are strictly positive for a certain household whereas for negative utility changes these indicators are strictly negative. If there is no change in the utility level of household h, both Hicksian welfare measures are equal to zero. They are thus reliable utility indicators.

In environmental valuation practice, the concept of compensating variation is often preferred to the equivalent variation because its interpretation as WTP for an environmental improvement and as WTA compensation for a negative environmental change is more intuitive than the respective interpretations of the EV. Furthermore, it is easier to convey this basic concept to politicians (usually the addressees of the valuation results) and individuals (the participants of valuation surveys). Therefore, in the following the consideration will be restrained to the compensating variation. Yet, it is clear that all theoretical arguments below also analogously refer to the equivalent variation.

In order to assess it empirically, the CV as specified in 2.5 can be broken down into several components. After adding the two terms $e_h(p^0, z^0, U_h^0) - e_h(p^0, z^0, U_h^0) = 0$ and $e_h(p^1, z^0, U_h^0) - e_h(p^1, z^0, U_h^0) = 0$, the CV of household h assumes the following form

$$\begin{aligned} CV_h^{01} &= e_h(p^1, z^1, U_h^1) - e_h(p^0, z^0, U_h^0) \\ &\quad + e_h(p^0, z^0, U_h^0) - e_h(p^1, z^0, U_h^0) \\ &\quad + e_h(p^1, z^0, U_h^0) - e_h(p^1, z^1, U_h^0). \end{aligned} \tag{2.7}$$

In this version, the different components of the CV become evident. The difference in the first row of 2.7 stands for the compensating variation resulting from the change in household income $I_h^1 - I_h^0$ and can thus be denoted with CVI_h^{01}. The difference in the second row is equal to the CV that is induced by the change in the price vector p for all market goods and can therefore also be written as CVp_h^{01}. Finally, the last row in 2.7 gives the compensating variation of the change in the level of provision of the environmental good alone, so an alternative expression is CVz_h^{01}. In doing so, it is possible to define a separate CV for each partial change: the changes in market prices Δp, potential income changes ΔI and the actual change in the level of the environmental good Δz. As a result, the sum of the three separate CVs is equal to the total CV according to

$$CV_h^{01} = CVI_h^{01} + CVp_h^{01} + CVz_h^{01}. \tag{2.8}$$

This additive nature of the total CV of a utility change triggered by an environmental project is very helpful because different techniques exist for the assessment of each of the three partial variations. The easiest is the valuation of the change in household income. Due to the money-metric nature of the expenditure function, which is the basis for calculating the compensating variation according to 2.5, CVI_h^{01} is equal to the absolute change in income $I_h^1 - I_h^0$. When it comes to the assessment of the CV of a change in market prices, well established techniques exist for its computation. Alternatively, CVp_h^{01} can be written as the integral of the Hicksian demand function in state 0 between the price vectors before and after the environmental project. Although the Hicksian demand function cannot be observed, either, techniques have been developed that make use of the observable Marshallian demand function to compute the CV of a change in market prices (cf. Vartia 1983).

The only remaining methodological challenge is the empirical assessment of the CV of Δz, the change in the level of provision of the environmental good. CVz_h^{01} can also be written as the integral over the shadow prices of the environmental good between the two states before and after the project is carried out. However, unlike Vartia's (1983) algorithm for changes in market prices, in this case there is no technique for the empirical computation of CVz_h^{01}. Therefore, other, more direct assessment techniques have to be applied. Before these techniques can be introduced in greater detail, it is necessary to come back to the aggregation problem. The question is, after assessing the Hicksian welfare measures for all households affected by an environmental project (i.e. the identification problem) how can these individual changes be aggregated into an indicator of the change in social welfare? If all individual utilities change into the same direction, the problem is trivial. It is either a clear Pareto improvement or a clear Pareto deterioration. The problematic case is a public project that causes both utility gains for some households and losses for others, i.e. winners and losers of the proposed project. In the realm of ordinal utility theory, Arrow (1951) has shown that there is no way to objectively and uniquely aggregate individual preferences. As a consequence, all approaches to aggregate individual preferences result in one way or another in inter-individual comparisons of utility. This is not consistent with ordinal utility theory. However, practical CBA relaxes these tight stipulations and usually applies the so-called Hicks-Kaldor criterion, also referred to as potential Pareto criterion. According to this criterion, the individual compensating variations of all affected households are simply added up and thus result in an indicator of the social welfare change. It holds that

$$\sum_{h=1}^{H} CV_h^{01} = \sum_{h=1}^{H} CVp_h^{01} + \sum_{h=1}^{H} CVI_h^{01} + \sum_{h=1}^{H} CVz_h^{01} \overset{<}{\underset{>}{=}} 0 \quad \Rightarrow \quad \Delta W \overset{<}{\underset{>}{=}} 0 \tag{2.9}$$

where ΔW denotes the change in social welfare between the states 0 and 1. The aggregate CV is the sum of all WTPs of the beneficiaries of the project ($CV_h^{01} > 0$) and the WTAs of the losers ($CV_h^{01} < 0$). A strictly positive balance of the aggregated WTPs and WTAs is an indicator of an increase in social welfare, whereas a negative balance indicates a lower level of social welfare as a result of the environmental project. The alternative name 'potential Pareto criterion' stems from the fact that in case the overall CV is positive, all beneficiaries could compensate the losers for their decreased utility. In this situation all households are as well off as before the environmental project and there would be at least one beneficiary who, despite paying the compensation to the losers, is still better off. Yet, in reality this compensation is never implemented, so the name is 'potential' Pareto criterion. It should be noted that applying the Hicks-Kaldor criterion constitutes a departure from ordinal utility theory and a step into cardinal utility theory because utility levels are summed across individuals and inter-individual comparisons of utility are made.

When it comes to practical CBA of environmental projects it is usually not feasible to assess all components of a change in social welfare according to 2.9. In order to do this, information of the income changes of all households (or at least a representative sample of them) as well as of all price changes and an estimation of the whole demand system of the economy would be required. Since this is both extremely costly and time-consuming, the practical CBA approach is simplified in the following way.[1] The overall cost of the environmental project can be calculated as the product of the vector of all input factors y and the vector of their respective prices q^1. This product simply represents the total input costs resulting from the implementation of the environmental project. Consequently, the cost-benefit formula can be expressed as

$$CB^{01} = \sum_{h=1}^{H} CVz_h^{01} - q^1 \cdot y \tag{2.10}$$

where CB^{01} is the cost-benefit balance of the environmental project. 2.10 is a direct and simplified comparison of the aggregate benefits ($\sum_{h=1}^{H} CVz_h^{01}$) and overall costs ($q^1 \cdot y$) of a certain environmental project. What follows from

1 For a more detailed illustration of these simplifications including the underlying assumptions refer to Ahlheim (2003, p. 27-29).

this simplification is that the assessment of the benefits in practical CBA applications focuses exclusively on the direct utility change induced by the change in environmental quality. To this end, a variety of valuation techniques have been developed, which will be introduced in the following subsection.

2.1.3. Environmental valuation in practice

Practical approaches to value non-market goods in general and environmental goods in particular can be conceptually separated into direct and indirect valuation methods. The most important indirect methods include the travel cost method, the hedonic-pricing method and the averting behavior method, whereas the contingent valuation method, attribute based choice modeling, and the participatory valuation method are the major direct valuation methods to be discussed in this subsection. The indirect approaches make use of actual consumption behavior of market goods to draw conclusions about the preferences of individuals for environmental goods. In a market where actual transactions take place, individuals reveal their preferences by the choices they make. Therefore, the indirect methods are also called revealed preference approaches. The direct valuation methods on the other hand have in common that they require individuals to indicate their preferences for non-market goods. Yet, since the preferences are not revealed by actual market behavior but only stated, these methods are also referred to as stated preference approaches. Another major difference between indirect and direct methods is that the former are only able to assess use values, whereas the latter can measure both use and non-use values. The reason for this is that the indirect methods merely observe use or consumption behavior and therefore only capture the use components of individuals' preferences (Ahlheim 2003). That means that only by means of the direct valuation methods can the total economic value of a certain environmental good be determined. Below the main indirect and direct valuation methods are introduced in turn.

Indirect valuation methods

The travel cost method (TCM) is often used for the assessment of the recreational value of certain areas like beaches, forests, or lakes. It was first employed by Clawson (1959) and refined by Cesario and Knetsch (1976). According to the original idea of this approach the costs that an individual is willing to incur to use a certain recreational site are an indicator of that individual's preference for it. So, when evaluating the utility generated by a river, a forest or a coastal area with a beach, this indicator is the cost that people incur for getting to these sites for fishing, trekking, or swimming. These costs include both the travel costs, which in turn comprise the opportunity cost of time for taking the trip and the cost for gasoline or public transport, and the costs for other equipment, such as fishing rods, trekking boots and swimwear, which is necessary to carry out certain recreational activities at these sites.

From a more general point of view, the revealed preferences for a market good like travel time or certain equipment for recreational activities provide information on an individual's preferences for the public environmental good (e.g. recreation at the beach). For this method to be able to work that way there must be a weakly complementary relationship between the observable consumption behavior of the market good and the preferences for the environmental good (Mäler 1974). According to Stephan and Ahlheim (1996) two conditions must be fulfilled for weak complementarity to hold. Firstly, the private good must not be essential. This means there must be a so-called choke price at and above which the demand for the good is zero. Secondly, in the range above the choke price for the market good, the marginal utility of the environmental good must be zero. Since an individual will not buy the market good if its price exceeds the choke price, the marginal utility of that good in this price range is zero. As in such a situation the environmental good is not consumed either, it is assumed that its marginal utility, too, is zero. If for example the environmental good is a mountainous area and the market good a set of trekking equipment, the area can only be used by means of the equipment. If, in a situation when the price for the equipment is above the choke price, no trekking equipment is bought, the mountain does not generate any utility. Therefore, if both conditions are fulfilled, the TCM can be employed to assess the use value of certain environmental goods by quantifying which cost people are incurring to use that good.

A major problem of the method is the exact valuation of time spent for accessing a recreational site. Obviously, a simple wage rate cannot be applied to value the travel time because the alternative to making the trip would not be work but leisure time (Ahlheim 2003). However, the fact that the price of leisure time is very hard to determine causes a considerable portion of uncertainty of values elicited by means of the TCM. Another problem is the fact that the fraction of the travel costs or expenses for equipment that is really associated with the environmental good is not clear. This problem arises for example, when a trip to a recreational site also serves other purposes like paying a visit to relatives, or the same equipment is used in connection with more than one environmental good (Loomis et al. 2000). In that case, the utility generated by the consumption of these environmental goods cannot be clearly inferred. Despite these short-comings, the TCM is still employed rather frequently (e.g. Du 1998, Fix and Loomis 1997, Hanley 1989).

The hedonic-pricing method (HPM) harks back to the work of Ridker (1967) and Rosen (1974). Detailed descriptions of this method including an introduction of the theoretical foundations and extensive discussion of econometric issues can be found in Palmquist (1991), Freeman (2003), and Bockstael and McConnell (2007). The basic assumption of the HPM is the idea that the price for a certain market good can be disaggregated into partial prices for the different characteristics of that good. Such goods are called heterogeneous goods. According to Rosen (1974, p. 34) such "goods are valued for their utility-bearing attributes or characteristics". So the price p of a certain good can be modelled as the function of its numerous characteristics $x_1, x_2, \dots, x_n$ according to

$$p = f(x_1, x_2, \dots, x_n). \quad (2.11)$$

If two varieties of the same market good only differ in one characteristic x_i, the price difference is an indicator of the tradeoff that people are willing to make to obtain this characteristic. The partial derivative of the price with respect to that characteristic $\partial p / \partial x_i$ is equal to the amount an individual is willing to pay for one additional unit of that characteristic, i.e. her marginal WTP (Palmquist 1991). If one of these n characteristics is the association of that good with an environmental good, its marginal price and thus its value can be determined by means of the HPM. This approach is applied for goods as different as environmental protection (Luttik 2000), agricultural land (Le Goffe 2000), or urban environmental elements (Jim and Chen 2006a), to name a few. A typical application of this method in the real estate market can be found in Jim and Chen (2006a). This study uses data on housing prices to assess the amenity value of urban green space, a typical environmental good with public good characteristics and thus without a market. Typical characteristics of apartments are size, number of rooms, number of bedrooms and bathrooms. In addition to that, certain characteristics associated with urban green space are identified, such as vicinity to a park or a water body or direct view of a park or green space. The study reveals which portion of the apartment price is determined by these features of the environmental good "urban green space" by estimating the price function as displayed in 2.11 and thus infers its value.

The most important problem of this approach is the fact that the number of combinations of characteristics of a good is limited. Therefore, not all households actually obtain their most preferred combination of characteristics but rather have to content themselves with what is available on the market. The above example of a real estate market illustrates this best. Here, only a limited number of different varieties of the good – an apartment – are available, so individuals do not have the choice over the full range of combinations and thus cannot freely express their preferences. Moreover, only if all households have the same preference ordering does $p = f(x_1, x_2, \dots, x_n)$ represent a function of household WTP. Yet, this is usually not the case since different households hold different preferences, which in their entirety result in the equilibrium market price. The data of a typical HDM study rather consists of point observations, which – combined with the limited number of combinations mentioned above – strictly does not allow for a generalization in form of a WTP function (Ahlheim 2003).

The so-called averting behavior method (ABM) considers costs that individuals or households are willing to incur in order to avoid the exposure to detrimental environmental influences as indicator of the value of environmental quality, i.e. the removal of those detrimental influences. This can include the complete avoidance of negative environmental influences or – where this is not possible – at least their reduction. The basic assumption behind this method is that a rational person will try to avoid a negative environmental influence as long as the expected damage caused by that influence is higher than the cost of averting that detrimental influence (Dickie 2003). A classic example is the valuation of improved water quality exemplarily documented in Abdalla et al. (1992). By employing a mail survey, this study quantifies the costs that households in an area with unsafe drinking water in the United States are willing to incur in order to avoid using unsafe tap water. This includes both direct cash expenditures and the time spent for such activities valued at the minimum wage of that area. Another classical example of costs of averting behavior is reported in Mansfield et al. (2006). This study assesses the WTP of households to prevent restrictions for children to stay indoors to avoid exposure to air pollution in the form of ozone. These WTP statements assess the value of avoiding negative health effects caused by staying outdoors and breathing air with excessive ozone concentration. The result is a lower bound of the value of improvements of air quality because an actual improvement would not only make the restrictions of being outdoors obsolete, but also entail other benefits such as existence or bequeath value aspects of clean air. Again it becomes obvious that this direct valuation method fails to assess non-use values.

All things considered, these approaches systematically underestimate the value of environmental goods because they are not able to assess the non-use value components of such goods. A comprehensive assessment of both use and non-use values can only be done by means of direct valuation methods. These methods are called direct because they do not rely on the inference of values from observed behavior but directly ask individuals for their valuation of environmental goods and amenities. Below, the three major direct valuation approaches are outlined.

Direct valuation methods

The most frequently employed and also most fervently debated direct valuation approach is the contingent valuation method (CVM). In addition to the field of environmental economics, it is also frequently used in transport and health economic analyses. Generally, it is a survey-based technique that directly asks a sample of respondents representative for a population affected by a certain public environmental project how they value this project in monetary terms. Since there is no market for environmental goods, and consequently no market prices can be used for their valuation, this approach constructs a hypothetical market situation and presents it to respondents in a survey. Basically, this method describes a certain public project that leads to the provision of an environmental good, such as the cleanup of a polluted river, the renaturation of an industrial wasteland, or steps to prevent the extinction of plant and animal species, and asks households how much they are willing to pay in order to get this project. On the basis of neoclassical welfare theory this WTP is interpreted as a measure of the change of utility of the individual household induced by the respective policy (cf. 2.1.2).[2]

The fact that the CVM is a survey-based approach is the source of numerous methodological flaws. Since the present study theoretically and empirically deals with one of these methodological problems and also practically employs a CVM survey, it will be discussed in greater detail in the subsequent section. However, before we get to that extensive presentation of the CVM's practical implementation, econometric procedures, and certain methodological problems, two alternative direct valuation methods shall be portrayed in brief.

An alternative method to directly value environmental goods is referred to as attribute-based choice modeling (ABCM). Conceptual reviews of different forms of this method include Adamowicz et al. (1998), Bennett and Blamey (2001), and Alriksson and Öberg (2008). According to this approach, alternative versions of an environmental good, which differ in the levels of one or several characteristics, are presented to the respondent. Subsequently, the respondent is asked to make a choice between these variations of that good. Similar to the case of the hedonic pricing method, such environmental goods are assumed to be heterogeneous goods which generate utility through their different characteristics, one of which is the price or the contribution necessary for the provision of that good. The level of provision of some of these characteristics can be modified and consequently different variations of the good can be formed. Practically ABCM evolved from so-called conjoint

2 Theoretically, also the willingness to accept compensation to forgo that positive utility change can be assessed, but in practical CVM applications mostly WTP is used.

analysis in marketing research and like CVM it is a survey-based method. Theoretically, this approach is based on Lancaster's (1966) characteristics theory of value stating that the value generated by a consumer good is the result of the utility of its manifold characteristics. The crucial aspect is that a certain good is defined by the specific combination of utility generating characteristics. Translated back to the case of environmental goods this means that a typical environmental good, say a reforested area, also consists of a range of characteristics, which determine the utility level individuals can generate from it. Such characteristics could be, for example, the number of tree species in the area, the number of animal species that can be protected, the existence of hiking trails and so on. The focus of this approach is on eliciting information on the preferences of respondents for the different characteristics rather than for the environmental scenario as a whole as applied in CVM where only one fixed scenario is evaluated.

More specifically, the literature distinguishes between several forms of ABCM, so-called choice experiments, contingent ranking, contingent rating, and paired comparisons (Hanley et al. 2001). Choice experiments (e.g. in Adamowicz et al. 1998, Boyle and Özdemir 2009, Hanley et al. 1998) can be regarded as a generalization of CVM because not only two cases (the status quo and an alternative environmental project) are presented to the respondent, but two or more cases, which are determined by varying levels of their characteristics and need not necessarily include the status quo (but usually do). After displaying all cases and the respective levels that the characteristics take in each of them, the respondents are asked to select their most preferred case. Contingent ranking (e.g. in Foster and Mourato 2000) goes one step further and has respondents rank all displayed cases instead of merely choosing the most preferred. A much less popular approach is contingent rating (e.g. in Alvarez-Farizo and Hanley 2002) where respondents are similarly confronted with a set of cases that differ in the level of the characteristics of the environmental good and are asked to rate them on a numerical scale. Since no direct comparisons are made there is no formal theoretical relationship between the ratings and economic choices, which requires much stronger assumptions for this method to be able to measure utility changes (Hanley et al. 2001). Eventually, paired comparisons (e.g. in Lockwood 1998) ask respondents to select one out of two cases and also indicate the strength of that choice on a numerical scale. Similar to the case of contingent rating the scale ratings render the results of the paired comparison approach inconsistent with economic theory.

Although some of these techniques appear very promising for the valuation of environmental goods they are not completely without problems. Most of all, the cognitive burden for respondents is higher when the choice modeling approaches are employed compared to contingent valuation (Hanley et al. 2001). Comparing more than two alternatives and at the same time making tradeoffs between different explicit characteristics is definitely more challenging than the single statement of WTP for a scenario to happen in ordinary CVM. Furthermore, the design of credible alternatives is often not an easy task for the researcher, because each combination of characteristics presented to the respondent must be equally plausible and feasible. The problem of a lack of consistency of results of rating models with economic theory has already been mentioned. Overall, preference elicitation data generated by the different ABCM approaches contain more information than CVM responses, but much more research is needed to overcome the manifold methodological shortcomings of these approaches.

The third major direct valuation method, which is nevertheless applied much less frequently than the two approaches introduced so far, is the participatory valuation method (PVM). The PVM, sometimes also referred to as "market stall" approach evolved as a result of certain problems of the interviewer process in traditional valuation studies, i.e. mostly CVM surveys. Typically, respondents are unfamiliar with environmental goods introduced in a survey interview, so the task of understanding and memorizing all features of the proposed project is considerable. Additionally, the survey interview might not be the right context for the expression of valuation statements, since some respondents might feel the need to explain their preferences a bit more in detail compared to putting it into merely one figure (Macmillan et al. 2002). These flaws can be solved to a certain extent by the PVM because more time for the evaluation of information as well as for the expression of a WTP is provided.

This approach, based on the application of focus groups, has a group of 10 to 15 individuals jointly evaluate an environmental project in a series of discussion meetings. During the first meeting, usually the environmental issue and specifics of the valuation approach are presented to and discussed with the participants. Before they reconvene for a second and even a third meeting, participants have the opportunity to review the information material at home and evaluate the proposed measure. Major advantages of this procedure are the opportunity of respondents to ask additional questions regarding the environmental issue and the informal social setting in which the evaluation is discussed. So, this approach takes into account the fact that respondents often do not have clearly defined preferences for environmental goods and consequently cannot express these within the tight timeframe of a traditional CVM interview. Although the existence of predefined preferences for goods valued in environmental surveys is taken for granted by neoclassical economic theory, several authors discuss the possibility that this assumption might not be justified (Bettman et al. 1998, Payne et al. 1999). If this is the case, the PVM offers an interesting alternative approach for the elicitation of environmental valuations because the process of preference construction is dealt with more carefully than in a survey interview.

Examples for applications of this approach can be found in MacMillan et al. (2002), Philip and Macmillan (2005), and Lienhoop and MacMillan (2007). Usually the PVM is based on the contingent valuation method but an increasing number of studies combine choice experiments and the PVM (e.g. Alvarez-Farizo and Hanley 2006, Alvarez-Farizo et al. 2007, Powe et al. 2005). A modified approach called citizens' juries, which is similar to the PVM except that participants only convene once for one or two days is the most recent development in this strand of literature (Robinson et al. 2009). Overall, this field of research is still emerging because many methodological problems have yet to be solved. Firstly, the time and effort of planning and organizing such group discussion meetings is considerable. Secondly, the number of participants is mostly quite limited and not comparable to sample sizes of usual survey studies. In addition, the people that are willing to take part in such discussion groups are likely to be better informed about the environmental issue than the general population in the first place and thus differ from the 'average' citizen in a community. Both problems might severely threaten the representativeness of the findings elicited by the PVM. Therefore, more research on the reliability and validity of these new approaches is needed.

2.2. The contingent valuation method

Since the contingent valuation method was chosen for the environmental valuation study in Southwest China and the investigation of the influence of socially desirable responding is the subject of this thesis, the theoretical background as well as current topics of CVM research will be reviewed in more detail in this section. The amount of literature on the CVM has been increasing in a breathtaking speed in recent years and decades. This includes applications and studies on methodological issues as well as conceptual works and extensive reviews. The most important of the latter are the edited volume by Cummings et al. (1986), the book by Mitchell and Carson (1989), and the chapter in the Handbook of Environmental Economics by Carson and Hanemann (2005). Literature adopting a rather critical perspective on the CVM is represented by Hausman (1993).

The idea of using direct interviews to elicit individuals' valuations of nonmarket environmental goods was first brought up in theory by Ciriacy-Wantrup (1947). Yet, Davis (1963) was the first researcher to practically apply the CVM in an effort to determine the recreational value of a forest area. He found similar valuation results compared to those calculated by means of the travel cost method for the same good. In his interviews he used the bidding-game format, which was also used by another influential study reported in Randall et al. (1974). This latter study was the first to explicitly stress the ability of the CVM to assess the existence value, which earlier had been shown to be a component of the total economic value of environmental goods (Krutilla 1967). During most of the 1970s and 1980s the number of contingent valuation studies rose steadily and besides the original form of the WTP question several new elicitation techniques were devised (c.f. section 2.2.1). The next major event for the development of this technique was the valuation of the environmental damage caused by the oil spill of the supertanker Exxon Valdez in 1989. A major study to value the damage of this substantial oil spill off the coast of Alaska (Carson et al. 1992) sparked a huge controversy over the validity of CV results. As a consequence, an expert panel organized by the United States National Oceanic and Atmospheric Association (NOAA) and superseded by Nobel Laureates Kenneth J. Arrow and Robert M. Solow scrutinized the CVM. The Panel concluded that non-use values are a legitimate part of environmental damage assessments and further established guidelines for the application of CV surveys (Arrow et al. 1993). It was also in the year of the Exxon Valdez oil spill that one of the most influential books on contingent valuation "Using surveys to value public goods: The contingent valuation method" by Mitchell and Carson (1989) was published. This book, which has been used as reference for the conduction of CV studies until today, was the first to provide a complete theoretical framework for this method. It discusses all elicitation formats as well as the problem of strategic behavior and other potential biases. Like the report of the NOAA Panel, these authors stress the importance of careful survey design in order to avoid such biases.

The subsequent section portrays some procedural aspects of the CVM in more detail. Different survey modes as well as the typical setup of a CVM interview are introduced. Thereafter, different forms of eliciting WTP statements and some relevant problems and criticisms of the method as well as selected current topics in CVM research are discussed. After that, section 2.2.2 deals with econometric techniques, which are necessary to actually arrive at evaluations of public goods, and section 2.2.3 reviews applications of the CVM in China.

2.2.1. Details of the CVM interview and questionnaire design

It was mentioned that the CVM is a survey-based method – WTP statements of respondents for non-market goods are elicited by means of direct questioning. Consequently, there are several modes of survey administration, namely in-person surveys, mail surveys, telephone surveys and internet-based surveys. Each of these administration modes has its advantages and shortcomings, which will be discussed shortly. A more detailed discussion of comparisons of CVM results of these different modes can be found in section 4.2 where the influence of social desirability on survey responses in the different survey modes is analyzed.

In-person surveys were the earliest administration mode of contingent valuation surveys (cf. Davis 1963, Randall et al. 1974) and were also recommended by the NOAA Panel (Arrow et al. 1993). CV scenarios are often rather complex and unfamiliar to the respondent, so the use of visual aids is very helpful. These can best be provided by an interviewer actively conducting the interview. Additionally, the presence of an interviewer raises the respondent's motivation and effort and assures that questions are answered according to the sequence in the questionnaire and in appropriate speed (Mitchell and Carson 1989). For instance, it can be prevented that the respondent jumps to questions at the end of the questionnaire without answering the first parts. Although telephone surveys also employ interviewers, the less personal nature of a conversation over the phone makes it more difficult to keep up the interest and motivation over a lengthy CVM interview. However, one important disadvantage of in-person interviews is potential interviewer effects, i.e. the fact that different interviewers receive systematically different responses. Closely related to this kind of bias is socially desirable responding. As will be introduced in chapter 3, one requirement for the occurrence of this form of bias is the presence of an interviewer. Consequently, this problem is especially important when CVM interviews are conducted in person compared to the other, less socially interactive interview modes. Finally, costs for surveys employing in-person interviews are relatively high because of the recruitment, training, supervision, transport, and payment of interviewers. Therefore it is obvious that the biggest advantage of mail and telephone surveys are the substantial cost savings compared to the conduction of in-person interviews. Although for telephone surveys interviewers are needed, there are substantial cost savings in transportation cost and time. Consequently, there are numerous applications of mail (e.g. Ahlheim et al. 2010, Bishop and Heberlein 1979) and telephone surveys (e.g. Davis 2004, Jorgensen et al. 2001, Whittaker et al. 1998). While in mail surveys, additional explanatory materials such as maps and photos can be used, this is not possible in telephone interviews. As a consequence of the need to properly present the sometimes very complex contingent valuation scenarios, in-person and mail surveys still prevail. Mail surveys are a form of self-administered surveys with no direct interaction of interviewer and respondent (Carson and Hanemann 2005). Consequently, there is no risk of biased data as a result of interviewer and interview effects. In telephone surveys on the other hand, these biases may exist because even over the telephone certain interviewer characteristics are perceptible from the perspective of the respondent and might thus exert biasing influence. One major shortcoming of mail surveys is the frequently reported low response rate and associated with this a self-selection bias (Messonnier et al. 2000, Whitehead et al. 1993). It may happen that the fraction of respondents that actually return the completed questionnaires have significantly different characteristics than that share of respondents who choose not to mail back the questionnaire. Typically respondents taking part in a mail survey are better informed about the environmental issue and have a higher interest in finding solutions to the respective environmental problem. If this is the case, the overall representativity of the resulting sample is no longer guaranteed. On top of that, mail surveys systematically exclude illiterate respondents. While this may not be a big problem in industrialized countries, the level of education and particularly the literacy rate in many developing countries is still quite low. This is one of the main reasons why the present study employs the in-person mode when conducting a contingent valuation survey in Southwest China (cf. chapter 5). The most recent development regarding survey administration modes makes use of the internet (e.g. Lindhjem and Navrud 2008, Marta-Pedroso et al. 2007, Nielsen 2011). Research in this field is still in its infancy, so little evidence regarding the reliability and validity of the internet as data collection mode for contingent valuation surveys could be collected so far. However, due to the increasing penetration of internet connections this field is definitely going to be a major field of methodological research with respect to the CVM.

The structure of a CVM interview

Usually a contingent valuation interview is made up of five parts. After contacting the respondent and introducing the survey the first part consists of some warm-up questions that deal with the respondent's familiarity with the environmental issue. Previous knowledge and attitudes towards the environmental problem are the major contents of this part. Subsequently, the scenario of the environmental project is introduced. The scenario is the most essential part of the whole interview process because it is on the grounds of this scenario that the respondent is asked to state her maximum WTP for the described environmental change to happen. To this end, in mail and in-person surveys visual aids, such as pictures, graphics or maps can be employed. Carson and Hanemann (2005, p. 897) emphasize that "the scenario must convey the change in the good to be valued, how that change would come about, how it would be paid for, and the larger context that is relevant for considering the change". The crucial challenge for the researcher is to craft a scenario that is both scientifically accurate and still comprehensible for the respondents who mostly have never been confronted with that topic before. The central point here is to find the appropriate amount of information, a task which is not easy considering the potentially very different original levels of information of respondents. Following the description of the project scenario is the so-called payment scenario. It is explained that all or some part of the costs for that project have to be borne by those who benefit from it, and that therefore the citizens are asked for their contribution. At this point respondents are informed that the environmental project will only be implemented if the sum of WTP statements by all households exceeds the total cost of the project. This piece of information is referred to as implementation rule. Following this, the payment vehicle is specified, i.e. the explanation of how the contributions for the proposed project would actually have to be made once it is implemented. This part is of equal importance relative to the scenario description because it is here that the tradeoff between benefiting from the environmental project and giving up a fraction of their budget has to be conveyed to the respondent in the most plausible and credible manner. Most surveys employ tax increases as payment vehicle, but fees or lump-sum payments are also used in applications of the CVM. The appropriateness of the payment vehicle with respect to the specific survey population has to be scrutinized by means of in-depth interviews and test interviews prior to the main survey, because the acceptability of taxes or fees, for instance, may vary across countries and cultures. Following the presentations of project and payment scenario, the respondent is then asked for her maximum WTP in order to make the presented environmental change happen. This elicitation question constitutes the fourth part and at the same time it is the core element of the interview. The researcher can choose between different formats of this elicitation question, which will be introduced below. In the final part, respondents are usually confronted with various types of attitudinal questions regarding for instance the motivations for their WTP statement, their views on environmental protection, on the specific project, on the performance of government, on life satisfaction or any other kinds of personal or political attitudes. In addition to that, a set of socio-demographic questions such as age, sex, household size, number of children etc. conclude the last part. These questions – in the same way as the attitudinal questions – yield a pool of covariates for identifying determinants of WTP.

Question formats for eliciting WTP statements

The topic of different forms of elicitation questions has already been touched above and will be outlined in greater detail here. Several forms of the WTP question have been proposed in the contingent valuation literature, with the oldest being the bidding game elicitation technique (Davis 1963, Mitchell and Carson 1989). According to this approach, a respondent is asked to answer yes or no to a certain bid amount. In case she answers yes, she is asked again with gradually increasing bids until she finally rejects a bid. Her WTP can consequently be placed in the range between the last bid that she agreed to and the first bid that she rejected. If she rejects the first bid, the follow up bids are gradually lowered until she accepts a bid. Analogously, her WTP falls into the interval between the last two bids. Being similar to an auction, this elicitation format both mimics a familiar purchase situation in the market (Venkatachalam 2004) and facilitates the respondents' selection process because for each bid only a choice between yes and no is required. However, the major flaw of the bidding game technique is the fact that responses might be influenced by the initial bid. Basis for this concept, referred to as starting-point bias, is the idea that respondents perceive the initial bid to contain information on the actual value of the proposed good (e.g. Frew et al. 2004). In addition to that, the bidding game format is not applicable in mail surveys because an interviewer has to actively decide whether and which follow up bids to ask (Loomis 1990).

As a reaction to concerns about starting-point bias in bidding game contingent valuation, the so-called open-ended (OE) elicitation technique was devised, whereby respondents are simply asked to name their maximum WTP for the proposed environmental project (e.g. in Walsh et al. 1984). Yet, the fact that respondents were not provided with any assistance in selecting their maximum WTP leads to a high fraction of non-response to this question. The reason for this is simply the fact that it is much harder to actively come up with an amount that one is willing to pay for an unfamiliar good than deciding whether one is willing to purchase the good at a predetermined price (Hanemann 1994). Due to that inadequacy of the OE format Mitchell and Carson (1981) came up with the payment card (PC) approach. Respondents are confronted with a list of possible WTP amounts or intervals and asked to select the amount they are at most willing to pay. Instead of confronting the respondents with one single bid amount, something more like a framework for selecting their WTP amount is given. This framework does not bias WTP statements as much as the initial bid in the bidding game format but at the same time provides more guidance than the OE format and thus reduces non-responses. In some applications, average contributions for other public goods are marked on the PC as reference (Mitchell and Carson 1989). However, biased statements cannot completely be avoided with this technique, either. The PC format is known to suffer from so-called range and centering bias meaning that WTP estimates significantly differ depending on the maximum or central amount on the PC. The idea behind this bias is that respondents are typically not familiar with the valuation of environmental goods and therefore seek information on the PC what an 'appropriate' WTP could be. In a health economic study to value provisions of cancer protection for example, Whynes et al. (2004) find a 30 percent higher mean WTP when using a PC with 1000 GBP as maximum amount than with 100 GBP. Despite these shortcomings the PC format has been frequently used until today and is also employed in the empirical part of this study.

The last major elicitation format is the so-called dichotomous choice (DC) format developed by Bishop and Heberlein (1979).[3] This approach involves confronting a respondent with only one bid amount and asking whether she is willing to 'buy' the proposed environmental good at this amount or not. Different respondents in the sample are randomly assigned different predetermined bid amounts. Rather than an exact WTP statement this approach elicits the boundaries of a range that includes a certain respondent's maximum WTP. Therefore, a single yes or no response in connection with the respective bid amount contains much less statistical information than OE or PC responses. In case a respondent rejects bid t, the researcher merely knows that her WTP is somewhere in the interval $[0, t)$. Analogously, a yes response indicates that the WTP falls into the interval $[t, \infty)$. As a consequence different statistical estimation techniques involving logit and probit regression (Hanemann 1984) and – most importantly – larger samples have to be employed with the DC format. Among all elicitation formats the DC approach most strongly resembles a real market situation and therefore facilitates the response task very much. In everyday life, consumers regularly have to decide whether to buy a certain good at a fixed price or not. As a result, the NOAA Panel strongly recommended employing this format. So it was the state-of-the-art approach in the years following that report but has gradually been taking a backseat in recent years. Another advantage of the DC format is its incentive compatibility "in the sense that a truthful response to the actual question asked constitutes an optimal strategy for the [respondent]" (Carson and Groves 2007, p. 184). Incentive compatibility only holds if the payments for the project, once it is implemented, are coercive (Carson and Groves 2007). So, by employing the DC format in

3 Alternative names for this approach are 'take-it-or-leave-it format' or 'referendum format'.

connection with the advice to respondents that in case of implementation, every household actually has to pay for the proposed project, strategic response behavior can theoretically be avoided.

A further refinement of the single-bounded DC format is the double-bounded DC format put forward by Hanemann (1985). According to this technique, upon responding to the initial bid the respondent is confronted with a follow up bid. This second bid is higher than the initial bid if the first response is yes and lower if it is no. The researcher obtains two binary responses from each respondent and can consequently narrow down the interval containing that respondent's WTP a bit more. Resulting from this is the fact that the double-bounded DC format is statistically more efficient than the single-bounded version, which is its major advantage (Hanemann et al. 1991, Kanninen 1993). On the downside, WTP statements elicited by means of both the single- and double-bounded DC techniques are very much prone to be influenced by starting-point bias (Ready et al. 1996). Similar to the case of the bidding game format, respondents might be looking for a clue of which amount would be an 'appropriate' WTP statement and thus interpret the initial bid as such a clue. In addition to that, both versions of the DC approach are likely to suffer from yea-saying, a tendency to agree to a question regardless of its content, because the responses are binary and not continuous like in the case of the OE and PC formats (Blamey et al. 1999). Finally, because of the binary nature of DC responses, more assumptions about the form of the underlying utility function than for the OE and PC formats have to be made in order to arrive at estimates of mean WTP (Mitchell and Carson 1989). Of course, the double-bounded DC format can also be extended to asking a second follow-up question, which results in the triple-bounded DC format (Bateman et al. 2001). Note that when the number of follow-up questions is not predetermined but contingent on the switch of responses from yes to no or vice versa, this elicitation technique is effectively a bidding game. Since the cognitive requirements and situational characteristics for respondents when answering to the above formats of the elicitation question may differ substantially, the empirical literature has found huge discrepancies in WTP estimates resulting from the different techniques. These differences are reviewed in further detail in section 4.2 when the traditional approaches to study the influence of socially desirable responding in CVM – the detection of mode effects – are discussed.

Methodological weaknesses of the CVM

It has already been mentioned in this chapter that the CVM is not without critics and that there is a wide range of procedural and methodological problems that threaten this method's reliability and validity. Since it is not meaningful and feasible to provide an extensive discussion of all problems of CVM, at least a short description of some important biases and recent approaches to deal with them is appropriate here. Two types of response bias that come with the use of the PC elicitation format, namely range and centering bias and starting-point bias in the DC format have already been mentioned above. In addition to these, there are several rather troubling irregularities that often occur in CVM studies. One of the most persistent criticisms of the CVM is the fact that both the valuation scenario and the respondent's WTP statement are hypothetical in nature. What is recorded in such a survey is not actual behavior but merely a statement of what the respondent would do if confronted with a specific situation. A definition of this bias can be found in Cummings et al. (1986) who describe hypothetical bias as potential divergence between hypothetical and real payments. The idea behind this phenomenon is that if the payment is not actually made, a respondent might have incentives to verbally state a higher WTP in order to increase the likelihood of the provision of the good in question (Harrison and Rutström 2008). A number of CVM studies comparing hypothetical and actual WTP find the former to be significantly greater (e.g. Botelho and Costa Pinto 2002, Christie 2007, Foster et al. 1997, Neill et al. 1994). Similarly, the vast majority of experiments listed in the review article by Harrison and Rutström (2008) find hypothetical WTP to exceed actual payments. Two main ways to remedy this bias have been proposed in the relevant literature. The first approach is to generally divide WTP statements by a certain factor in order to correct the overstatement caused by the hypothetical nature of the valuation task (Fox et al. 1998). Yet, this mitigation strategy is problematic because the factor of such a calibration might be contingent on the good to be valued and the specific situation of the survey (Murphy et al. 2005). Therefore, a general rule for the calibration of WTP results cannot be derived. Secondly, so-called 'cheap talk' has been found to reduce the extent of hypothetical bias. Cheap talk refers to giving the respondent explicit instructtions about the problem of hypothetical bias and to directly ask her not to engage in it. There is mixed success in eliminating the difference between hypothetical and actual payments by means of this procedure (cf. Cummings and Taylor 1999, Morrison and Brown 2009). Somehow related to cheap talk is the insight that the payment scenario must be credible from the point of view of the respondent. It has been found that designing the valuation task as a referendum makes the transaction appear to be more realistic, which in turn raises mean WTP estimates (Polome et al. 2006). The fact that the statement of WTP is hypothetical and that misreporting is not associated with a change in actual behavior is one of the reasons for investigating SDR in contingent valuation surveys as discussed in section 4.2.

Another form of distortion, so-called strategic bias occurs when a respondent misstates her WTP for strategic reasons regarding the provision of the public good to be valued (Mitchell and Carson 1989). According to Venkatachalam (2004), this bias can generally have two forms, either free riding or overpledging. Free riding occurs when a respondent intentionally understates her true WTP because she expects others' payments to be sufficient for the provision of the public good. This type of strategic behavior occurs most notably when respondents believe that upon implementation of the project payments really have to be made according to stated WTP. That way, the respondent would end up paying less than others but would still receive the benefits of the public good. This idea harks back to Samuelson's (1954) concerns about free riding in situations where public goods have to be financed. Overpledging occurs when a respondent intentionally overreports her WTP in order to influence the decision about the provision of the public good. For overpledging to exist it is necessary that the respondent believes that future contributions to the good are not based on the WTP statements. If this is the case, her excessively high WTP statement would unduly influence the decision whether to implement the project but she would end up paying just as much as any other citizen. In order to overcome the problem of deliberate misstatement of WTP a strand within the CVM literature deals with incentive properties of the different elicitation formats (cf. Carson et al. 2001, Carson and Groves 2007). The objective of these efforts is the development of an incentive compatible elicitation mechanism that induces respondents to report their true WTP. While it is clear already that binary elicitation formats such as single-bounded DC theoretically provide sufficient incentive for respondents to reveal their true WTP (Carson and Groves 2007), a mechanism that also generates incentive compatible responses empirically still has to be devised (cf. Schläpfer and Bräuer 2007). However, many studies find that from the empirical perspective strategic bias is not such a severe problem, if measures are taken to avoid any mentioning of the hypothetical nature of the elicitation question (Griffin et al. 1995, Schulze et al. 1981). It is argued that respondents would need a much greater extent of information than is usually supplied in a CVM scenario in order to behave strategically.

Related to the strategic misrepresentation of WTP is another issue largely unresolved so far: the identification of protest responses (cf. Dziegielewska and Mendelsohn 2007, Halstead et al. 1992, Meyerhoff and Liebe 2006). Some respondents may state a zero WTP merely because they oppose the idea of putting a price on nature or any feature of the project and payment scenarios and not because they really do not value the good at all. Others may state an unrealistically high WTP for the same reason, which, too, cannot be counted as meaningful WTP response. These positive outliers also distort estimates of mean WTP. Respondents who intentionally state an exaggerated WTP amount to express protest influence the sample mean in an overproportinal way, which leads to the wrong estimate of an environmental good's social value. What is usually done in such situations is to identify the protest respondents, discard them from the survey sample and recalculate mean WTP (cf. Jorgensen et al. 1999). The potentially resulting selection bias can be avoided by applying appropriate sample selection models (cf. Strazzera et al. 2003). However, no consistent and objective procedure for the identification of protest respondents has been developed until now. The main reason for this is that the meaning of protest beliefs may vary with the elicitation format, the good to be valued and certain demographic characteristics of the respondent (Jorgensen and Syme 2000). Usually a set of attitudinal questions is employed to detect protest responses. By this technique, the researcher hopes to identify those respondents who hold views opposing the valuation technique, the payment vehicle or any other methodological feature of the survey and therefore falsely state a WTP of zero ("protest zeros"). However, the interpretation of these so-called protest beliefs is often difficult and thus the exclusion of protest respondents becomes rather arbitrary. Although some strategies for the identification of protest respondents have been put forward, there is still no agreement in the literature on which procedure effectively achieves this objective. Dziegielewska and Mendelson (2007) for instance only use those protest beliefs which differ between those who accept and reject a certain bid. These authors classify only those respondents as protesters who reject all DC questions in that survey, respond zero to the follow-up OE question and agree with statements which are recognized as protest beliefs on both a theoretical and empirical basis. In contrast to that, Meyerhoff and Liebe (2006) find that discarding certain respondents on the basis of some protest beliefs is indefensible. These authors still observe a lack of "established protocols for excluding protest responses" (p. 585). They investigate the motivations underlying protest beliefs and find that these do not differ between respondents who are willing and not willing to pay. Therefore they conclude that excluding respondents by means of such protest belief questions should not be applied. Overall, these examples demonstrate that the question of how to deal with protest responses remains controversial among CVM practitioners.

The influence of psychological and sociological concepts on CVM surveys

In recent years, an increasing fraction of CVM studies has applied psychological and sociological approaches to investigate remaining flaws and drawbacks of the method. Researchers applying psychological concepts with practical valuation surveys aim at a better understanding of the processes within a respondent leading to the statement of WTP (e.g. Fischer 2003, Frör 2008, Loomes 2006). Many of these authors challenge the assumption that respondents in a contingent valuation survey behave in a fully rational manner. Yet, this assumption underlies the welfare theoretical basis of environmental valuation by means of WTP statements (cf. section 2.1.2). Both Loomes (2006) and Frör (2008) contest that the assumptions of conventional economic theory hold for respondents in CVM surveys and claim that the discrepancy between assumption and reality is the source for many biases frequently found in such studies. Loomes (2006, p. 716, 719) distinguishes between two kinds of irregularities in valuation surveys: "excessive sensitivity to theoretically irrelevant factors" and "insufficient sensitivity to theoretically relevant factors". Irregularities of the first category include starting-point and range bias, but any type of situational influences would also go under this label, such as interviewer effects and social desirability. Insufficient sensitivity to theoretically relevant factors refers to part-whole bias, also called embedding (cf. Cummings et al. 1986, Heberlein et al. 2005, Kahneman and Knetsch 1992). This bias describes the observation that elicited valuations in the form of WTP do not vary sufficiently with respect to the quantity of the good being evaluated. Many studies have found that mean WTP estimates for a certain good and another good that contains this good as one part do not differ significantly (e.g. Bateman et al. 1997, Desvousges et al. 1993, Kahneman and Knetsch 1992), which – according to conventional economic theory – they should as long as the marginal utility of that good is strictly positive. Consequently, Loomes (2006) calls for a psychological perspective on CVM that explicitly takes into account the cognitive shortcomings of human-beings when asked to evaluate unfamiliar environmental amenities.

In a somewhat more practical approach, Frör (2008) uses a psychological question inventory to classify the type of information processing of respondents when answering a WTP question. By means of this inventory respondents can be categorized to either apply an intuitive-experiential or an analytical-rational information processing mode. While intuitive-experiential respondents in this model strive for a minimization of cognitive effort and make use of heuristics and past experience, analytical-rational respondents base their WTP statements on systematic and thus slow information processing. The data of this empirical study reveal that both factors have a significant impact on WTP statements and that especially the intuitive-experiential factor is associated with a series of protest beliefs. In a related approach, Fischer and Hanley (2007) are able to identify another dimension of psychological factors which are at work when respondents answer WTP questions. These authors categorize respondents to a CVM survey with a consumer economics background as "cognitive", "emotional", or "reactive". By identifying these decision types, the authors develop a tool to filter out those respondents who do not answer according to neoclassical economic theory. Similar approaches can be found in e.g. Andersson and Svensson (2008), Arana and Leon (2008), or Sauer and Fischer (2010). One common characteristic of all these studies is the psychological point of view on CVM. Rather than assuming that respondents always behave according to neoclassical economic theory, these studies question those assumptions and succeed in empirically detecting response patterns which are different from the conventionally rational patterns. In addition to that, most of these studies employ psychological question inventories to assess cognitive, emotional, or habitual factors that potentially affect WTP statements. In the empirical part of this study, this procedure is applied, as well (cf. chapter 5).

The discussion of rational and non-rational behavior in general, and in particular within the framework of survey-based environmental valuation, has also found its way into sociological research. Liebe (2007) makes the case for a sociological perspective on the valuation of public environmental goods by means of surveys. His main point is that a consistent model of behavioral theory to account for the wide range of biases in CVM studies is not provided by any branch of economics but by sociological models of behavior instead. Consequently, he provides an overview of the implications of some very influential sociological theories of behavior and highlights their relationship with the assessment of WTP statements in CVM surveys.[4] When CVM survey results are analyzed the theoretical point of view can be broadened beyond the rather narrow interpretation of WTP statements as indicators of utility changes of households, which is propagated by neoclassical welfare economics. By stating a WTP for an environmental project a respondent might also express a certain attitude not only towards the good itself but also towards the process of its provision, the interview process, or even other aspects of society or government. The sociological perspective on CVM interprets the survey interview as a situational decision task that should be analyzed by taking into account all behavioral demands and motivations of that situation. In accordance with these theoretical advances, several studies have already empirically investigated the influence of social norms (Blamey 1998) or environmental attitudes (Kotchen and Reiling 2000) on WTP statements in contingent valuation surveys. The present study takes up this perspective on the process of responding to WTP questions and in chapter 3 develops a theoretical model of response behavior. While this model has its roots in sociology, the question inventories for the assessment of the factors of the model originate in psychological research. In this respect, the approach of

4 These approaches include the theory of planned behavior (Ajzen 1991), the low-cost hypothesis (Diekmann and Preisendorfer 2003), and the norm-activation model (Schwartz 1977).

this study combines both sociological and psychological perspectives on the behavioral determinants of WTP statements.

This section gave an overview of certain methodological challenges of the CVM. Certain types of biases are associated with the specific form of the elicitation question. While starting-point bias might occur with the DC or bidding game format, the payment card approach potentially suffers from range and centering bias. Additionally, hypothetical and strategic bias are forms of misrepresentation of WTP statements that might occur with any elicitation format. Another unresolved issue in CVM research is the existence of protest respondents. If some respondents falsely state a zero WTP because they oppose some technical feature of the project description or survey process, it is very difficult to separate these from true zeros. Finally, this section introduced several attempts of CVM researchers to make use of psychological and sociological concepts. Analyzing the task of stating a WTP for an environmental good in a survey from an interdisciplinary perspective might help to remedy some of the biases discussed above. This idea is taken up again in chapters 3 and 4 when the importance of socially desirable responding in CVM surveys is discussed.

2.2.2. Econometric approaches to assess environmental values

In the following, practical econometric estimation techniques of WTP and its determinants will be displayed. However, before the specific models can be introduced, a note on some sampling issues in contingent valuation studies seems appropriate at this point. The CVM is a sample survey technique (Mitchell and Carson 1989), which means that not all households in a certain study area are interviewed but that a sample of households is selected, which are representative of the whole population. While for testing purposes convenience sampling may be applied, the only permissible (and therefore most frequent) sampling technique for actual survey implementation is probability sampling (Arrow et al. 1993, Carson and Hanemann 2005). This approach implies that every household of the population of interest has a positive and equal probability of being selected into the actual sample. This also means that this probability must not depend in any way on the choices that respondents make. This is often the case when users of a public park for instance are intercepted at the park entrance and asked to be interviewed. In this case only individuals that access the park have a chance to be interviewed, but those who do not enter it are systematically excluded. In case the target population is the general public, this would result in an impairment of the representativeness of the survey sample.

If the survey is to cover a big geographical area, stratified sampling can be applied. According to this approach, different subsamples in certain locations are defined according to the characteristics of the population in those areas. The aggregation of those subsamples then yields a sample representative of the overall population. Sometimes also cluster sampling is employed, whereby households in the vicinity of one location are interviewed to lower transportation costs of interviewers. The drawback of this approach, however, is the reduction in statistical efficiency of the resulting sample (Carson and Hanemann 2005). That means inferences of findings with respect to the general population cannot be made as conveniently as by means of probability sampling.

When it comes to the practical estimation of WTP and its determinants, one basically has to distinguish between continuous WTP data on the one hand and binary and interval data on the other. Continuous data result from the open-ended elicitation format and are rather easy to deal with as discussed in the first part of this subsection. Binary data originating from dichotomous choice questions and interval data elicited by the payment card approach require a more sophisticated estimation model, which is presented below. All those estimation models usually serve two objectives. One is the calculation of mean WTP of a sample of households, and the other is the analysis of determinants of WTP, such as a respondent's socio-demographic characteristics, political and environmental attitudes, and so on. The latter objective is important to assess the validity and reliability of a certain CV study and to characterize those groups in society that benefit most or least from an environmental project. Hypotheses about the influence of certain characteristics of the household on WTP can be tested in this way.

When the open-ended elicitation format is being employed, the estimation of mean WTP from a sample and determinants of WTP is very simple. Since for each respondent a precise figure of stated WTP is recorded, the sample's mean WTP is equal to the arithmetic mean of all individual WTP amounts. The 95%-confidence intervals of this mean WTP estimator can easily be computed according to well-established textbook techniques. The mean WTP is necessary to calculate the overall WTP of a population. Since this amount is an average over all respondents in the representative sample, it can simply be multiplied by the total number of households in the affected area. This results in the aggregated WTP of that population, which is usually interpreted as the social value of a proposed environmental project. Very often it is also meaningful to report the median WTP, the calculation of which is equally straightforward. The median WTP is that amount that splits an increasing list of all WTP statements exactly into two equal halves. In other words it is the WTP statement which exactly 50% of all respondents would support because their WTP is either equal or higher than that amount.

Unlike the mean, the median is not influenced by positive (or negative) outliers, i.e. WTP amounts that by far exceed the range of amounts stated by the majority of respondents. Therefore, the median is a valuable indicator for policymakers and other potential addressees of CVM surveys alike. Typically the median is lower than the mean WTP estimator due to the fact that the distribution is not symmetric, which in turn results from the high number of zero responses (e.g. in Kahneman and Knetsch 1992). In order to arrive at the second objective, the identification of determinants of WTP statements, regression techniques with WTP as dependent and a set of socio-demographic and attitudinal characteristics as explanatory variables are employed. However, because of the high fraction of zero responses a regression approach employing ordinary least squares (OLS) is inappropriate. Using this approach in spite of the large number of zeros would yield biased parameter estimates (cf. Amemiya 1984). Instead censored regression techniques, such as the tobit model are necessary for this computation (Halstead et al. 1991, Tobin 1958).

The more interesting case is the analysis of WTP from dichotomous choice and payment card data. Both the calculation of mean WTP and the identification of determinants of WTP require estimation models which are a bit more sophisticated than for the case of OE data. The basic model was developed by Hanemann (1984) for the single-bounded DC case and Cameron and Huppert (1989) for PC data. Despite the existence of several good texts that deal with this topic, the discussion freely follows these two fundamental papers as well as the exposition in chapter two of the book by Haab and McConnell (2002). Since the empirical analysis of the present thesis deals with procedural aspects of CVM it does not seem necessary to discuss different statistical models in detail. Instead the most basic approach to estimate mean WTP, the so-called random utility model (RUM) with linear income will be employed.

In contrast to OE responses, the DC format produces binary data that indicate whether a household with certain characteristics accepts or rejects a certain bid amount. Therefore, a decision model based on the characteristics of that household is needed, for which the welfare theoretical background displayed in section 2.1.2 provides a natural starting-point. It is assumed that household h has the following indirect utility function

$$v_h = v_h(I_h, z_i, s_h). \tag{2.12}$$

For the two possible states of the environmental good z_i, $i = 0$ is the original situation and $i = 1$ is the situation after the CV scenario has been implemented. Further, I_h denotes the household's discretionary income; s_h is the vector of all the household's demographic and socio-economic characteristics as well as attitudinal and interview variables. Since z_i denotes a public good, the consumption level of which is equal for each household by definition, it is not indexed with h but only with i because it changes as a result of the environmental project described in the scenario. When confronted with the question whether it is willing to pay the bid amount t_h for the proposed project, household h answers 'yes', if the utility level in the final state $i = 1$ is still at least as high as in the original situation $i = 0$, i.e. if

$$v_h(I_h - t_h, z_1, s_h) \geq v_h(I_h, z_0, s_h). \tag{2.13}$$

Note that on the left-hand side of the inequality, which describes the utility level after the proposed project has been implemented, the household's income is reduced by the amount of the bid t_h. The problem of the researcher is that she cannot directly observe the indirect utility function of the household. Therefore, in order to derive an estimation model for the analysis of WTP statements the utility function in 2.13 is modeled as a random variable consisting of a deterministic and a stochastic component. It follows that

$$v_h(I_h, z_i, s_h) = \hat{v}_h(I_h, z_i, s_h) + \varepsilon_{ih} \tag{2.14}$$

with ε_{ih} representing the stochastic part of the indirect utility function. While the deterministic component $\hat{v}_h(\cdot)$ is a function of the observable characteristics of the household, such as income I_h, the state of the environmental good and all socio-demographic attributes, and can therefore be modeled by the researcher, the stochastic term ε_{ih} is unknown to the researcher. Included in the latter term are all kinds of private information of the respondent. With this stochastic extension the model becomes a random utility model (RUM). The framework for the analysis of such models was developed by McFadden (1974). What is also observable by the researcher is the actual binary response, i.e. whether the household accepts or rejects the bid t_h. With this information the probability that a certain bid t_h is accepted and thus 2.13 holds is given by

$$\Pr(yes_h) = \Pr(v_h(I_h - t_h, z_1, s_h) \geq \hat{v}_h(I_h, z_0, s_h)). \tag{2.15}$$

Applying the RUM form of the indirect utility function according to 2.14, the probability of household h stating a 'yes' response reads

$$\begin{aligned} \Pr(yes_h) &= \Pr(\hat{v}_h(I_h - t_h, z_1, s_h) + \varepsilon_{1h} \geq \hat{v}_h(I_h, z_0, s_h) + \varepsilon_{0h}) \\ &= \Pr(\hat{v}_h(I_h - t_h, z_1, s_h) - \hat{v}_h(I_h, z_0, s_h) \geq \varepsilon_{0h} - \varepsilon_{1h}). \end{aligned} \tag{2.16}$$

The interpretation of 2.16 is as follows. The household accepts the bid t_h if the observable utility difference between the two states before and after the implementation of the environmental project is at least as great as the difference between the error terms in the two states. In order to further rearrange the notation, the utility difference can alternatively be expressed as $\Delta\hat{v}_h = \hat{v}_h(I_h - t_h, z_1, s_h) - \hat{v}_h(I_h, z_0, s_h)$ and the difference of the error terms simply as $\varepsilon_h = \varepsilon_{0h} - \varepsilon_{1h}$, which is also a random variable. Following this and specifying $F_\varepsilon(\cdot)$ as the cumulative distribution function of ε_h the probability that the household accepts the bid reads

$$\Pr(yes_h) = \Pr(\varepsilon_h \leq \Delta\hat{v}_h) = F_\varepsilon(\Delta\hat{v}_h). \tag{2.17}$$

The next step is the specification of a functional form of the utility function as well as the choice of a probability distribution of the random term ε_h. The simplest approach of specifying the utility function is to assume a form that is linear in income and other observable characteristics of the household s_h. For now, these other variables are aggregated in α but a model to explicitly include these variables will be introduced below. The deterministic observable utility difference can thus be expressed as

$$\Delta\hat{v}_h = [\alpha_1 + \beta(I_h - t_h)] - [\alpha_0 + \beta I_h] \tag{2.18}$$

$$= \alpha - \beta t_h \tag{2.19}$$

with $\alpha = \alpha_1 - \alpha_0$. It should be noted that this is the easiest specification to be found in the relevant literature. There is a variety of other functional forms of indirect utility, for instance in Haab and McConnell (2002, p. 36ff) and Hanemann and Kanninen (1999). However, since the focus of this study is not the effects of different econometric approaches on WTP estimates but issues regarding survey methodology, it seems sufficient to employ this simple approach.

Having specified the form of the indirect utility function, the next step is to say something more about the form of the distribution of the error term ε_h. Again, to keep the model as simple as possible, it is assumed that this variable is independently and identically distributed. On top of that it is assumed that ε_h is normally distributed. In this case, it holds that $F_\varepsilon(\Delta\hat{v}_h) = \Phi(\Delta\hat{v}_h)$ with $\Phi(\cdot)$ being the standard normal cumulative distribution function. Since this assumption also implies that the error terms are normally distributed with mean of 0 and a variance of 1, i.e. $\varepsilon_h \sim N(0,1)$, the resulting estimation model is a probit model. In order to estimate this model, the parameters α and β have to be normalized to α/σ and β/σ due to the normal distribution of the error terms. Consequently, the probability of household h accepting bid t_h is $\Phi(\alpha/\sigma - (\beta/\sigma)t_h)$. Alternatively, instead of the standard normal distribution of the error term the standard logistic distribution can be assumed. In this case, the likelihood of stating a 'yes' response is

$$F_\varepsilon(\Delta\hat{v}_h) = \left(1 + e^{-\Delta\hat{v}_h}\right)^{-1} = \left(1 + e^{-\left(\frac{\alpha}{\sigma} - \frac{\beta}{\sigma} t_h\right)}\right)^{-1}. \tag{2.20}$$

However, the only difference between the two distributions is the fact that the logistic distribution has fatter tails, so the results of the two estimation approaches only differ very slightly. Therefore, the present illustration continues to assume the standard normal distribution of the error terms. So, with the above parametric specification the calculation of the WTP is very straightforward. If the WTP of household h is exactly equal to the bid, i.e. $WTP_h = t_h$, the utility difference between the two states before and after the implementation of the environmental project is zero. Consequently, it holds that $0 = \alpha - \beta \cdot WTP_h$ which can be rearranged into

$$WTP_h = \frac{\alpha}{\beta}. \tag{2.21}$$

One useful consequence of the assumption of the standard normal (or standard logistic) form of the distribution of the error terms is that the WTP measure in 2.21 is both the mean and the median. This is the result of the symmetry of the standard normal (or standard logistic) distribution function.

In order to fill these functions with data and practically estimate the parameters α and β the maximum likelihood approach is employed. Therefore, the likelihood function of the single-bounded DC elicitation format reads

$$L(\alpha,\beta|t_h) = \prod_{h=1}^{H} \left[\Phi\left(\frac{\alpha}{\sigma} - \frac{\beta}{\sigma} t_h\right)\right]^{yes_h} \left[1 - \Phi\left(\frac{\alpha}{\sigma} - \frac{\beta}{\sigma} t_h\right)\right]^{1-yes_h}. \tag{2.22}$$

In this form, $yes_h = 1$ indicates that household h accepts bid t_h and $yes_h = 0$ stands for a rejection of that bid. Since the multiplicative form of the likelihood function is somehow hard to compute, what is normally used is the log-likelihood function of the form

$$\begin{aligned} \ln L(\alpha,\beta|t_h) = \sum_{h=1}^{H} yes_h \cdot \ln\left[\Phi\left(\frac{\alpha}{\sigma} - \frac{\beta}{\sigma} t_h\right)\right] \\ +(1 - yes_h) \cdot \ln\left[1 - \Phi\left(\frac{\alpha}{\sigma} - \frac{\beta}{\sigma} t_h\right)\right]. \end{aligned} \tag{2.23}$$

Again, $yes_h = 0,1$ is an indicator of the household accepting or rejecting the bid. Through an iterative process those parameters of α and β are determined that maximize this function.

The same log-likelihood function can be derived for the case when the PC format is used to elicit WTP statements. Employing this elicitation format, the lower and upper limits of the payment card interval that the household chooses can be interpreted as two bids. Applying the logic of the DC model, the household accepts the lower bid t^{low} because its WTP is greater than that bid. At the same time it rejects the upper bid t^{high} because if its WTP exceeded that bid it could as well have chosen the next higher PC interval. In this case the log-likelihood function has the form

$$\ln L\left(\alpha, \beta \middle| t_h^{low}, t_h^{high}\right) = \sum_{h=1}^{H} \ln\left[\Phi\left(\frac{\alpha}{\sigma} - \frac{\beta}{\sigma} t_h^{high}\right) - \Phi\left(\frac{\alpha}{\sigma} - \frac{\beta}{\sigma} t_h^{low}\right)\right]. \quad (2.24)$$

In the empirical part of this study the PC format will be used exclusively, so 2.24 is the log-likelihood function that is used for the computation of α and β, which in turn serve to calculate mean WTP. The calculations of the empirical investigation reported in chapter 5 are executed by means of the statistical software package LIMDEP, version 9.0 (cf. Greene 2007). Note that at this point one could argue that with PC data the researcher could as well calculate the midpoints of each PC interval and simply perform a tobit regression like for OE data. However, Cameron and Huppert (1989) demonstrate that this approach leads to biased estimators of mean WTP and that also the extent of that bias depends on the specification and size of the intervals on the PC. Therefore, these authors argue, the maximum likelihood approach to compute willingness to pay estimates from PC data should be used.

For the case of this maximum likelihood model the computation of the 95%-confidence intervals of the WTP estimators is not as straightforward as with the employment of OE data in the tobit model. Instead, in order to arrive at boundaries of the confidence intervals for DC and PC data, the so-called bootstrapping method must be applied because the estimators are ratios of random variables. Several of these approaches have been developed (cf. Cooper 1994), and the present study will employ the procedure devised in Park et al. (1991).[5] According to this approach, 1000 WTP values are artificially computed on the basis of the estimated parameters of α and β. Subsequently, these WTP values are ordered and the first and last 25 values (corresponding to the upper and lower 2.5% tails of the distribution) are cut off. The remaining first and last values of the list of computations are the lower and upper boundaries of the 95%-confidence interval.

---

5 Note that Park et al. (1991) develop the bootstrapping method for WTP estimates derived by means of logit regression. Yet, the same approach can be used in connection with probit regression, which is applied in this study.

In order to arrive at the second objective of the analysis of CVM data generated by the DC or PC formats, the identification of determinants of WTP statements, the linear specification of the utility difference model in 2.19 has to be extended by a set of potentially influential explanatory variables. So, the linear utility difference model becomes

$$\Delta\hat{v}_h = \alpha - \beta t_h + \gamma_j s_{hj} \tag{2.25}$$

with the j-dimensional (column) vector s_h denoting J characteristics of household h and γ_j representing the j-dimensional (row) vector of J coefficients of these characteristics. By means of the maximum likelihood model specified above, parameters for the coefficient vector γ are estimated in the same way as α and β are computed. Depending on their respective sign, those coefficients with a sufficient level of significance are then an indicator of a positive of negative impact of their respective characteristics s_{hj} on WTP. In the empirical part of this study in chapter 5, both the computation of mean WTP estimators and the identification of determinants of WTP by means of 2.25 will be applied.

2.2.3. Contingent valuation in China

In China, the history of the CVM is comparatively short and almost exclusively limited to the last decade. Accordingly, the number of empirical applications in the Middle Kingdom is increasing but still manageable, especially regarding English language publications. Environmental goods valued in such surveys include reduced air-pollution (Hammitt and Zhou 2006, Wang and Mullahy 2006, Wang et al. 2006, Wang et al. 2007), different kinds of ecosystem services (Xu et al. 2003, Xu et al. 2006, Yang et al. 2008), urban biodiversity conservation and recreation amenities (Chen and Jim 2010, Jim and Chen 2006b), water quality (Day and Mourato 2002, Du 1998), ground water resources (Wei et al. 2007), and basic health insurance of informal sector workers (Bärnighausen et al. 2007). Beyond CVM, Zhai and Suzuki (2008) is the only study to be found in the literature that applies choice experiments in a Chinese context. Their survey elicits WTP statements for environmental management including water quality and pollution control in a coastal area in Northern China. In addition to that, there are also an increasing number of studies published in Chinese journals (e.g. Lin and Chen 2005, Niu et al. 2005, Zhang et al. 2003, Zhao et al. 2005). Survey topics cover a wide range including for example the valuation of urban mass transit service or ecosystems services of an urban river. However, except the studies by Xu and colleagues (Xu et al. 2003, Xu et al. 2006) and Wei et al. (2007), all quoted CVM studies are conducted in major cities in the more industrialized eastern and central parts of the country. Applications of survey-based valuation studies in rural areas of West and Southwest China cannot be found so far. Wei and colleagues conduct a CVM survey in the North China Plain, a rural region located around the capital Beijing. Their data reveal a very low mean WTP for in situ groundwater and an overall very low level of education of respondents. The authors regard the finding that valuation estimates by far fall short of actual protection and restoration costs as evidence for the inappropriateness of employing the CVM in rural areas of China. This shows the need for more research on the applicability of the CVM in rural contexts such as the background of the survey presented in this study.

Most studies quoted above merely aim at the valuation of environmental goods and scrutinizing the applicability of the CVM in China. Only very few studies tackle methodological problems. Xu et al. (2006) for instance compare different forms of the elicitation question in a survey conducted in rural Northwest China. Their results show that mean WTP estimates using the single-bounded and double-bounded DC approach exceed those elicited by means of a PC by a factor of seven to nine. The authors hold excessive yea-saying responsible for this striking discrepancy. In a study to value water quality improvements in an urban lake in the central Chinese city of Wuhan, Du (1998) compares contingent valuation and travel cost estimates and finds similar results. Regarding the survey administration mode, CVM surveys in China rely exclusively on in-person interviews. No application employing mail, telephone or internet-based techniques could be found in the literature.

CVM research in China – very much like all types of survey research – faces certain challenges that differ from surveys in Western countries and also in other developing countries. Firstly, since the CVM and all survey research is associated with asking questions and this in turn involves personal interactions of some kind, the cultural context is of importance for such studies. The impact of cultural differences on survey responses has long been acknowledged in many scientific fields (cf. Middleton and Jones 2000) but appears to be insufficiently taken into account in survey-based environmental valuation. The particular cultural background of China is dealt with in section 3.2.4, and implications for the use of surveys to value environmental goods will be discussed in more detail. Secondly, conducting CVM studies in transformation countries might be more challenging than in well-established market economies. Due to the legacy of the centrally planned economy in pre-reform China, respondents might not be as experienced with the concept of market prices and the information that they convey. Therefore, asking for a WTP for some environmental amenity might work differently in such societies than in Europe or North America where the CVM was originally devised. These concerns add to the above rationales for launching a conceptual study to investigate the influence of socially desirable responding on CVM responses in the Chinese context.

2.3. Summary

This chapter provided an introduction to environmental valuation and the contingent valuation method in particular. Rationales for the economic valuation of environmental goods were provided and the concept of total economic value (TEV) was introduced. The TEV of an environmental good consists of both use and non-use values, which in turn can be broken down to more subtle categories of value. Subsequently, environmental values from the perspective of neoclassical welfare theory were discussed and on this basis the concept of the Hicksian Compensating Variation as a measure of utility changes induced by environmental projects was derived. The Compensating Variation can be interpreted as the willingness to pay of a household for a public environmental project. The assessment of such a WTP is the objective of the CVM, which – after briefly portraying a variety of direct and indirect valuation methods – constituted the focus of the rest of the chapter. Therefore, in the second part of this chapter the CVM was introduced in detail and practical issues such as questionnaire design, administration mode, and different elicitation formats were discussed. Subsequently, the basic econometric approaches for analyzing CVM data were introduced. This included the discussion of sampling issues as well as the derivation of practical estimation models for mean WTP and WTP determinants. These models will be used in the empirical part of this study to investigate the influence of socially desirable responding on WTP statements. Due to the practical application of a CVM survey in Southwest China reported on in this study, this chapter closed with a short overview of the development of this field of research in China.

Chapter 3

Social desirability

3.1. Outline of the chapter

Social desirability bias is one of the most frequently quoted response biases in the social sciences and is regularly held responsible for distorting any kind of survey data. Therefore, this response bias is addressed in many different disciplines, and the approaches for its definition, identification and mitigation are manifold. Originally located in the field of socio-psychological research, the exact nature and conditions of the occurrence of socially desirable responding were soon also investigated by sociologists and survey methodologists. Today, concerns for the biasing influence of SDR can be found in almost every discipline that employs surveys as a means of data collection. Yet, the importance of SDR for many different scientific disciplines has also brought about a wide range of different definitions and conceptualizations of this phenomenon. Thus, this chapter introduces the concept of socially desirable responding (SDR) and its components both from the socio-psychological and sociological point of view. As will become clear in the course of the chapter, several factors jointly constitute the phenomenon labeled as SDR. The first of these factors is need for social approval, the concept of which is discussed at length in section 3.2. Opposed to this conceptualization of SDR as a persistent characteristic of the respondent's personality, so-called trait desirability is identified as another component of SDR. This component is rather dependent on the topic of a survey question and describes the level of desirability of certain response options.

While psychologists are more concerned about the definition of the phenomenon and methods for its measurement, sociological research in this field rather deals with the question to what extent SDR constitutes measurement error in question inventories that have other objectives. Sociological research is reliant upon survey data about people's behavior. Since both sociologists and CVM practitioners are trying to assess certain behavior of individuals by means of self-reports, the discussion of SDR in sociology stresses the relevance of this bias for environmental valuation. As the overall objective of this study is to investigate the influence of SDR on responses in contingent valuation surveys, the relationship between the different conceptualizations of SDR and the stating of WTP amounts is discussed at several points in this section.

Subsequently, in section 3.2.4 the role of social norms for the existence of SDR is analyzed. As will become clear in that section, social norms are the basis on which individuals judge certain responses or patterns of behavior to be desirable or undesirable. It is with the knowledge about the importance of social norms that conjectures of the existence of SDR in specific surveys can be made. It has to be scrutinized if there are sufficiently clear and widely known social norms that govern attitudes and behavior associated with the natural environment and environmental protection. If this is the case, concern for the occurrence of SDR in contingent valuation surveys is warranted. Similarly, since the empirical part of this study is based on a survey conducted in Southwest China, the question of how notions of desirability change across cultures has to be discussed. As social norms change from culture to culture, so do the perceptions of social desirability. This discussion will serve as justification for the modification of existing SDR question inventories developed by Western researchers in section 5.2.

Another focus of sociological research on SDR is the question of which components actually make up that construct. After presenting several early empirical approaches to investigate the joint influence of several components of SDR on survey responses, the second main part of the chapter, section 3.3, develops a behavioral model of socially desirable responding. As will become clear through the discussion of the basic socio-psychological concepts in section 3.2, SDR consists of three factors – need for social approval, lack of total anonymity of the interview situation and a perceived difference in the desirability level of different response options (trait desirability). By employing the theory of rational choice a decision model of the respondent is developed that provides a framework to explain how the factors work together. The exposition of that behavioral model closes with a detailed introduction of the three factors and the specification of their relationship. The non-compensatory nature of this relationship is the basis for the multiplicative model of SDR that is developed in chapter 4 and empirically tested in chapter 5. Eventually, section 3.4 provides a summary.

3.2. Socially desirable responding

3.2.1. The concept of socially desirable responding

The survey interview is one major tool of data collection in the social sciences including the valuation of non-market goods. However, when individuals in interview situations are asked to give reports about their own behavior, attitudes, intentions or valuation of certain goods or amenities, it is likely that their responses are triggered not only by the actual question stimulus. Instead, other factors such as the interview situation, their current mood, social and cultural norms, and the presence and specific appearance of the interviewer might influence their answers. Following this logic, a response bias is defined as the "systematic tendency to respond to a range of questionnaire items on some basis other than the specific item content" (Paulhus 1991, p. 17). This means that these other factors together with the actual "item content" or "question stimulus" jointly determine the response. According to Paulhus (1991, 2002) there are two forms of response bias. If the bias is consistent over different situations over time, it is labeled *response style*. If the response bias is a temporary phenomenon being the result of a situational demand it is referred to as *response set*.

One of the most frequently analyzed response biases[6] in social sciences is socially desirable responding (SDR).[7] Defining this concept is not easy, since many different definitions have been put forward, and Helmes (2000) even argues that a formal definition is completely missing. According to this author, the lack of such a formal definition has been fuelling the debate over both theoretical conceptualizations and practical approaches in social desirability research for decades. However, in the following paragraphs an overview of approaches to define and describe this phenomenon is given and its relevant features are discussed.

In a very profound overview of advances in social desirability research up to that point in time, DeMaio (1984) assembles several definitions of this concept. The author's quintessence from these descriptions results in two assertions. Firstly, she sums up that statements by respondents to survey interviews can somehow be classified as "good" or "bad", and secondly, that the wish to be perceived in a good way makes individuals choose to report "good" statements rather than "bad" ones. Of course good and bad are very hazy descriptions of behavior, but it is at the point where these notions have to be defined that social norms enter the stage. Social and cultural norms are the basis, on the grounds of which statements about characteristics or behavior can be judged as "good" or "bad". This becomes apparent when the

6 Acquiescence, another often studied response bias, is not subject of this study because, in contrast to SDR, it is content independent (Esser 1991), that means respondents give an answer regardless of the item content. Wiggins (1964) further mentions extreme response style. The difference of SDR and these concepts is discussed below.

7 In the literature the term social desirability (SD) is used most frequently and denotes the same concept. However, throughout this study this phenomenon will be termed socially desirable responding (SDR).

same author quotes Stricker (1963, p. 320) saying that “norms favor the reporting of approved behavior and opinions and the denial of disapproved ones”. This indicates the role of social norms which separate a set of possible responses to a question into “approved” or “good” ones on the one hand and “disapproved” or “bad” ones on the other. Furthermore, two strategies in which to respond in a socially desirable manner become apparent at this point, i.e. overly claiming approved behavior or characteristics and completely rejecting disapproved ones. The role of social norms and their connection to social desirability as well as a further elaboration of the two strategies mentioned above is discussed in a more detailed manner below.

Another very simple and catchy definition of SDR is given by Paulhus (1991, p. 16) describing it as "the tendency to give answers that make the respondent look good". Although the question of what is “good” is not addressed in this definition either, it contains the idea that the intention of a respondent when answering a survey question is not (only) the conveyance of some specific response content but also the pursuit of other goals (Gove and Geerken 1977). With DeMaio’s (1984) definition of the concept as “the overall tendency of a person to respond in a desirable manner”, the idea becomes somewhat clearer. Again, not only does the content of a question determine how it is being answered, but other factors influence the form of the response. One of these other factors or potential goals that the respondent might want to attain is termed *social approval* by Crowne and Marlowe (1964). It is these authors that first describe SDR as the *need for social approval*. The relationship between the pursuit of social approval and the biasing of a response is given by the fact that certain statements are perceived as more and others as less socially desirable. By complying with what social desirability demands, an individual is able to receive approval from the outside, i.e. from a group of bystanders, from the interviewer, or from her fellow citizens. Thus, what Paulhus (1991) refers to as “look good” is in fact an answer that complies with what is socially desirable, and this in turn is determined by social norms and beliefs. This is further reflected in Hebert et al. (1997, p. 1046) who define social desirability as “the defensive tendency of individuals to respond in a manner consistent with societal norms or beliefs”. To sum this up, when factors other than the semantic question content jointly trigger an individual’s response, response bias is at work. If these factors are social or cultural norms that are perceived by the individual and make certain self-reports or patterns of behavior appear more desirable than others such a response bias is referred to as socially desirable responding (SDR).

For all of the authors mentioned so far, SDR is a response style in that it is a personality characteristic of the individual respondent, which is consistent over time and situations. Opposed to this view is the interpretation of SDR as an item characteristic, i.e. the tendency to give a socially desirable response depending on the specific item content (which corresponds to the conceptualization as response set). Consistent with this view is the definition of SDR by Mick (1996, p. 107) as "a temporary reaction to a situational demand such as time pressure or expected public disclosure of answers". Another term for this interpretation of SDR often found in the literature is *trait desirability* or *SD beliefs*, which is introduced in more detail in subsection 3.3.2. At this point it becomes clear already that when both the individual disposition of the respondent and the specific item content potentially trigger SDR, a possible measure or control instrument for SDR must incorporate both sources (Nederhof 1985). We will come back to the idea of a multi-dimensional SDR measure later.

For the moment, two main research questions arise. Firstly, to what extent does a respondent comply with social norms when answering to questionnaire items, i.e. how strong is the individual influence of social desirability? Secondly, which factors trigger compliance with social norms, i.e. which factors influence the strength of SDR? The present study sets out for the development of a tool to assess socially desirable responding in the framework of survey-based economic valuation of environmental resources. According to the main questions above, both individual differences in SDR and relevant factors of such behavior shall be measured and integrated into one theoretical model. Before these questions can be tackled, the concept of socially desirable responding has to be demarcated from some seemingly similar concepts first.

Differentiating SDR from acquiescence and warm glow

It was mentioned above that SDR is but one type of response bias in surveys.[8] Another frequently observed bias is acquiescence or yea-saying (Couch and Keniston 1960, Cronbach 1950). Paulhus (1991, p. 46) refers to this phenomenon as the "tendency to agree rather than disagree with propositions in general". While this description of acquiescence is correct, it does not cover the entire concept. Its decisive feature is the fact that the likelihood of agreeing to a question is not related to the specific content – acquiescence makes respondents agree to survey items regardless of what is asked (Bachman and O'Malley 1984, Moum 1988). Similarly there is also the tendency to negate items without making any reference to their content, which is named naysaying. The relevant literature is not very clear about the conceptualization of acquiescence as response style or response set (Bachman and O'Malley 1984), which is why it is likely to be both permanent and situational. Krenz

8 Response biases that will not be looked at in this study are extreme response bias (Greenleaf 1992) or midpoint bias. A very good overview of response biases in behavioral research can be found in Podsakoff et al. (2003).

and Sax (1987) describe it as an interaction of a general inclination to agree, which corresponds to the permanent response style, and an impulse to endorse certain item content, which is equivalent to the rather situational response set. Similar to SDR, acquiescence is therefore obviously triggered by both personality and situational factors. Further, Paulhus (1991) accumulates evidence that this bias is more severe for attitudinal questions than for personality tests. The fact that statements in attitudinal surveys are rather complex compared to personality measurement increases the fraction of respondents who are uncertain, and such uncertainty has been observed to result in yea-saying (Krenz and Sax 1987).

At first glance, acquiescence looks very similar to SDR because both phenomena make respondents agree to statements even if they do not entirely (or sometimes even *not at all*) support their content. The difference between the two, however, lies in the specification of yea-saying as *regardless of item content*. For acquiescence to work a respondent has to completely blind out the item content, whereas it is just this very content that social desirability derives its biasing influence from. SDR can only influence response behavior if the item topic is sensitive in the sense that there are social or cultural norms referring to it and which at the same time are perceived by the respondent. The influence of acquiescence works explicitly without relying on reference to question content; it is therefore *content independent* (Esser 1991, Krosnick 1999).

When it comes to survey-based non-market valuation, acquiescence is mostly a problem in dichotomous choice contingent valuation (Blamey et al. 1999). This type of bias might explain why mean WTP from surveys that employ the DC format usually exceed that elicited by means of other question formats such as OE and PC (Frew et al. 2003, Kealy and Turner 1993, Ready et al. 1996, Ryan et al. 2004). In a survey valuing a wetlands improvement program with the DC approach, Kanninen (1995) finds one fifth of the respondents to engage in yea-saying. When the OE or PC approaches are employed, the influence of this bias can be neglected as a result of the specific form of the elicitation question. This claim is supported by the evidence of higher mean WTP in DC contingent valuation discussed in the previous chapter. It should be noted that in contrast to the psychological and sociological literature on yea-saying, studies in contingent valuation also hold social pressure responsible for the occurrence of acquiescence (Blamey et al. 1999, Mitchell and Carson 1989). Since it was defined that acquiescence works regardless of item content, social pressure cannot result from sensitive questions but merely from social conventions that prescribe positive answers independent of item content.

In contrast to that, the concept of warm glow of giving will be excluded from further analysis. This phenomenon, which can simply be referred to as warm glow, describes the fact that certain respondents to a CVM survey derive utility simply from the act of giving something for a good cause, such as the provision of a public environmental good. The theoretical model of this concept can be found in Andreoni (1989, 1990). The utility generation from the act of giving is the result of some moral satisfaction that respondents feel when they support that good cause. This phenomenon has also been found to work in the context of practical contingent valuation where it might distort WTP statements (cf. Hackl and Pruckner 2003, Kahneman and Knetsch 1992, Nunes and Schokkaert 2003). According to this theory, a stated WTP amount does not necessarily reflect the change in utility of a household but is rather a symbolic contribution to the environmental good. The fact that this symbolic contribution is independent of the scope of the environmental good relates warm glow to embedding, i.e. the purchase of moral satisfaction might be an explanation for the embedding effect (cf. section 2.2.1). Kahneman and Knetsch (1992) call attention to the fact that the degree of moral satisfaction that can be derived from contributing to a public good may differ between goods. These authors hold "community values" responseble for these differences. These values are basically social norms. This makes clear one common feature between warm glow and SDR – both are the result of the public good being highly charged with social norms that prescribe a certain pattern of behavior or certain attitudes towards that good. If social norms strongly call for support of the provision of a public good in form of an environmental project (Kahneman and Knetsch (1992) mention "saving the panda" as an example) both warm glow and SDR will predict a higher WTP than for a public good where social norms are less clear-cut. So, are warm glow and socially desirable responding related?

A closer observation of the two phenomena reveals that there are two crucial differences between them. Firstly, for warm glow of giving to be able to generate extra utility for the respondent in a CVM survey no interviewer is necessary. The respondent feels better about herself even if nobody notices her contribution; both the statement and the actual contribution can be completely anonymous and still provide the respondent with extra utility through moral satisfaction. This is not the case for SDR where the presence of an interviewer (or any other outside institution that perceives the WTP response) is critical for this bias to work. It is only such an outside institution that can grant social approval sought for by the respondent. This is not to say that the perception of the contribution by others cannot intensify the effect of warm glow. Hackl and Pruckner (2003) mention "gaining social approbation" as potential source for respondents to feel the warm glow of giving. Yet, this aspect is not critical for warm glow to generate utility in the first place. Further, this feature is not included in the theoretical concept of warm glow as modeled by Andreoni (1989, 1990). In that model, the contribution directly (and positively) enters an individual's utility function, which renders it independent of others' perceiving the act of giving. This aspect is fundamentally different for the case of SDR. Secondly, while SDR is a form of response bias that does not reflect actual economic values, warm glow is part of the utility gain that is generated by the whole process of contributing to and enjoying the benefits of the public good, and therefore part of its value. Since for the measurement of the total value of a public good there is no limitation of what type of 'ingredients' can generate utility, moral satisfaction may very well be one of them (cf. Carson et al. 2001). This is not the case for SDR, which bears no relationship with the actual contribution to and provision of the public good but is merely a methodological artifact arising from the interview situation. Therefore, it does not form part of the value of a public (environmental) good elicited by a contingent valuation survey but merely constitutes a type of measurement error that must be corrected. Even if social approval resulting from a socially desirable WTP statement is interpreted as utility it does not count as portion of the utility change that CVM intends to measure. The above considerations demonstrate why the concepts of warm glow of giving and SDR might look somewhat related at first glance but still differ in some fundamental features. This is why the following analysis will not further investigate the effects of warm glow and exclusively focus on the impact of SDR.

3.2.2. SDR research in psychology – in search of a measurement tool

In the field of psychology, research on social desirability has from its start always been concerned with the definition of the phenomenon and the development of appropriate tools for its measurement. Thus, when looking at the evolution of this concept in this discipline over the last 60 years, it follows that together with differences in the theoretical conceptualization of this phenomenon, different measurement tools focus on different aspects of the concept. Two main theoretical cleavages that never ceased to be discussed in the psychological SDR literature are the following. Firstly, as indicated above, SDR can be interpreted as a persisting characteristic of an individual's personality or as merely momentarily triggered by confronting an individual with certain item content, i.e. being a function of the item rather than of the nature of the respondent. The dualism of personality versus item characteristic is one of the main aspects that have been discussed in social desirability research for decades both in the theoretical field and in the practical application of questionnaire inventories. Secondly, social desirability can be regarded as a meaningful psychological concept in its own right or just as "a source of irrelevant error on a test that should be minimized if not eliminated" (Helmes 2000, p. 21). Theorists have been arguing to what extent different social desirability scales measure a response style, i.e. some measurement error, or just truthful personality characteristics of an individual. After reviewing main landmarks in the historical development of the concept of socially desirable responding in psychological research, these cleavages will be illustrated one by one in greater detail.

Concern about possible response bias and untruthful self-reporting mainly in personnel assessment contexts was raised as early as during the 1930s (Bernreuter 1933), but it was not until the mid-1950s that the first question inventory explicitly constructed for the measurement of the tendency to give socially desirable responses was developed by Edwards (1957). In this study, ten judges were asked to indicate whether yes or no was the more desirable answer to each of the 150 items of the Minnesota Multiphasic Personality Inventory (MMPI), a question inventory of personality assessment originally developed during the 1940s (McKinley et al. 1948). After selecting the 79 items which were unanimously rated by the group of judges, the inventory was further shortened to a 39-item scale, named Edward's Social Desirability Scale (Edwards 1957, Paulhus 1991). According to DeMaio (1984) this measurement tool conceptualizes both the personality characteristic and item characteristic dimensions of social desirability, but stresses the latter. That means this scale only fulfilled its purpose – to measure inter-individual and not inter-item differences in SDR – only partially. It was also Edwards who had shown in a previous study (Edwards 1953) that the social desirability rating of personality statements of the MMPI was highly correlated with the likelihood of them being endorsed by respondents. It was the first time that the relationship between the social desirability level of a self-descriptive statement and the greater probability of its endorsement was empirically investigated (Millham and Jacobson 1978). This finding forms the basis for the conceptualization of SDR as item characteristic (referred to as trait desirability).

Edward's pioneer measurement tool was soon criticized for its psychopathological item content because the items were taken from the MMPI, a tool for the diagnosis of mental illness. In addition to that, many authors were concerned about the high correlations of Edwards' Social Desirability Scale with a wide range of personality tests, especially subscales of the MMPI measuring mental illnesses such as depression or schizophrenia (Millham and Jacobson 1978). Since it obviously did not make sense that only social desirability would explain the most part of inter-individual variance in those personality tests, it was Marlowe and Crowne (1960, 1964) who developed an alternative question inventory that "focused instead on ordinary personal and interpersonal behaviors" (Paulhus 1991, p. 28). These authors paid much attention to reduce the psychopathological implications of item content (DeMaio 1984) in purposely avoiding the use of items of the MMPI. The 33 items of the resulting Marlowe-Crowne Social Desirability Scale consist of either socially desirable but very uncommon or socially undesirable but commonly observed traits and patterns of behavior. In the Marlowe-Crowne Scale, respondents are asked to indicate if a statement is either "true" or "false" regarding themselves. Thus, an individual excessively claiming to possess socially desirable but very uncommon and overly denying socially undesirable but very common traits or patterns of behavior is likely to have biased her responses, i.e. to have a response style. It is Marlowe and Crowne who explicitly focus on the personality characteristic of the SDR concept when they coin the term *need for social approval* (Crowne and Marlowe 1960, 1964, DeMaio 1984) and claim the new scale to be able to measure this construct. According to their conceptualization of need for social approval, individuals differ to the extent that they rely on the evaluative judgements of others, and that in turn these judgements present an incentive to conform to relevant social norms (Millham and Jacobson 1978). Generally speaking, individuals with a high need for social approval can be expected to be more prone to social influence, be it from a single interviewer, from a group of people or society as a whole. The Marlowe-Crowne Social Desirability Scale remains one of the major tools of assessing this phenomenon until today.

Yet, a major shortcoming of this scale was its lack to account for the theoretical and empirical separation of two components within its measurement range, since it was only after its development that advances in social desirability research brought about this theoretical distinction. Basis for these advances in conceptualizing social desirability is the following reflection on the fundamental logic of the Marlowe-Crowne Scale. The goal of receiving social approval can either be reached by claiming socially desirable characteristics for the self or by denying undesirable characteristics. Since the groundbreaking work of Paulhus (1984) these two concepts have gone under the names of *enhancement* and *denial*. It is also clear that these two phenomena do not necessarily have to be perfectly correlated or influence individual behavior to the same extent. In an overview of applications of the Marlowe-Crowne scale during the 1960s and 1970s, Millham and Jacobson (1978) report much empirical evidence that support the assertion that these two phenomena are not equivalent.

A further modification of the concept of social desirability that came up at the end of the 1970s was the distinction between biased statements in front of others and biased statements which even the individual herself believes to be true. Even researchers who had been investigating SDR earlier had already suggested this distinction (Damarin and Messick 1965, Wiggins 1964). For instance a study by Wiggins (1964) reports on a factor analysis that yielded two distinct factors labeled Alpha and Gamma.[9] A theoretical interpretation of these two factors was given by Damarin and Messick (1965) who described them as autistic bias in self-regard and propagandistic bias, thus stressing the different addressees of such response behavior. This is one of the first pieces of evidence of the theoretical distinction between what was later called self-deception and other-deception. This early distinction between alpha and gamma factor was taken up again by Sackheim and Gur (1979) who developed two question inventories to empirically assess these phenomena. However, their so-called self-deception questionnaire and the other-deception questionnaire were never published or widely used in psychological research. Instead, the other-deception questionnaire served as a basis for Delroy Paulhus who refined and modified the items and came to a major breakthrough in social desirability research. In a very influential study (Paulhus 1984), he empirically tested two different two-component models of social desirability. The first model was supposed to empirically distinguish between other-deception and self-deception, which based on earlier work by Wiggins (1964), Damarin and Messick (1965), and Sackheim and Gur (1979) described above. Paulhus introduced the terms *impression management* and *self-deception,* which basically equal the alpha and gamma factors that already Wiggins (1964) had identified. The terms impression management (IM) and self-deception (SED) have been widely used since then. In this context, impression management refers to the presentation of a favorable picture of the self to some outside audience, whereas self-deception describes the overly positive (but not necessarily correct) unconscious self-presentation, which even the respondent herself believes to be true. The term impression management was preferred to other-deception because the latter conveyed the meaning of deliberate lying, which is not meant by this concept. Instead, the IM concept also covers the "habitual presentation of a specific positive public impression" (Paulhus 2002, p. 56) and is therefore more of a personality characteristic than an act of intentional cheating that has to be detected.

The results of this study that factor-analyzed data generated by a wide range of existing social desirability scales[10] clearly supported the impression management versus self-deception model (Paulhus 1984). It could even be demonstrated that those scales that were most strongly associated with the impression management factor (the other deception questionnaire and Wig-

9 A good overview of the development of SDR as a multidimensional concept, which includes all studies quoted in this paragraph, can be found in Paulhus (2002).

10 Paulhus (1984) employed the Marlowe-Crowne SD Scale, Edward's SD Scale, the self-deception questionnaire, the other-deception questionnaire, Wiggins' SD Scale and a subscale of the MMPI, the so-called Lie Scale. It was not until the second out of three reported studies in this paper that he explicitly designed the BIDR.

gins' SD scale) were significantly higher when the degree of anonymity was reduced. On the contrary, the self-deception factor was not influenced by such modifications in test administration. Considering the direction of IM towards an outward audience and SED towards the self, this difference in sensitivity to modifications of the level of anonymity clearly supported the theoretical considerations of SDR as a two-dimensional construct. It is on the grounds of this piece of research that the one-dimensional conceptualization of social desirability was abandoned.[11]

Based on the work of Millham and Jacobson (1978), in a second model Paulhus tried to separately assess the enhancement and denial components of social desirability. Earlier studies (e.g. Millham 1974) had already categorized items of the Marlowe-Crowne SD scale into enhancement and denial, i.e. into items that contain desirable behavior and are thus overly claimed by individuals with a high need for social approval on the one hand and items with undesirable content which are thus denied by such individuals on the other. To this end Paulhus (1984) reversed several items of Sackheim and Gur's (1979) self-deception and other-deception questionnaires to arrive at an inventory with the same number of enhancement and denial items. This new measurement tool is called the Balanced Inventory of Desirable Responding (BIDR) (Paulhus 1984, 1991, 1998). It consists of 40 items, made up of two 20-item subscales measuring IM and SED separately. Additionally, the positively and negatively keyed items are balanced within the subscales, so that enhancement and denial items are equally represented. Similar to the items in the Marlowe-Crowne SD scale, the statements describe patterns of behavior or character dispositions which are either socially desirable but unlikely to occur or socially undesirable but very common.[12] Respondents are asked to rate to what extent they associate a certain statement with themselves on a 5-point or 7-point Likert scale. In order to tap only those respondents who give answers which point into a socially desirable direction in an extreme manner, only the extreme answers are counted and summed up to yield a test score. That is, the negatively keyed items are first reversed, and then one point is added to the score for each extreme response ("5" on the 5-point and "6" or "7" on the 7-point Likert scale). The BIDR was tested and applied under various circumstances and its

11 This has implications for how to control for SDR in survey research, since Paulhus (1991, p. 23) suggested only controlling for impression management since self-deception "is inextricably linked to content variance". This aspect will be discussed in more detail when choosing a measurement tool for SDR in a non-market valuation context below.

12 An example for the former is the item "I don't gossip about other people's business"; an example for the latter is "There have been occasions when I have taken advantage of someone".

reliability and validity have been sufficiently demonstrated (Paulhus 1991).[13] Although this second model of enhancement versus denial was not as strongly supported by the data in Paulhus (1984), the separation between enhancement and denial is still an important aspect for the measurement of desirable responding. Dividing SDR along the two dimensions described above results in four components displayed in table 3.1.

Table 3.1: Two two-component distinctions of SDR – four potential components

	Enhancement	Denial
Impression management	Impression enhancement	Impression denial
Self-deception	Self-deceptive enhancement	Self-deceptive denial

Following this milestone in SDR research, further studies attempted to determine the relationship of the different factors introduced above. It could be demonstrated in several studies employing factor analysis that the distinction between enhancement and denial empirically manifests itself only within the self-deception dimension (Paulhus and Reid 1991). Within the impression management dimension these two phenomena load on the same factor. Consequently, the concept of SDR can only split up into three components empirically. This finding is challenged, however, by studies with Chinese respondents (Li and Li 2008). These authors also find a distinction between enhancement and denial within the IM dimension. Since in the empirical part of this study a modified version of the impression management subscale of the BIDR is employed in a survey in Southwest China, this question will be further elaborated upon below.

The substance versus style debate

As mentioned above, Paulhus (2002, p. 50) emphasizes the requirements of a good measure of SDR by pointing out that SDR is defined as "the tendency to give overly positive self-descriptions" and that SDR is at work only if such a description is "a departure from reality". Thus, a set of questions for the assessment of SDR must be capable of separating positive but truthful responses from overly positive (and therefore untrue) responses. This question of response *style* versus response *content* and which of them is actually measured has been accompanying the debate on SDR measurement invento-

13 The empirical analysis reported below is employing a modified version of the impression management subscale of the BIDR, cf. chapter 5.

ries throughout. To some researchers, SDR is not merely a form of response bias that distorts the correlations between other variables primarily under investigation. These researchers rather regard it as a concept in its own right, a character disposition of an individual that can be – both theoretically and empirically – linked to other dispositions to describe an individual's character or personality (Borkenau and Ostendorf 1992, McCrae and Costa 1983, Pauls and Stemmler 2003, Smith and Ellingson 2002, Zerbe and Paulhus 1987). These researchers doubt the notion of SDR contamination in personality assessment when for instance the Big Five personality dimensions are assessed (McCrae and Costa 1983). That means they doubt that a high correlation between an SDR scale and the variable of interest is interpreted as evidence for contamination with this response bias. Instead they plead for an interpretation of SDR as representing a personality trait of its own rather than being measurement error. McCrae and Costa (1983) compare self-reports on personality traits with ratings by so-called informed others, in this case spouses. Their results show that a correction for SDR as measured by the Marlowe-Crowne Scale does not increase correlation between the respondents' self-ratings and those of their spouses. The spouses confirm many of the claimed traits by individuals scoring high in SDR. The authors conclude that this is because SDR constitutes a substantive personality trait and not measurement error impairing validity. Similar results regarding the agreement of self and peer ratings were obtained by e.g. Borkenau and Ostendorf (1992) and Pauls and Stemmler (2003). From the theoretical perspective, Zerbe and Paulhus (1987) hold that if there is a conceptual link between social desirability and the variable under investigation, SDR should not be controlled for. These authors give an example when this might be the case. If psychic health is the variable of interest, self-deception should not be regarded as contamination of the measurement inventory because individuals who honestly hold a positively biased view of themselves are psychologically more stable. The two concepts psychic health and self-deception are obviously related so that the latter is an expression of the former.

In sum, the debate of substance versus style is most relevant only for personality assessment. Therefore, in all other disciplines which are concerned about response bias – including survey-based environmental valuation such as CVM – SDR should still be regarded as systematic error that should be either avoided or at least controlled. Further, while for the case of personality tests McCrae and Costa (1983) conclude that only inter-individual differences in SDR are a problem because those tests do not measure absolute values, the situation is different in environmental valuation. It is clear that the fact that respondents are affected by SDR differently is a severe threat to the validity of CVM results. Yet, since what is measured is the absolute WTP of a household to support a certain environmental project, even if all respondents' statements are biased by SDR in the *same* way this should still worry the researcher. Finally, the above proposals to interpret SDR as a personality variable of its own all rely on a theoretical relationship between this variable and other constructs of interest. Such a relationship does not plausibly exist in environmental valuation where the variable of interest is the valuation of the non-market good by the respondent. Building on the above illustrations, the present study employs the conceptualization of SDR as enhancement and denial and as self-deception and impression management following Paulhus (1984). It is assumed that only IM potentially distorts WTP statements. The study further regards SDR entirely as measurement error, the extent of which must be gauged and the effect of which must be controlled. So in the following, the relationship of this conceptualization with the theoretical foundations of the willingness to pay of a respondent in a CVM survey as a measure of utility will be discussed.

The two distinctions and stated WTP

When a measure of incentives for social desirability responding is employed in a contingent valuation survey as is done in the empirical study reported in chapter 5, it is necessary to reflect on the effects that the different components of the construct identified above may have on WTP responses. Concerning self-deception and impression management the case is very straightforward in that only the latter should be controlled for. The reasons for such a procedure come from both psychology and economic theory. Paulhus (1991) points out that controlling for self-deception in personality assessment has been found to lower the predictive validity of numerous measurement inventories and thus concludes that this component of SDR is closely related to the content that these inventories are supposed to measure. Therefore, only the influence of impression management can be regarded as measurement bias. This argument also makes sense from the point of view of economic theory when one recalls that self-deception is a view of the world that the respondent herself believes to be true (but that does not necessarily have to be true objectively). As introduced in the previous chapter, contingent valuation strives to measure changes in individual utility, which is based on individual preferences. These preferences are constructed with the private information of an individual, i.e. they are subjective. So if the self-deceptive exaggerations are part of this private information set they form the basis for that individual's preferences and are thus part of her utility. Following this logic, in a contingent valuation context only conscious misreporting of information, i.e. impression management, constitutes a threat to validity, while self-deception is an integral part of what the analyst wants to measure (utility). It is due to these theoretical considerations that in the empirical part of the present study merely the IM subscale of the BIDR is employed.

When it comes to the distinction of enhancement and denial, the two possible strategies to gain social approval, the effects of these components on stated WTP are not that obvious. It will turn out that reliable predictions of how the two different components affect stated WTP cannot be made. For the sake of the following considerations it is assumed that the WTP question from the perspective of the respondent can be broken down into two parts: the first part concerns the decision whether to state a zero or a positive WTP, and the second part concerns the respondent's choice of the specific amount she is willing to pay. Since the denial construct assesses the tendency to deny negative personality traits or patterns of behavior, respondents showing this tendency are more anxious not to appear too negative in the eyes of the interviewer. Therefore, it is conceivable that respondents who have a true WTP of zero eventually state a positive but small WTP as a result of the social interaction process and the SDR concerns of the interview situation. That means that denial effectively drives some respondents out of the 'zero WTP' category into some other (small) amount. Their intention is to avoid social disapproval that might be associated with too low a response (according to what is demanded by social norms or social pressure in the interview). Similarly, a respondent who believes that her true and positive WTP is below the social norm biases her statement upwards in order to escape social disapproval that might result from telling the truth. If, however, a respondent deems her true WTP to be higher than what she thinks is socially desirable, a tendency to deny negative traits might make her state a lower WTP. This is due to the fear of social disapproval caused by stating an (as she thinks) excessive WTP amount. This illustrates that the denial component of SDR can be expected to bias stated WTP upwards for rather low WTP amounts and work the other way round in the range of very high amounts. The latter case is certainly less frequent than the upward bias. Yet, since the perceived social norm of how big a contribution is desirable certainly differs across respondents, this reference point is very hard or even impossible to determine empirically.

Enhancement on the other hand measures the tendency to exaggerate one's positive personality traits or even to claim positive traits or patterns of behavior that one actually does not possess. Regarding contingent valuation, respondents scoring high on enhancement should be more likely to exaggerate their stated WTP in order to appear overly concerned for the public (environmental) good and overly willing to contribute. This exaggeration could take the form of a simple increase of an originally positive WTP or of a switch from a true zero WTP to a positive amount. Unlike the case of denial, the influence of enhancement should be a positive bias regardless of the absolute WTP levels.

When it comes to the relative strength of the impact of the two components on WTP responses, another theoretical approach appears to be relevant. The distinction between enhancement and denial and their relative behavioral importance can be analyzed by means of prospect theory (Kahneman and Tversky 1979). This theory was devised as an alternative to classical expected utility theory to analyze decisions under risk. Since the gain or loss of social approval also bears risky characteristics because it is dependent on the evaluation of an individual's behavior by the outside institution (e.g. the interviewer) that perceives it, the application of prospect theory to the comparison of enhancement and denial appears justified. Within the bigger framework of this theory, it is assumed that individuals have a so-called value function that evaluates all possible outcomes of their actions in a decision situation with respect to a reference point. This reference point is the status quo, so the outcomes are split up into positive changes (gains) and negative changes (losses) from the reference point. The first new idea about this value function is that it is not final states that are valued but rather the changes in welfare which are triggered by certain behavior. The psychologists Daniel Kahneman and Amos Tversky find that individuals are not so much capable of evaluating absolute states rather than appraise changes between such states. The second new idea about this value function is its S-shaped form. While it passes through the zero point (i.e. remaining on the status quo has a value of zero), its negative branch is steeper than its positive part. This special shape is an expression of the fact that losses are valued stronger than equivalent gains. Since it is by means of the value function that individuals evaluate all possible actions and choose the one with the highest expectancy value, losses consequently have stronger behavioral implications than gains. In other words, the fear of losses exerts a greater motivation on people than the prospect of potential gains. This is what can be expected in a similar way from enhancement and denial. The potential to bias responses to surveys, such as WTP statements, is greater for the tendency to deny negative characteristics than for the tendency to exaggerate one's positive features. The reason for this is as follows. The denial of negative characteristics is motivated by the fear of losing social approval, whereas people enhance their self-representation in order to gain more social approval. If the findings of prospect theory also hold for the case of social approval, the denial component can therefore be expected to influence response behavior more strongly than enhancement. In chapter 4, this idea will be taken up again and lead to the formulation of hypothesis 3.

The above considerations show that only very hazy predictions regarding the differing effects of enhancement and denial on WTP statements can be made from the theoretical perspective. Overall, scoring high on one or both of these subscales should be the condition for a respondent to be sensitive for prevalent social norms. If, in addition to the high denial or enhancement score, she also perceives stating a high WTP as socially desirable, it is very likely that her responses are biased. Therefore, in the empirical part of this study the effects of all three possible measures of need for social approval (denial, enhancement, and the sum of both) will be analyzed.

Consequences for psychological SDR research in China

Since the empirical study reported on in chapter 5 is located in China, the natural question at this point is what can be expected of Chinese respondents with respect to the completion of a social desirability inventory. When looking at the most obvious cultural differences between Eastern and Western societies (cf. 3.2.4), it seems that SDR might be a very serious problem in survey-based environmental valuation studies in Eastern cultures and in China in particular. Therefore at first glance, scores on a need for approval scale of Chinese respondents can be expected to be comparably high. In contrast to that, the inclination to be more critical about oneself and the cultural tendency to avoid standing out within the group of peers (Liu et al. 2003) makes rather low SDR scores plausible. In order to be able to form a more precise expectation of the extent of SDR of Chinese respondents, in the following the respective research in China is reviewed.

Both intercultural research on this topic and investigations on SDR in China have a much shorter history than in Western countries. Yet, despite this short history, some psychologists and sociologists have been active in this field in recent years. Both the Marlowe-Crowne SD Scale (Chen 2008, Dai and Zhang 2007, Liu et al. 2003) and the BIDR (Bai et al. 2004, Guo et al. 2006, Li and Li 2008) have been employed with Chinese samples. Dai and Zhang (2007) investigate the relationship between SDR as measured by the Marlowe-Crowne SD scale and self-esteem. They find significantly different SDR scores for university students of different majors with scores of social science students exceeding those of natural science students. In a similar way Chen (2008) studies the relationship between need for social approval and self-evaluation among different groups of students. Likewise, the use of the BIDR in China is also restricted to student samples so far. Guo et al. (2006) relate the scores of a slightly modified Chinese version of the BIDR of college students in Northeast China to certain personality inventories. Their data show the existence of SDR as a strategy to present oneself among students who are asked to complete questions to evaluate certain personality characteristics. Furthermore, Bai et al. (2004) employ a shortened version of the IM subscale of the BIDR and find evidence for SDR in a student sample in Beijing.

Although empirical evidence is still scarce, there are several studies indicating that the relationship between enhancement and denial in Chinese samples is somewhat different from what was found in Western cultures. While Western researchers hold that this distinction is of no importance within the impression management dimension of SDR (Paulhus and Reid 1991), a factor analysis conducted by Li and Li (2008) actually detects four factors within the social desirability construct, indicating that both IM and SED are split into enhancement and denial, respectively. The findings show that Chinese respondents answer modestly to the enhancement items but show stronger denial regarding negative content. These authors consequently reject the three-dimensional conceptualization by Paulhus and Reid (1991). In another study, Liu et al. (2003) find a dilemma situation in Chinese college students when being confronted with incentives to answer in a socially desirable manner. These authors claim that on the one hand action according to social norms and impression management are salient characteristics of Chinese culture. On the other hand, they refer to Confucianism which classically stresses values such as modesty and honesty, i.e. motivations that contradict SDR, especially the strategy to falsely claim overly positive characteristics. Their findings reveal that Chinese respondents solve this contradictive situation in favor of self-enhancement when it comes to desirable items and in favor of the honest option when undesirable items are concerned. Although the overall tendency goes towards self-enhancement rather than honest reporting, these findings also call for a measurement instrument, which is able to distinguish between enhancement and denial. Therefore, in the empirical part of the present study where only the level of impression management of respondents is assessed, it is also investigated if the enhancement and denial dimensions of SDR exert different influence on WTP statements in a CV survey. While Liu et al. (2003) find the influence of enhancement to be stronger than denial within the impression management construct, Li and Li (2008) report just the opposite results. However, all above studies use student samples as source of data. So far there is still no investigation of this subject matter employing non-student samples. Furthermore, similar to Western countries there is thus far no research on the impact of SDR on survey concerning the natural environment and environmental valuation in particular. In these respects, the present study enters new territory.

A consequence of the different socio-cultural background of China compared to Western societies where the question inventories for the assessment of SDR were developed, these instruments might have to be modified for application in China. The social norms that form the basis for certain question inventories might not exist in that form in China, which involves the danger of rendering certain items useless. If this is not scrutinized and Western question inventories are simply adopted one-to-one severe measurement bias is likely to result. Therefore, in the empirical part of this study, the existence of social norms governing the behavior described in the items of the BIDR among the Chinese survey population is scrutinized and several items are modified accordingly (cf. section 5.2).

When it comes to the trait desirability dimension of social desirability it is clear that this factor surely has to be assessed in an environmental valuation survey. Most Western researchers take a bias towards a higher willingness to pay as socially desirable for granted. However, this might be different in China. The precondition for SDR to distort statements of WTP for environmental projects is that a biased statement generates greater social approval for the respondent than the true answer. Consequently, the topic of contributing to the provision of public goods in the environmental sector must somehow be subject to certain social norms, which are perceived by the respondents. As will be demonstrated theoretically in section 3.3, only if stating a higher (or lower) WTP than one's true valuation is more socially desirable, does a respondent have the chance to raise the likelihood of obtaining social approval for such a response by the interviewer or any other outside party that perceives her response. Thus, the belief whether or not a higher WTP statement with respect to an environmental project is regarded better by society has to be assessed for each respondent.

3.2.3. SDR research in sociology – to what extent does SDR bias survey results?

While SDR research in the field of psychology has mostly dealt with the definition and description of the concept and the development of tools for its measurement, sociologists are rather interested in the influence of SDR on other variables under investigation in survey research (Gove and Geerken 1977). The question to sociologists in this respect is whether and to what extent social desirability is a threat to the validity of the measurement of other variables, i.e. if and how much it influences the relationship between explanatory and dependent variables in a survey. If it does it is a systematic error, which has to be corrected for in order to obtain valid and reliable results; if it does not, i.e. only influences either the dependent or independent variable, it is merely random noise. The latter case was assumed by sociologists until the mid-1960s, when they were still hoping that this kind of error would not be systematic and thus cancel itself out if only the number of interviews was sufficiently great (Hyman (1954, p. 221) as quoted in Gove and

Geerken 1977). It was only during the 1960s that concerns about the influence of the different dimensions of the social desirability concept on the responses to mental health surveys were raised (Dohrenwend 1966, Dohrenwend and Dohrenwend 1969), which made obvious the need for models to predict the existence of SDR. These concerns triggered more profound research on the circumstances that foster the occurrence of SDR and on the relative strength of the different components of that phenomenon. Researchers investigated the multidimensional nature of the SDR phenomenon and attempted to develop new models for the prediction of the existence of socially desirable responding.

The idea behind a model for the prediction of the existence of SDR is the need to control for this kind of measurement bias. A great number of authors acknowledge that the survey interview used to be and still is the most widespread tool of data collection in the social sciences (Esser 1991, Phillips and Clancy 1972) and in this way a shortcut to assessing human behavior. Asking people about how they think they are and how they (would) behave in certain situations is much cheaper and less burdensome than designing methods to actually observe such behavior. This is especially true for non-market valuation where researchers elicit a respondent's preference for a certain good through her stated willingness to pay (or willingness to accept) instead through the observation of actual market behavior. In this field, however, the reason for relying on stated preference methods (or to put it into the sociological term, relying on "self-reported behavior") is not so much the cost-saving argument of the survey but rather the nonexistence of markets for those goods where observable actions could take place. As discussed in section 2.1, a revealed preference approach to the assessment of non-use values is impossible per definition.

When it is accepted that the correlation between an SDR score and a variable of interest constitutes a kind of SDR contamination of this variable, there are several ways how the latter could change the correlations between variables in a data set. The most influential sociological model of the impact of social desirability on survey data was developed by Ganster et al. (1983). These authors specify three ways of how socially desirable responding alters the relationship between dependent and independent variables in a data set. Firstly, it is conceivable that SDR creates a spurious observed correlation between two variables which are actually not correlated. This problem might arise when two variables of interest both correlate with the SDR variable but not with each other. If the researcher only considers the two variables of interest but is ignorant of SDR, it falsely appears as if the two variables are correlated. The proposed remedy is partialing the SDR variable from the other two. Secondly, it is possible that a real correlation between two other variables might be suppressed by the SDR variable and therefore remains undetected. The authors give the following example for this case. In companies, self-reports of effort or motivation by employees often do not correlate with actually observed performance. A very likely explanation for this finding is the contamination of the self-report variable with SDR, because employees might exaggerate their effort when reported in the survey. If this exaggeration is corrected for (again by partialing out the SDR variable), the two variables self-report of effort and actual performance should be (more likely to be) correlated, i.e. the correlation is not suppressed anymore. A third model proposed by Ganster et al. (1983) is the so-called moderator model which describes an interaction effect between the SDR variable and some other independent variable. This situation might arise when two groups of respondents (those scoring high and low in the SDR variable) exhibit different relationships between two other variables. Imagine the case when the correlation between variables A and B for respondents high in SDR is negative and for those low in SDR is positive. If the influence of the SDR variable is not controlled for, the different signs of the correlation coefficients neutralize each other over the entire sample and no correlation between variables A and B is found. If, however, the interaction effect of the SDR variable is accounted for, both its moderating effect and the real relationship between A and B can be detected. This discussion highlights the importance of detecting potential influence of SDR on survey data.

Which components constitute SDR?

Following the concerns in Dohrenwend (1966) and Dohrenwend and Dohrenwend (1969) and in order to investigate the validity of a certain mental health question inventory, it was Phillips and Clancy who systematically assessed both trait desirability and need for social approval (Phillips and Clancy 1970, 1972). In their 1970 study, these authors found that the desirability of certain mental health inventory items (i.e. trait desirability) influences the relationship between a respondent's demographic variables and her mental health status as revealed by means of this inventory. They were concerned about the fact that finding an individual to suffer from a mental disorder in this way might be more a result of a certain response style – in this case social desirability and/or acquiescence – than of the actual existence of such a disorder. Yet, their data also show that the relationship between demographic characteristics and a possible mental disorder is not entirely accounted for by the existence of trait desirability. That means that trait desirability is not the only explanation of these survey results but still poses a substantial threat to the validity of that question inventory.

In the second study (Phillips and Clancy 1972), the same authors show that both components – need for approval and trait desirability – independently influence the rating of several self-reports such as visiting a doctor, overall happiness or religiosity. The authors made subjects judge the desirability of several human characteristics or patterns of behavior and to report to which extent they themselves possess such characteristics. Their data revealed that need for social approval as measured by the Marlowe-Crowne Scale is not related to evaluations of the desirability of certain personality traits. When investigating the effect of these two variables on the responses to self-reports it became evident that those who regard a trait as desirable claim themselves higher on that trait. This supports earlier findings on trait desirability indicating that the desirability of a certain trait is closely related to the likelihood of claiming to possess it (Edwards 1953). Further, it was found that both trait desirability and need for social approval can bias survey responses on their own. These biases take the form of a distortion of the relationship between sexual status of the respondent and her responses – for some questions the two SDR variables modify the magnitude and sometimes even the direction of the original relationship between the independent demographic variables and the dependent variable, the reported behavior. Finally – and contrary to the authors' expectations – the assessment of neither component is biased by the other and vice versa, that means that respondents with a high need for social approval cannot be shown to persistently give higher trait desirability ratings. This result is rather surprising because it seems very plausible that respondents who feel a strong need for social approval also tend to rate those traits that are demanded by social norms, such as frequently going to see the doctor or to be happy with one's life, as more desirable. In the empirical part of this study, this type of interaction between the two factors will also be examined (cf. chapter 5). Another influential study investigating the influence of those two components of SDR was done by Gove and Geerken (1977). In addition to the above two components, these authors also assess a respondent's tendency to yea-say or nay-say in a mental health survey. Contrary to Phillips and Clancy (1972) these authors can find but very little systematic distortion of the relationship between dependent variables in three mental health question inventories and common demographic variables. They conclude that acquiescence, need for social approval and trait desirability are all merely random noise instead of systematic distortions. So, up to this point, empirical evidence regarding the relationship of different components of SDR is very ambiguous and it was only during the 1980s that a new approach was devised.

DeMaio (1984) also discusses the question of conceptualizing SDR as either personality or item characteristic. After reviewing the relevant literature up to that point (consisting mainly of the studies presented above), she finally supports the idea of a joint influence in what she calls social desirability response effect models. This refers to a type of model developed by another branch of (mostly German-speaking) sociologists who, from the mid-1970s onwards, began to simply regard a respondent to a survey as an individual that seeks to maximize her utility by rationally selecting one out of a set of possible actions (Atteslander and Kneubühler 1975, Esser 1986, 1991, Steinert 1984). The main idea of this approach, which set out to design a formal theory of response bias in interviews, is to interpret the survey interview (regardless of its form in an in-person, mail, telephone or internet-based survey) as a type of social interaction between the respondent and some other institution taking the specific environment of the interview into account. This 'other institution' can be the interviewer, the institution administering the survey, or even a third party who listens to the interview – or all of them at the same time. According to this conceptualization the respondent uses all perceivable characteristics of the interview, including question stimulus, appearance and behavior of the interviewer, the location and time of the interview and many more that might arise from the interaction of those basic characteristics to select a response that best supports the pursuit of her objectives. These objectives in turn can also consist of different motivations, such as the revelation of the true answer, the preservation of a positive picture in front of the interviewer or the minimization of cognitive effort. This theoretical framework that comes very close to DeMaio's SDR response effect model consists of the following components.

To begin with, Atteslander and Kneubühler (1975) identify three main criteria that qualify a conversation as a survey interview. An interview (a) serves some scientific purpose, it is (b) characterized by an orderly procedure, and (c) it implies a stimulus-reaction-model. The first criterion distinguishes the interview from other forms of conversation such as an interrogation or a journalistic interview. It also sets the overall objective of this specific type of exchange of information. This is the collection of data in order to support or refute scientific hypotheses. The second criterion focuses on the structure of the interview. This structure determines the topic and the possible behavior during the interview process and the type of answers that can be given. The level of orderliness can vary according to the type of information that is to be assessed and the associated theoretical requirements. The motivation to administer a highly orderly interview, such as the standardized survey interview, is to reduce the number of stimuli that impinge on the respondent and potentially trigger her (response) behavior. This idea is related to the third criterion, the stimulus-reaction model that is implicitly assumed to be at work (Orne 1962). According to Atteslander and Kneubühler (1975), this characteristic is closely connected to the scientific purpose of the interview. A respondent is made respond by means of a specific question stimulus. Since the objective of a survey is to compare responses to a certain question stimulus across respondents, this stimulus should be the same for all respondents. Only if this condition is met, is it possible to attribute the difference in responses to differences in the respondents' true attitudes and characteristics and not to the difference in stimuli. The stimulus-reaction concept highlights another feature of the survey interview. The stimuli are not restricted to the specific question content but include characteristics of the interview situation like the above mentioned time, location, appearance and behavior of the interviewer, tone of voice, etc. If these entire aspects sum up to the set of stimuli that trigger the respondent's reaction, but if the researcher is only interested in the reaction to one of these aspects (the specific question stimulus) the resulting data are biased systematically.

This line of thought is the foundation for the drafts of guidelines of interview practice which usually aim at a standardization of interviews by holding many of the above aspects constant across interviews and respondents. Yet, two problems render perfect standardization impossible. Firstly, interviewers remain human-beings and, as well as the interview situation, are unique in their characteristics and can never be completely reproduced in different interview situations. Secondly, the impact of this set of stimuli on the respondent does not depend on their objective configuration but rather on the respondent's subjective perception of these. It is obvious that different respondents may perceive even the same situation differently. The result of these limitations is a persistent and systematic bias which cannot be completely erased even with the most sophisticated interview techniques (Atteslander and Kneubühler 1975). However, if it is possible to gauge the extent and direction of some of the remaining stimuli, they could be controlled for during data analysis.

In order to account for a larger set of stimuli on the respondent and thus reduce the set of uncontrolled stimuli, this approach explains systematic error in an interview as the result of the respondent's rational choice over different behavioral options. The main idea is that the respondent takes all these stimuli into account when she selects the response that best supports her overall goal, i.e. "to act according to her personal interests and thereby to strive above all after social approval" (Esser 1991, p. 63). These situational stimuli serve to construct a categorization of the interview situation, which in turn activates associated norms and habits from the point of view of the respondent. For instance the respondent regards the interviewer as a representative of government and subsequently behaves as an obedient citizen who discharges her civic duty of providing accurate information. Another possible interpretation is the perception of the interviewer as an intruder into the private space of the respondent, which would most likely result in the respondent being reluctant to cooperate. A third example could be a feeling of pity for the "poor fellow" of interviewer who has to be assisted in doing such a burdensome job (Steinert 1984). The resulting response behaveior and level of cooperation of the respondent may obviously be very different in all these cases.

Like indicated above, this approach implies a utility maximization problem of the respondent. As such, from the perspective of the respondent the interview constitutes a problem and utility maximization is her way to solve it (Esser 1991). Basis for the solution of this maximization task is the respondent's attitudes, beliefs and preferences on the one hand and her perception of the entire interview situation on the other. This interpretation is supported by the famous quote by Manning, which reads "The respondent never lies – accurate interpretation of what he says depends on the skill of the analyst" (Manning (1966) as quoted in Esser (1991) p. 59). This means that a reduction of attention to the mere question stimulus and the explanation of responses by only that stimulus are inappropriate. The effects of all other stimuli – as long as they are measurable – have to be included in the analysis, as well. If the question stimulus is not the only influence on the respondent, it is clear that the revelation of a true response is not her entire motivation for action in that situation either. Rather the statement of a response becomes a simple means of attaining a more general goal.[14]

The model introduced and rudimentarily sketched here will form the theoretical basis for the development of an empirical tool to assess the existence of socially desirable responding in a contingent valuation survey. Therefore, the foundations of rational choice theory will be reviewed and the above model will be illustrated in greater detail in section 3.3. This will eventually lead to the development of a three-factor model of SDR, which will be applied in a CVM survey in rural China in the empirical part of this study.

In addition to the field of sociology, there are concerns about the distorting influence of SDR in several other disciplines. The field that constitutes the origin of the psychological research on this topic is personality assessment and personnel selection (Bernreuter 1933). These two fields are related because employers typically seek for an assessment of the applicant's personality but at the same time have to rely to a great extent on the latter's self-reports during the recruiting process. Incentives to misreport in surveys exist also in branches of business research, such as organizational research (e.g. Berry et al. 2007), marketing (e.g. Fisher 2000, King and Bruner 2000), as well as the fields of sexual behavior research (e.g. Meston et al. 1998, Tan and Grace 2008), nutrition science (Hebert et al. 1997), ethics research (Randall and Fernandes 1991) to name but a few. Virtually all of the above

14 An interesting implication of this point of view is that there is no true or false answer on the part of the respondent because any kind of response serves to reach her objective – utility maximization.

studies conceptualize social desirability as a one-dimensional construct as *need for social approval* and attempt to measure it with the established social desirability scales. What is often neglected is the impact of other features of this phenomenon such as level of anonymity perceived by the respondent and trait desirability. It should be clear that it is especially the factor trait desirability that entirely depends on the specific content of questions, surveys and whole branches of research. Social norms vary greatly in their direction and intensity between subjects such as sexual behavior, environmental conservation, or consumer attitudes. Looking at this broad variety of fields that usually gather survey data it is therefore more than likely that incentives for SDR work differently in different thematic contexts. As a consequence, not accounting for the influence of trait desirability – both independently and as an interacting factor with need for approval – means neglecting one major pillar of the whole concept. The investigation of independent effects also contradicts early theoretical advances in SDR research, as DeMaio (1984) already advocates an "item-centered approach" to social desirability assessment. According to this approach, the level of social desirability of an item or a question should be "a function of [its] loading on social desirability and the respondent's need to respond in such a manner" (DeMaio 1984, p. 264). This is exactly the description of a conceptual linkup of these two (or more) components of SDR that will be the guiding principle for a rational choice-based model of SDR to be developed in section 3.3.

3.2.4. The role of social and environmental norms

If it is accepted to describe SDR as the tendency of a respondent to give answers that make himself look good (Paulhus 1991), the question arises which institution determines what is good and what is not. This further poses the question of what is the source of SDR – is it exclusively inside the respondent, does it stem from the interaction between interviewer and respondent, or does society have an influence, too? The key to answering this question lies in the existence of social norms, which forms the basis for a respondent to behave in a socially desirable manner.

In the first part, this subsection provides an overview on the phenomenon of social and internalized norms and the difference of these and notions such as habits and conventions. Subsequently, the theoretical relationship between social norms and social desirability is discussed. It is shown that norms form the basis for incentives to respond in a socially desirable manner. Finally, two special cases which are relevant for the present study are examined. The question of which norms govern pro-environmental behavior will be discussed in order to highlight the potential for SDR in surveys regarding the natural environment, including environmental valuation. Eventually, approaches in SDR research in China are presented. The discussion about differences in social norms between different cultural contexts serves as justification of a modification of a Western measurement inventory for the application in China.

To begin with, a social norm is defined as a rule of behavior that is enforced by social sanctions (Coleman 1990). Two characteristics stand out in this definition. Firstly, a norm prescribes a certain type of behavior and prohibits another. That means it provides clear instructions regarding how to behave in a certain situation and is thus – which is apparent from the word itself – normative. Secondly, an acting individual feels some coercion to comply with this behavioral instruction and this coercive pressure originates in the potential punishment in case of a lack of compliance. Such punishment is not necessarily physical in nature but rather takes the form of social disapproval (or in the opposite case reward takes the form of social approval). It is apparent that the right to punish misbehavior as specified by the norm is with another person or institution. Thus, a norm is defined to exist "when the socially defined right to control the action is held not by the actor but by others" (Coleman 1990, p. 243). These others possess the power to exert punishment to the actor in case she does not comply with the norm. Thereby this author makes clear that a norm does not belong to an individual actor but always to an entire social system. For such a social system norms determine which actions, attitudes or patterns of behavior are appropriate or correct and which are not. At this point it becomes apparent already that by imposing some outside control of an action a social norm suppresses or at least limits an actor's free choice of behavior. Another consequence of the norm being part of a social system is that norms potentially differ between such systems. It is therefore very plausible that different norms exist and affect individual behavior in different cultural contexts. Consequently, the occurrence of socially desirable responding potentially differs across cultural spheres. This idea was touched on when the question of SDR in China was discussed in subsection 3.2.2, which is relevant for the empirical application in this study.

Yet, before we continue and look at how norms affect individual behavior[15], the nature of internalized norms has to be discussed and this concept has to be distinguished from notions such as habits or conventions. The potential of outside punishment was defined as a feature of a social norm above. However, there are types of norms that individuals adhere to even if

15 There is a branch of sociology that investigates the processes of how social norms evolve and are formed (cf. Coleman (1990), chapters 10 and 11), yet this is not relevant for the present argument. For the sake of this analysis, social norms are taken as given, since it is rather their influence on human behavior that is studied here.

nobody is able to observe the action. If individuals still act according to a social norm even though this happens in complete privacy, this is referred to as an internalized norm. Lindbeck (1997) defines the difference of norms on the one hand and habits and conventions on the other in that the former are able to produce (positive or negative) "social rewards" e.g. in the form of individual feelings of satisfaction, shame, or guilt. That means that even if an individual complies with norms that are internalized, is there a positive feedback effect such as satisfaction. The possibility that rewards or punishment as a result of norms are "internally generated" is also mentioned by Coleman (1990). That explains why potential external sanctions are not necessary when such internal rewards are caused by internalized norms. Habits and conventions, however, do not produce any of these feedbacks when individuals act in accordance with them. Further, contrary to social norms, which were defined to belong to a social system, habits are private (Elster 1989), i.e. they emerge from individual behavior and affect the behavior of only this individual.

Focusing on the potential to generate positive or negative rewards, a virtual contradiction in the literature can be solved. When defining characteristics of social norms, Elster (1989) describes them as not outcome oriented and thus contrasts them to rational action which is motivated "by the prospect of future rewards". According to this author, the social norm itself is not future-oriented and is not concerned with outcomes, it rather influences behavior by triggering strong emotions in the minds of individuals, such as the above mentioned guilt, shame, or anger and not by the rational expectation of some future outcome. He contrasts this to economic incentives which influence individual behavior through rational expectations. If, however, individuals are assumed to anticipate the social or internal reward caused by acting in accordance with a norm, social norms and rational action can be regarded as similar in that both trigger purposeful behavior that generates utility (Lindbeck 1997). This idea has a long tradition in economic theory where the anticipation of social approval or disapproval is traditionally modeled as motivating pro-social behavior (cf. Becker 1974, Holländer 1990, Olson 1965). From this perspective, both economic incentives and social norms promise certain rewards, which can also be interpreted as utility. This is in line with Arrow (1951) stating that whatever increases people's well-being – in this case the accomplishment of a certain goal set by either economic incentives or being prescribed by a social norm – is part of their utility. These considerations indicate how the influence of social norms on individual behavior can be modeled in a model of rational choice and utility maximization.

As indicated above, there is strong agreement in the social sciences that norms govern behavior (Mohr 1994, Sunstein 1996). In economic theory, the standard approach of modeling the influence of social norms is to incurporate social approval into an individual's utility function (Akerlof 1980, Holländer 1990). This is an expression of the fact that individuals have preferences for approval – be it external social approval or private rewards like satisfaction to comply with a norm (Rege and Telle 2004). This way, the motivating influence of anticipated satisfaction, shame or guilt mentioned above can be tackled theoretically. Further, the relative importance of this additional argument in each utility function may differ across individuals, which expresses the facts that on the one hand individuals perceive social norms to different degrees and on the other that there are differences in the inclination to comply. As will be demonstrated in further detail below, the degree of norm perception and the inclination to comply is what is being empirically assessed as trait desirability and need for social approval.

Norms as a basis of SDR

After introducing the concept of social and internalized norms and investigating how it affects behavior, the focus now turns to social norms as basis for socially desirable responding. Stricker (1963) establishes a link between norms and social desirability stating that "the behavior and opinions which these items describe have associated with them social norms reflecting the approval or disapproval that our society attributes to these behaviors and opinions" (Stricker 1963, p. 320). This implies that it is the item content that evokes the respective norm. According to this conceptualization and in line with e.g. Elster (1989), it is the norms that determine the appropriateness or inappropriateness of certain patterns of behavior or opinions. Thus these norms "favor the reporting of approved behavior and opinions and the denial of disapproved ones" (DeMaio 1984, p. 258).

At this point, the question of who or what determines which norms are at work in an interview situation has to be raised. DeMaio (1984) reports on a dispute as to which standards govern the desirability, that means who determines which norms are invoked and perceived. Is it the respondent herself, the interviewer, or the whole interview situation that triggers certain norms and influences the degree of perception by the respondent? First and foremost, as indicated above the question content certainly determines which norms are activated. Usually, social desirability research focuses on sensitive survey questions such as sexual behavior or mental illness (Meston et al. 1998, Phillips and Clancy 1970). It is in such topics that instructions about which patterns of behavior are socially approved and which are not are most clear-cut. When the respondent can choose between several response options, the norms triggered by the question content determine which options are more or less socially desirable.

Secondly, the interviewer and the institution that she represents are likely to influence norms, as well. Sociological studies on interviewer effects usually find interviewers with different characteristics such as gender, ethnicity, or age to systematically elicit different responses. Many studies have found so-called race bias (e.g. Campbell 1981, Hatchett and Schuman 1975) and demonstrated empirically that respondents to surveys conducted in the United States answer differently to white or African-American interviewers. Campbell (1981) can even show that these effects only occur for topics that are related to race-issues, while they could not be detected for topics unrelated to race. In an interesting survey investigating interviewer effects in a WTP study by Loureiro and Lotade (2005), a white American and an interviewer of African origin elicited WTP for eco-labeled products (fair-trade and organic coffee). The results showed a significantly higher WTP for fair-trade coffee when elicited by the interviewer of African origin. This difference between interviewers could not be found for organic coffee. The social norm in this case would read that it is appropriate to pay a higher price for fair-traded products because fair trade with developing countries should be supported. Obviously, the presence of the interviewer from Africa made this norm more salient, which made respondents state a significantly higher WTP for that product only in this setting. This is a classic example for a social norm which is invoked and reinforced by a specific interviewer.

Finally, many other characteristics of the interview are conceivably influencing the perception of social norms by a respondent. These might be the location or time of the interview as well as specifics of the interview protocol including speed, language style, or comments by the interviewer. A consequence of the many potential sources of influence on social norms in interview situations is the usual call in survey manuals and guidelines for interviews to be as standardized as possible. However, such methodological concerns only call for a standardization of interview characteristics from the part of the interviewer. What is often neglected is the fact that even the same features of an interviewer or an interview situation might trigger different norms (or the same norm but less obvious) form the perspective of different respondents. Which norms are perceived by the respondent to govern relevant response behavior is therefore determined to a large extent by item content and appearance of the interviewer, but the interaction of other interview(er) and respondent characteristics might as well play a role. Further, it is conceivable that item content and several interviewer characteristics interact (Steinert 1984). While in a survey on sexual behavior the gender of the interviewer might influence the respondent most, this might be the interviewer's age in a survey that deals with adolescents' prejudices against the elderly. In a survey dealing with the provision of public goods by government, such as contingent valuation, the respondents' perception of the interviewer representing a governmental institution or not could influence responses.

What has been shown so far is that in order to bias behavior or the reporting of behavior or attitudes into a socially desirable direction, norms relevant in a survey interview must both exist and be perceived by the respondent. If these two conditions are met, there is a "competing tendency" to either modify one's response according to the respective norm or to give a truthful response (Stricker 1963). The incentive to answer truthfully is itself the result of a norm – the social norm against lying. Therefore, in such a situation, a respondent might find herself confronted with a dilemma to either answer truthfully and thus comply with the norm against lying or bias her response in order to be in accord with the norm governing the content of the question (for example deny the consumption of alcoholic beverages on a daily basis). This competition of incentives induced by competing social norms will be theoretically modeled in a rational choice approach of response bias in section 3.3. Further, this model will be extended to incorporate different sources of SDR. In that model, the variety of influences of salient norms in survey interviews is the justification of a multi-factor model of incentives for SDR as it is developed in that section.

This discussion also demonstrates that social and internalized norms are a prerequisite for the existence of SDR since it is the norms that determine what kind of behavior is actually desirable. The anticipation of social sanctions as a result of disobeying the perceived social norm works as incentive for an individual to behave in accordance with the norm. Similarly, the expectation of feelings such as satisfaction or shame motivates compliance with internalized norms. In both cases, the fact that the individual perceives a certain type of behavior as being in line with the norm constitutes the desirability of this behavior. From this point of view, social desirability is a subjective feeling of an individual when acting in a social sphere. It is here that Lindbeck (1997) sees the similarity between social norms and economic incentives mentioned above. Rege and Telle (2002) refer to social desirability as a "channel for social norms". That means that the social desirability of a certain type of behavior or a certain response option to a survey question is an expression of the approval or disapproval that would result from a certain action (Stricker 1963). Thus social desirability represents the potential positive or negative consequence of a certain action or survey response. This idea serves as the justification of modeling incentives for SDR as expected utility in section 3.3.1. In addition to that, some authors claim that the reaction of a reference group – the sanctioning institution – does not need to be actual and explicit, since even "the suspicion that someone dislikes one's behavior may constitute a significant cost for somebody disobeying a social norm" (Rege and Telle 2004, p. 1626). This stresses again the finding that it is not the actual sanction (external or internal) that triggers norm compliance but merely the anticipation of positive or negative rewards. Therefore, the sanctioning of a lack of norm compliance must be both credible and important from the perspective of the respondent. If a respondent does not care about how her behavior or response is being evaluated by the interviewer or some other outside actor, the social norm does not exert any influence. In this case, the respondent does not incur any cost (in the form of shame, guilt, etc.) when she impinges upon the norm. The respondent's sensitivity to a potential sanction is expressed by the concept of need for social approval. This personality construct forms one main – and even indispensable – factor in the model of incentives for SDR that is developed below. Before this model is introduced, two special cases will have to be illustrated. These are firstly norms related environmental concern and environmental protection and secondly the intercultural aspects of social norms with a focus on China.

Environmental norms and environmental concern

Since this study is concerned with survey-based environmental valuation, it has to be investigated to what extent norms regarding environmentally friendly behavior and conservation efforts exist in society and influence survey results. Until the early 1970s, environmental protection was not a major concern of governments and society in the Western world. People still believed in unlimited growth and progress, and the restraints that the limited availability of natural resources imposes on economic development were still not realized. This "anti-ecological dominant social paradigm" has since then been challenged by what was termed the "new environmental paradigm (NEP)" (Dunlap and Van Liere 1978). After initially merely gaining popularity in academic circles, this new world view has been increasingly shaping public debate and policy making. The need for radical changes in the present economic system and the way of living has become more and more apparent even to ordinary citizens in industrialized countries as is reflected in much scientific work to measure the endorsement of pro-environmental orientation (Dunlap et al. 2000, Kaiser 1998, Kaiser and Wilson 2000, Scott and Willits 1994). As a result, a positive attitude towards environmental protecttion and sustainable economic activity has been the major paradigm during the last decades. At the same time, the existence of such a new and strong paradigm changes social norms by laying out new or at least modified guidelines for human behavior (Mohr 1994). With the number of people who realize the need for environmental protection increasing, environmentally friendly behavior becomes gradually more socially desirable whereas environmentally unfriendly behavior, such as littering, wasting water or energy, or excessive travelling by plane is more and more regarded as unacceptable. It is therefore undisputed that today strong social norms exist which call for both pro-environmental mindset and behavior.

At the same time, it has long been acknowledged that the relationship between environmental attitudes and environmental behavior is not very strong (Scott and Willits 1994). Usually the latter lags behind the former. One of the main reasons for this discrepancy is the potential contamination of measures of environmental attitudes with SDR (Kaiser 1998). The desirability of showing environmental concern and presenting oneself as ecologically conscious is a direct consequence of the prevalent environmental or even ecological paradigm introduced above. After demonstrating that social norms influence behavior and even bias survey responses on the one hand, and that today there are clear social norms when it comes to environmental attitudes and behavior on the other, the need for a rigorous control of SDR in surveys related to the natural environment is obvious.

Such a gap between attitudes and actual behavior poses an extremely dangerous threat to the validity of direct methods of environmental valuation such as the CVM, as well. What is elicited in a CVM interview is the amount of a hypothetical payment, i.e. a verbal statement of intent. If, however, pro-environmental attitudes and action diverge, WTP statements in CVM interviews cannot be taken at face value. On the contrary, the more clearly a respondent perceives social norms that call for pro-environmental behavior the more likely it is that her response is biased in that direction. For the specific case of a contribution to support a public policy measure to increase environmental quality, one would expect an upward bias in WTP. These considerations are the – often implicit – basis for researchers to suspect SDR to be at work in environmental valuation surveys (e.g. Laughland et al. 1994; Leggett et al. 2003).

A practical approach to account for the discrepancy of attitudes and behavior regarding the protection of the natural environment is the development of the concept of environmentally desirable responding (EDR) (Ewert and Galloway 2009). The main rationale for developing a question inventory to measure this new construct is the fact that this scale would be domain-specific, i.e. that it is directly linked to survey content. This is the foundation for the development of the Environmentally Desirable Response Scale (EDRS) by Ewert and Galloway (2009). These authors doubt that a general inclination to respond in a socially desirable manner as assessed by the traditional scales, such as the Balanced Inventory of Desirable Responding (BIDR) and the Marlowe-Crowne Scale, would completely translate to environmental topics. Therefore, the new tool is supposed to gauge a respondent's inclination to overly respond in a pro-environmental way, i.e. to exaggerate her pro-environmental attitudes and intentions. The new scale incurporates items from both the BIDR and the Marlowe-Crowne Scale. Item content is modified to represent attitudes and patterns of behavior that deal with the natural environment. Yet, for several reasons the present study is not making use of the EDRS. Firstly, the validity of the new tool was tested only by means of student samples in the United States, Australia and Japan. Evidence for the validity and reliability of this measure in other contexts has not been reported yet. Secondly, the authors fail to demonstrate that the new scale is more effective in explaining the attitude-behavior gap in environmental topics than the traditional SDR scales. They even frankly acknowledge that their "research does not indicate whether the EDRS is more or less effective in determining the presence of environmentally desirable responding when compared to the more general measures" (Ewert and Galloway 2009, p. 67). Thirdly, the authors interpret a high correlation between the new scale's three factors (self-deceptive enhancement, self-deceptive denial, and impression management) and established SDR scales as evidence for convergent validity. Yet, if these correlations are high, EDR is closely related to general SDR, and thus assessing merely the latter should be sufficient to control for this response bias even in environmental surveys. This high correlation deprives so to speak the new scale from its right to exist. Fourthly, the present study is conducted in a medium-sized town in Southwest China where it can be doubted that respondents are able to respond to items as sophisticated as in the new EDR Scale. As is reported in greater detail in the fifth chapter, the impression management subscale of the BIDR has to be modified for application in rural Southwest China because certain items simply do not apply to the relevant survey population. It can therefore be expected that the more specific item content of the EDRS would cause even bigger problems among those respondents. Finally, Ewert and Galloway's approach was only published while the survey in this study was already being conducted. In sum, the idea of developing a content-specific SDR scale concerning the natural environment is certainly worth exploring. However, at the current stage, the measurement tool put forward by Ewert and Galloway (2009) turns out not to be applicable, especially not in the socio-cultural context of rural Southwest China.

Social norms in China

If it is accepted that social norms are the precondition for SDR, the tendency to engage in such behavior should then potentially differ across cultures when also norms differ. What kind of statements and patterns of behavior is socially acceptable and desirable and what is not differs between cultures. A definition of culture in this respect is made as a "collective programming of the mind which distinguishes the members of one group or society from those of another" (Hofstede 1984a, p. 82). This common way of thinking of a group is being transferred over generations and determines how members of that group interpret and judge their environment. This is what Hofstede (1984a) refers to as values and collective beliefs, which are shared by the group. Values in this respect are defined as "what they [the group members] consider as 'good' and 'evil'" while collective beliefs are defined as "what they consider as 'true' and as 'false'" (Hofstede 1984a, p. 82). From these definetions it is apparent that these notions of "values" and "collective beliefs" are nothing else than what was discussed above as social and internalized norms, i.e. normative rules that assist people in categorizing behavior, actions, and states as good/bad, positive/negative, or desirable/undesirable. Another definition of culture can be found in Smith et al. (2006, p. 273) as "a set of shared constraints and affordances, both ecological and societal, which influence human social behavior, values, beliefs, attitudes, self-construals and personality factors". This definition makes even more obvious that the standards which categorize desirable and undesirable behavior differ across cultures. When these standards, i.e. the social and internalized norms, vary between cultures, so do the attitudes and behavior which is deemed right, good, or desirable. Therefore, it is possible that what is desirable within one cultural sphere is completely undesirable (or at least neither desirable nor undesirable) in another cultural context. This in turn makes the investigation of social norms and standards an indispensable precondition of any research regarding SDR in a new cultural context. This is especially true for the contrast between the cultural sphere that has witnessed the most intensive degree of SDR research (the Western culture) and that cultural sphere where the empirical investigation of this study is conducted (the Eastern, or more precisely, the Chinese culture). Most – if not to say all – practical SDR measures where developed by European and North American scientists and most of the empirical literature in this field was produced in this region of the world. Any measurement of the tendency of a respondent to answer in a socially desirable way to be employed outside this region has thus to be adapted according to the specific social norms and standards prevalent in the new cultural context. Therefore, in the following relevant notions of cultural difference between Western and Eastern cultures as well as their consequences for SDR will be discussed. Together with the display of SDR research in China, this serves as justification of the modification of an existing question inventory to measure need for social approval. An overview of environmentalism in China will conclude this subsection.

In cross-cultural research it is common to distinguish between cultural spheres and dimensions of cultural variability. One of the most heavily investigated dimensions of differing value orientation between cultures is the dichotomy of individualism and collectivism (Hofstede 1984a). People with an individualistic value orientation tend to stress independence, relying on oneself, and being unique. In a predominantly individualistic society, social action is mostly triggered by its individuals' goals, intentions, and attitudes because the focus is rather on the self than on others. Since in such societies the right or the tendency to express oneself constitutes a crucial cultural value, the deliberate shaping of one's views and attitudes merely in order to fit in with prevalent standards and norms is not that likely to occur. Therefore, individualism is expected to bear no or little relationship with the impression management dimension of SDR, which is just the very expression of fitting one's attitudes and behavior to comply with relevant standards and norms (Lalwani et al. 2009). Contrary to this, collectivistic value orientation emphasizes the role of the individual within the group, harmonious interdependence between its members, and the pursuit of common objectives. Collectivism underlines the importance of the group relative to the individual unlike individualism that places more weight on the role and goals of the individual. Therefore, the focus of the collectivistic cultural value orientation is rather on the group than on the self. Further, it is striking that features such as maintaining face, avoiding disapproval, and improving social relations are known to be distinctive for both collectivism and impression management (Lalwani et al. 2009). These conceptual similarities are further reflected in the original definition of need for social approval by Crowne and Marlowe as the tendency of a respondent to answer in a "culturally sanctioned and approved" manner (Crowne and Marlowe 1964, p. 27). In sum, it becomes clear that acting in accordance with prevalent social norms and standards, which is the defining characteristic of need for social approval and thus impression management, is stronger in collectivistic societies than in more individualistic cultural spheres. This dichotomy of individualism and collectivism is the most frequently quoted theoretical basis to distinguish between individualistic Western (i.e. European and North American) and collectivistic Eastern (mostly Japanese, Chinese, and Korean) cultural contexts.

Apart from this, there are three other frequently mentioned dimensions of differing value orientation that constitute differences of culture including (a) power distance, (b) uncertainty avoidance, and (c) masculinity-femininity (Hofstede 1984a). As part of an effort to explore intercultural differences in SDR, some researchers (Bernardi 2006, Middleton and Jones 2000) employ this typology to separate Eastern and Western cultures. In this framework, power distance refers to the degree of unequal distribution of power, wealth and prestige that is accepted within a society. According to Middleton and Jones (2000) Eastern cultures show a higher degree of power distance in that hierarchies are steeper, subordination is more explicit and that therefore individuals can be expected to respond in a more socially desirable way. The second dimension is called uncertainty avoidance and describes the question of how societies deal with uncertainty about the future. Rather liberal and free societies are characterized by a high uncertainty of the individual about her and the society's future. This is related to a high level of anxiety (Hofstede 1984b). Authoritarian societies can thus be explained to be a response to this kind of anxiety and an attempt to reduce uncertainty by limiting individual freedom. This is why Middleton and Jones (2000) expect individuals in Eastern societies that typically exhibit strong tendencies to avoid uncertainty to respond in a more socially desirable manner. Such responses are likely to be approved by a large fraction of society and thus individual uncertainty is reduced. Finally, the masculinity-femininity dimension describes the degree to which gender roles are defined within a society (Middleton and Jones 2000). In this respect, societies that stress the equality of the sexes are referred to as "feminine", while those with distinct gender differences are called "masculine". Middleton and Jones (2000) describe people from feminine societies as being sensitive to relationships with and concern for others. On the contrary, Eastern cultures are categorized as moderately masculine and Western cultures as strongly masculine. The authors argue that the more masculine a culture the more influenced the responses are by one's own ambitions, i.e. the less affected by social desirability. In sum, employing the above dimensions of cultural value orientation yields a rather clear distinction between Western and Eastern cultures (cf. table 3.2). By going through these dimensions according to Middleton and Jones (2000), SDR can be expected to be a much more severe problem in Eastern than in Western samples.

Table 3.2: Four dimensions of cultural value orientation according to Hofstede (1984a)

Dimension	Western culture	Eastern culture
Individualism / Collectivism	Individualistic	Collectivistic
Power distance	Low	High
Uncertainty aversion	Low	High
Masculinity / Femininity	Strongly masculine	Moderately masculine

There is a branch of cross-cultural sociology and psychology that investigates the influence of cultural differences on response behavior and response bias empirically. One of the main objects of study is the differential effect of individualistic and collectivistic value orientation on SDR manifested in the difference of response bias and psychological characteristics of Western and East Asian subjects (Bernardi 2006, Keillor et al. 2001, Lalwani et al. 2006, Lalwani et al. 2009, Middleton and Jones 2000). The overall question is – are collectivists dishonest and overly presenting themselves in a socially desirable manner and are individualists responding candidly? Or are collectivists closer to truthful reporting and individualists exhibiting stronger distortions in self-evaluation? More and more findings in this field indicate that the need to view oneself in an overly positive light, i.e. self-deceptive enhancement, is a characteristic aspect of the North American culture and not that prevalent in Eastern cultures, especially in Confucian cultures such as the Chinese, Japanese, and Korean (Heine and Hamamura 2007, Heine et al. 1999, Liu et al. 2003). Heine et al. (1999) claim that positive self-regard is not a universal concept. While it can be found throughout Western cultures, Japanese subjects in their study do not exhibit this psychological characteristic. Similarly, Japanese students usually evaluate themselves even less positively than others, whereas American students view themselves significantly better than they are viewed by others (Heine and Renshaw 2002). In all of these studies it is the Westerners who deviate more from truthful reporting in order to self-enhance than Eastern subjects do this in order to meet social norms and manage their impressions on others. Also, they indicate that while Western subjects are self-enhancing, Japanese subjects are rather self-critical.

Concerning the impression management dimension, many studies report Eastern subjects to exhibit significantly higher scores than their Western counterparts. The study by Middleton and Jones (2000) compared response sets by undergraduate students of both Eastern and Western origin. Their results indicate that the above cultural dimensions have an influence on SDR. Namely, Eastern subjects coming from societies with typically higher power distance, higher uncertainty avoidance, and collectivism were found to support socially desirable responses and to deny socially undesirable statements in a stronger way than Western subjects. These findings further support the criticism in intercultural research that such differences in SDR scores might be the result of differences in the interpretation of the item content. Another series of studies has found that individualism is indeed related to self-deceptive enhancement while collectivism is related to impression management. Lalwani et al. (2006) report evidence that Singaporeans and Asian Americans on the one hand scored higher on IM and lower on SED than Americans and European Americans on the other. Similarly, Bernadi's (2006) investigation reveals that country-level collectivism is strongly positively correlated with individual IM scores as measured by the BIDR. The same finding is reported by Ewert and Galloway (2009) who find that Japanese respondents scored significantly higher on the IM subscale of the Environmentally Desirable Response Scale (EDRS) than Americans and Australians but significantly lower on the two measures for SED. Finally, the data in Lalwani et al. (2009) support the above findings that individualists exhibit more self-deceptive enhancement and collectivists engage more in IM.

Two lessons can be learned from the above discussion. Firstly, it is very likely that impression management – and therefore also SDR – in contingent valuation surveys is a much bigger problem in Eastern than in Western cultures. When applying this method in the socio-cultural context of China, it is therefore necessary to empirically scrutinize the existence of this response bias. This is the main justification of the research objective of the empirical part of the present study (cf. chapter 5). Secondly, the difference of social norms across cultures shows that the assessment of individual incentives for SDR among Chinese respondents must not exclusively be done by means of question inventories developed in Western countries, such as those introduced in section 3.2.2. Instead, the applicability of these inventories has to be tested and where necessary modifications have to be made. Practically this means that reliability and validity of the existing or adapted question inventories have to be documented prior to their application with a CV survey.

Environmentalism in China

Certainly, the result of an assessment of trait desirability for the contribution to an environmental project is influenced by the environmental policy of government and the level of environmental consciousness within the respective society. For the case of China, the rapid economic development in recent decades has caused unprecedented pollution and environmental degradation. After these problems were widely neglected and even deliberately aggravated in an attempt to form nature according to human will during the first three decades of the People's Republic (Shapiro 2001), the initiation of the policy of reform and opening up beginning in 1979 has brought about an ever increasing level of environmental regulation accompanied by growing environmental consciousness among citizens. So, as initial form of environmental policy the classical command and control approach that matched very well with the planned economy at the time was dominant from the mid-1970s to the mid-1990s. Over the same period, the number of environmental laws and regulations gradually increased. Today, environmental protection is one of the most prioritized fields of government attention in China. This is reflected by the fact that in 1998 the State Environmental Protection Agency became ministry-level agency and in 2008 was finally transformed into the Ministry of Environmental Protection (MEP). In the last decade, local branches of the MEP on each administrative level have been given larger degrees of freedom in dealing with environmental problems. Together with the transformation of the whole economic system towards a market-oriented model, environmental policy also employs more market-based instruments especially since the early 1990s (Mol and Carter 2006). Therefore, environmental policy in China today includes market-based instruments of pollution control such as subsides, taxes and other financial models mixed with command-and-control measures like for instance the national logging ban, which are enforced by local government authorities. Until the mid-1990s the environmental reform of China was almost exclusively led by the state and there was virtually no public participation in goal setting and policy formulation (Martens 2006). This is reflected by the fact that environmental non-governmental organizations (NGOs) only started to exist from the mid-1990s (Mol and Carter 2006). Since then, the number of such NGOs has been steadily increasing and public debate concerning environmental policy issues has certainly been increasing within the scope of governmental control.

All these developments are accompanied by increasing media coverage, especially by newspapers as representatives of state-controlled mass media as well as by the internet as a more liberal arena of dissemination of knowledge and attitudes (Yang and Calhoun 2007). Environmental issues are not regarded as sensitive topics anymore, which gives newspapers and TV channels the chance to report on environmental accidents and scandals very openly. Also the links between Chinese mass media such as press and television on the one hand and environmental NGOs on the other is very close so that the latter are more and more able to use these media as a platform of information and discussion. In addition, environmental education has been identified on both the part of the state institutions and the NGOs as a key strategy to induce more environmentally friendly behavior of citizens and firms (Mol and Carter 2006). This includes both large-scale campaigns like e.g. the protest against a dam project on the Nu River described below or the central government's attempt to publicize the concept of green GDP in 2004 (Economy 2006). There is also a growing number of environmental awards and prizes that are intended to raise the population's awareness for the importance of this topic (Mol and Carter 2006). This transition of environmental governance in China as outlined above has been described as "greening of the state" (Yang and Calhoun 2007). The tendency of more environmental protection activities and rising environmental awareness originates in a shift of government policy in the reform era. Only as a consequence of this institutional shift and mostly under control of the state has the atmosphere for environmental NGOs entering the scene become more and more favorable. This explains the now considerable number of environmental NGOs in the otherwise still very restricted arena of Chinese politics.

How does this institutional development translate into the public sphere and the perception of environmental issues from the perspective of citizens? What is certainly the most important factor for the emergence of social norms and codes of conduct regarding environmental protection – and is quasi the result of the above mentioned "greening of the state" – is the rise of a "green public sphere" (Yang and Calhoun 2007). These authors find three factors for such a green public sphere to be existent in China, the first of which is a new language or "greenspeak" consisting of neologisms that shape environmental consciousness. Notions such as "environmental protection" (*huanjing baohu*), "sustainable" (*kechixu*), or "biodiversity" (*shengtai duoyang xing*) – just to name a few – have been newly created and are now being used by politicians, newspapers and TV channels. This leads to the remaining two factors for a green public sphere, namely a public that can consume and create greenspeak and media as a channel of dissemination. All three factors have been gradually emerging in China over the last 15 years, so that today such a green public sphere can really be said to exist. According to Yang and Calhoun (2007, p. 215) "greenspeak promotes new moral visions and practices" and advertises environmentalism as a "new way of life" that emphasizes the harmony between man and nature. Exemplary for this development is the 2008 regulation to ban plastic bags in supermarkets and shops that directly affects the habits of all citizens. Chinese people realize that environmental protection starts from their everyday life and are taught that it can only succeed when everybody contributes their share. This most clearly stresses the emergence of environmental norms that call for active involvement and contribution of the whole society.

The fact that citizen action can indeed result in advances in enhanced environmental protection is demonstrated in several widely recognized cases of public protest against economic development programs. One of the most prominent is the public debate and citizen protest that made the central government finally halt the project of damming the Nu River in the northwestern part of Yunnan Province. In August 2003 the National Development and Reform Commission approved a plan to build 13 dams on the section of the Nu River running through Northern Yunnan. Immediately upon announcement of the plan several environmental NGOs started to publicize a campaign against it, surprisingly even backed by the State Environmental Protection Agency. The campaign included discussion forums with scientists and environmentalists in Kunming, the provincial capital, and Beijing. As a result of the rising public pressure on the central government and the increasingly pronounced protest, the dam project was abandoned 9 months after approval in April 2004. All these actions were extensively covered by national media, especially newspapers. Such campaigns – with more or less overt government support – have shaped awareness of environmental problems among Chinese citizens particularly emphasizing the role and responsibility of the individual relative to the state.

Although the discussion so far shows that environmental norms and rules of behavior are already very clear, actual pro-environmental behavior of

Chinese citizens in everyday life can only be described as very ambivalent (Harris 2006). Since other objectives like economic development, social stability, or poverty alleviation are prioritized both by government and society, environmental concern of citizens mostly only equals lip service. Only when environmental problems affect people directly in space and time and benefits are associated with the awareness of such problems and taking action, does pro-environmental behavior emerge (Harris 2006). This discrepancy between growing verbal support for environmental protection and emerging social norms in this field on the one hand and sometimes still environmentally destructive behavior by individuals and firms on the other characterize China today. Such a societal atmosphere provides the perfect hotbed for the existence of SDR in surveys dealing with environmental topics. It is consequently highly probable that SDR is a major source of distortion in contingent valuation surveys in China in general. When adapting this method to the socio-cultural background of China the existence of this bias should therefore be empirically investigated. This is necessary even more because social norms and codes of conduct with respect to environmental protection do not work in the same way in different areas of this huge country (Mol and Carter 2006). Local conditions, such as state of the environment, level of education and economic development, or cultural aspects (especially in the minority areas) are definitely influencing the strength and degree of perception of such norms.

3.3. The three-factor model to measure incentives for SDR

It has been mentioned at several points in this text that social desirability can be conceptualized both as a personality and as an item characteristic, i.e. both as a response set and a response style. The SDR phenomenon might thus be regarded as being triggered by a set of factors rather than having a single source that affects the likelihood of occurrence and strength of incentives for socially desirable responding. Apart from the characteristics of the respondent, these factors may also include a wide array of interview variables, such as the degree of anonymity, the time and location of the interview, and the whole range of interviewer characteristics. This section takes up the idea of SDR as a multidimensional phenomenon.

In response to the rather inconsistent findings concerning the interaction of the different components of SDR introduced in section 3.2.3, a consistent theoretical approach to incorporate the different factors into one model for the prediction of the existence of SDR is developed by Esser (1986, 1991). His rational choice approach to model response bias is inspired by earlier works that regard the survey interview as a social situation (Phillips 1971, 1973), in which respondents act as individuals guided by their self-interest and strive to maximize their respective expected utility which is (partly) determined by social approval (Esser 1986, 1991). This means that when confronted with a survey question a respondent finds herself with alternative response options that she can evaluate with respect to the above goal – utility maximization by means of full control over her appearance in the face of the interviewer. The respondent will then choose the option with the highest expected subjective utility. The final response is thus a result of a cost-benefit analysis by the respondent.

The rational choice approach to response behavior serves as a framework for the systematic inclusion of different factors that potentially trigger socially desirable responses. Subsequent to the exposition of the theoretical model potential factors are discussed. It is demonstrated that especially the factors "need for social approval", "trait desirability", and the "degree of anonymity of the interview situation" have to be included in a model to prognosticate the occurrence of SDR. This three-factor model of socially desirable response behavior forms the basis for the empirical analysis conducted in the subsequent two chapters.

Note that the following rational choice model of response behavior is not the only approach of modeling theoretically the process of deliberate misreporting in surveys. Tourangeau et al. (2000) also mention misreporting out of concerns about privacy and confidentiality and misreporting to avoid embarrassment. According to the first approach the fear of the disclosure of interview responses to the researcher, to other members of the household, or to any third party are the reasons for respondents to deviate from reporting true answers. The second approach stresses the impulsive and emotional nature of stating distorted responses. A strategy of respondents for avoiding the embarrassment of making statements concerning sensitive topics is simply to lie. As will become clear below, the basic ideas of both alternative approaches can also be found in the rational choice model of response behavior, which shall be developed in the following subsection.

3.3.1. Response behavior as rational choice

The following model constitutes the formalization of the basic idea of the interview as a social situation with a wide range of stimuli triggering the respondent's behavior, which is already touched on in section 3.2.3. This special form of a social situation is the result of the interaction of respondent and interviewer in the survey interview. It has been mentioned that respondents do not only react to the very stimulus of a survey question but are prone to be influenced by characteristics of the interview situation, such as the location, the interviewer, and the interaction with her. This range of influencing factors is the reason why the respondent might not only be concerned with the revelation of the true answer to a certain question but is rather trying to cope with the interview situation as a whole. In section 3.2.1 this idea is used to define response bias as the "systematic tendency to respond [...] on some basis other than the specific item content" (Paulhus 1991, p. 17). So, in order to understand the incurrence of response bias in general and SDR in particular, the entirety of characteristics of the interview situation have to be regarded as a problem or task to be solved by the respondent with respect to her objectives. Against this background the response behavior of the person being interviewed can be considered the result of some problem solving process in which the respondent seeks to maximize her utility. Since the factors influencing the response behavior in a survey interview are manifold, a theoretical model has to be developed that allows for a structured analysis of the relationship of these factors with the resulting response as well as among each other. The necessary theoretical framework to model such a decision problem from the perspective of the respondent is provided by the theory of rational choice (cf. Diefenbach 2009, Riker and Ordeshook 1973, chapter 2). This model will allow the inclusion of all kinds of influences, such as salience of question content, need for social approval, trait desirability, interviewer effects, and degree of anonymity into one well-structured decision problem of the respondent.

The rational choice approach to response behavior

The rational choice approach of response behavior regards the respondent in a survey interview as being able to rationally evaluate different response options (including the "don't know" or non-response options) and choose the one that maximizes her subjective expected utility according to her individual objectives. This model is in the tradition of the von-Neuman-Morgenstern rationality because the respondent is assumed to choose the option that maximizes her expected utility (von Neumann and Morgenstern 1947). So, the actual rationality in the behavior of the respondent rests in the orderly process of response selection based on the evaluation of certain factors (Riker and Ordeshook 1973). However, while this approach employs the conceptual idea of von-Neuman-Morgenstern expected utility theory, it deviates from it in some marginal technical assumptions as will become apparent during the following exposition.

The following illustration is mainly based on Esser (1986, 1991). Assume a respondent in a certain interview situation can choose between *m* response options A_i, with $i = 1, \dots, m$. At the same time she has knowledge about certain outcomes that are the consequences of her responses as a result of her desire for social approval, truthfulness, or other motives. The realization of any of these outcomes provides a certain level of utility U_j. Since the respondent knows all $j = 1, \dots, n$ possible outcomes and their respective utility levels resulting from them in advance, U_j can also be referred to as objective of the respondent – or rather an objective evaluated by the individual utility function.[16] If the anticipated utility level is high, the respondent is motivated to realize the respective outcome. Thus the realization of that outcome and the associated utility level can be regarded as a motivational factor of the respondent's behavior. Each response option A_i is linked to several objectives U_j with a certain probability that this option might cause one of these objectives. This likelihood is denoted with p_{ij}. So for instance, response option A_i might trigger objective U_1 with p_{i1} and objective U_2 with p_{i2}. Note that the sum of the p_{ij} for one response option A_i across all $j = 1, \dots, n$ objectives is not necessarily equal to 1 because it is conceivable that an action could be without any consequences. This can also mean that there might be certain objectives that the respondent cannot reach with a specific option A_i. However, the sum of all p_{ij} for one objective U_j across all response options $A_1, \dots, A_m$ must equal 1. The reason for this is the fact that a certain objective U_j of the respondent must either be reached by option A_1 or A_2 or by each of them with respective probabilities that add up to 1.

What is to be explained by this model is why the respondent selects the response option A_i with respect to the specific characteristics of the situation. These characteristics are the utility levels of the objectives and the probabilities that action A_i causes the respective objectives (p_{ij}). The process of evaluating different response options with respect to the objectives they might entail is simply a summation of the utility levels of all objectives multiplied with the respective probability. That means, the subjective expected utility SEU of option A_i is calculated according to

$$SEU(A_i) = \sum_{j}^{n} p_{ij} U_j. \qquad (3.1)$$

This calculation can be done for all possible actions in the action vector A and results in m SEU values. The basic idea of this approach is that an individual will select that option A that is connected to outcomes that are

16 The direct use of the utility terms can be regarded as a short-cut because that utility can only be generated from the outcomes of an action. The evaluation of an outcome O_j by means of the individual utility function of a respondent would be $U_j = u_j(O_j)$. For notational convenience, we look at the utility levels U_j directly.

highly valued and that are very likely to result from this response option. In case an objective U_j is connected to the response options in a mere random manner, all p_{ij} for that option are equal to $1/m$. Consequently, from the perspective of the respondent it is equally likely for each response option to trigger that specific objective.

According to this approach, the process of response selection consists of three steps (Esser 1991). In the first step, referred to as *cognition*, the respondent perceives the interview situation. This includes the visible and audible characteristics of the interviewer, the institutional context of the survey, the degree of anonymity, and of course the question content. The perception of these characteristics is the basis for a categorization of the interview situation by the respondent according to well-known stereotypes. As will be further discussed below, it is in this step that the values of different p_{ij} and U_j are influenced and determined. The second step is the *evaluation* of the response options. This is done by calculating the subjective expected utility levels for each option according to 3.1. In a third step, the *selection*, the respondent chooses a response option A_i according to a certain decision rule. It is assumed that this rule is utility maximization, so that the response option with the highest subjective expected utility $SEU(A_i)$ is chosen.

This simple framework of the theory of rational choice can be employed to categorize different situations that a respondent to a survey might be confronted with and thereby explain the conditions that lead to a certain pattern of response behavior. The factors that make up these conditions in the case of a survey interview can be twofold – on the one hand they can originate in the characteristics of the situation (i.e. characteristics of the interview like time or location and of the interviewer, such as sexual status, outward appearance, age, etc.) and the specific question content on the other (Esser 1986). If those factors and their influence on response behavior can be identified the existence of potentially biased responses can be prognosticated. This is the main objective of the following approach.

Imagine a respondent has already decided to take part in the survey and to respond to a question at hand.[17] In such a situation, she has to select one of two response options A_1 and A_2. Furthermore, the respondent has certain objectives that she wants to attain by selecting one or another response option. In the framework of this model we assume she has two objectives: either to report the true answer or to make a socially desirable statement and gain social approval. Each of the two objectives generates certain individual utility to the respondent. Firstly, the utility level that results from reporting the true answer is that of being in accord with one's personal identity

17 Note that the following considerations can also be applied to the decision whether to participate in the survey or not, or to answer a specific question or not. That means this approach applies to any kind of decision problem in a survey interview.

because the true answer is part of that identity. This is the utility derived from the satisfaction of telling the truth and thus expressing oneself truthfully in the face of the interviewer, which is denoted with U_t. The clearer and deeper rooted the respondent's true answer to a specific question the greater the value of U_t because the more satisfaction can be gained from actually expressing that true answer. Analogously, if she does not have a true answer to the question, possibly because the survey topic is entirely new to her or she does not understand the question, it holds that $U_j = 0$ because there is no potential utility gain from truthful responding. Secondly, the sensitivity of the respondent to the situational and social desirability constitutes a potential level of satisfaction when she actually complies with what she feels is desired by the situation or by society. The utility level U_s, which results from stating a socially desirable response covers this satisfaction. The higher the need for social approval of a respondent and the perceived trait desirability of the specific question content the higher is the potential satisfaction generated by stating the socially desirable response. Esser (1986) refers to these two factors as the "motivational basis of socially desirable reactions" from the part of the respondent. Thus, U_s is an expression of these two factors in this model. This idea is the basis of the development of a three-factor model of social desirability in the subsequent subsection.

According to the specific characteristics of the respondent or the interview situation these utility expressions can vary in their level and thus motivate different behavior. Following the basic rules of rational choice theory, the respondent calculates the subjective expected utility for the two response options according to

$$\begin{aligned} SEU(A_1) &= p_{1t}U_t + p_{1s}U_s \\ SEU(A_2) &= p_{2t}U_t + p_{2s}U_s. \end{aligned} \tag{3.2}$$

This simple model can now be used to illustrate the influence of certain characteristics of the interview situation on the decision process of the respondent. Esser (1991) emphasizes that both the transparency of the interview situation and its categorization according to stereotypes are preconditions for the elements of the matrix of expectations p_{ij} to assume values different from zero. Transparency in this respect means the level of understanding of a respondent regarding the question content, as well as the perceptibility of interviewer and interview characteristics. If in a telephone interview, for instance, the outward appearance or the ethnicity of the interviewer is not visible from the perspective of the respondent, there is no perceived relationship between action A_i and objective U_s. Since the respondent does not know this special characteristic of the interviewer, she is not able to form a probability whether or not the selection of A_i will result in the expected utility of gaining social approval (U_s). That means the subjective probability p_{is} is equal (or close) to zero. It is thus clear that this interview(er) characteristic cannot affect her response in any way because even if the respondent has a high need for social approval (large U_s), does this not translate into a high level of subject expected utility because that product is (close to) zero. In addition to transparency, stereotypes of what the respondent actually perceives during or prior to the interview are important because they activate certain norms or guidelines for role behavior. These stereotypes determine the way behavior is influenced when a certain type of interview situation is perceived by the interviewer. Thus, transparency and a stereotypical categorization of the interview situation are preconditions for the respondent to construct a link between her response options and the objectives of her actions, i.e. $p_{ij} > 0$. Concerning the anonymity of an interview situation, the perceived level of anonymity lowers the value of p_{ij}. For a respondent who believes her responses will not be made public and thus do not help her gain social approval, the relationship between a certain response A_i and the social desirability objective of that action U_s is weaker. This is expressed by a lower value of p_{is}.

In order to specify even further the typical conditions of a survey interview within this theoretical framework the following variations of the elements of the above model are conceivable. For these variations, each of the four summands in 3.2 can basically assume two values – zero and non-zero. The model possesses the four following basic elements:

1. The existence of a "true answer": This is expressed by a U_t which exceeds a certain minimum value, i.e. is sufficiently different from zero.
2. The subjective probability p_{1t} that leads to the realization of the utility of the true answer U_t. This link makes option A_1 stand for "giving the truthful response".
3. There is a positive situational demand U_s perceived by the respondent. This element is driven by need for social approval, sensitivity of question content, and trait desirability.
4. The subjective probability p_{2s} that option A_2 leads to the realization of the utility of the socially desirable answer U_s. This link makes option A_2 stand for "giving the socially desirable response".

Elements one and two yield the subjective expected utility $p_{1t}U_t$ of reporting the true answer A_1, whereas the third and the fourth element constitute the subjective expected utility $p_{2s}U_s$ of responding in a socially desirable manner (A_1). By combining these two elements four stereotypical situations can be characterized and are displayed in table 3.3. The following detailed discussion of these types illustrates how the situational and personal factors of a survey interview influence response behavior. Furthermore, it is assumed that there is no anonymity towards the interviewer and that there is a difference between the true answer and the response demanded by social desirability concerns. If this was not the case, a response even though it is biased by SDR would still represent a respondent's true answer and the respondent could simultaneously realize the utility levels U_t and U_s. In order to rule out this case, the above assumption is made.

Table 3.3: Typology of interview situations to be analyzed by the rational choice model. Source: Esser (1986; 1991)

	Type I	Type II	Type III	Type IV
	Indifference	Validity	Situational effects	Inconsistency
$SEU(A_1)$	"0"	$p_{1t}U_t$	"0"	$p_{1t}U_t$
$SEU(A_2)$	"0"	"0"	$p_{2s}U_s$	$p_{2s}U_s$

Imagine first a situation (type I) in which the respondent is influenced neither by the question content nor the interview situation. This is the consequence firstly of the respondent's lack of a true answer ($U_t = 0$) and/or a low level of transparency and categorization of the situation ($p_{1t} = p_{2t} = 1/m = 0.5$). The level of utility for the true answer equaling zero can be the result of a question concerning a topic the respondent has never thought about before and has thus no idea what to respond. The low level of transparency may result from a very unclear formulation of the question or impaired understanding on the part of the respondent. Although she might have a true answer about this topic, the question is so unspecific and unclear that she is not able to link that answer to this question. Secondly, this situation results from a lack of a situational motivation ($U_s = 0$), i.e. low need for social approval and low trait desirability and/or a vague definition of the situation ($p_{1s} = p_{2s} = 1/m = 0.5$). Again the latter refers to a low level of transparency so that the respondent cannot anticipate which response option will lead to the realization of the utility from socially desirable behavior. Biasing her answer would thus not generate any utility. This level of utility, however, is also very low ($U_s = 0$) because as a result of low need for approval and trait desirability, the respondent cannot gain anything, no matter which response she chooses. In this situation, the expected utility values for the two response options are both very similar and close to zero (symbolized by the "0" in table 3.3), and therefore the respondent is indifferent regarding the selection of an option.

The type II situation is characterized by a respondent with a deep-rooted and well-defined true answer and very clear question content. The question is highly unambiguous and refers to a latent and already existing opinion, value or answer in the respondent. That means $U_t > 0$ and p_{1t} close to 1 because the link between response option A_i and this objective is very close. This results in a high value of $p_{1t}U_t$. At the same time the respondent does not feel any motivation to engage in SDR ($U_s = 0$) and due to a lack of transparency concerning U_s she cannot categorize the situation sufficiently ($p_{1s} = p_{2s} = 1/m = 0.5$). Expressed in terms of equation 3.1, this type is characterized by

$$\begin{aligned} SEU(A_1) &= p_{1t}U_t + 0.5U_s \\ SEU(A_2) &= 0 + 0.5U_s \,. \end{aligned} \tag{3.3}$$

In this situation the subjective expected utility of the first response option, answering truthfully, by far exceeds that of the second option, so the respondent has strong incentives to always report the true answer (A_i). This type – the ideal setting from the point of view of the survey researcher – is labelled "validity" because response bias is virtually non-existent and both the reliability and validity of the resulting survey data is ensured.

The opposite case is displayed as type III and referred to as "situational effects". Like in the type I situation the intensity of the objective to state the true answer is very low ($U_t = 0$), i.e. the respondent is lacking a latent "true" opinion or answer regarding the specific question content. Similarly, the transparency concerning question content is again very low, which is expressed by $p_{1t} = p_{2t} = 1/m = 0.5$. In this case, however, the transparency and the level of categorization with respect to the situational demand, as well as the need for social approval (and sensitivity of the question and trait desirability) are very high (large U_s, and p_{2s} close to 1). The basic equation therefore is modified to

$$\begin{aligned} SEU(A_1) &= 0.5U_t + 0 \\ SEU(A_2) &= 0.5U_t + p_{2s}U_s \,. \end{aligned} \tag{3.4}$$

The subjective expected utility of the second response option, giving the socially desirable response, is now by far greater than that of the first resulting in the selection of option A_2. Consequently, situational effects determine response behavior to a large extent and the validity of the resulting data is low. The reason for the poor validity of the responses in this case is twofold. Firstly, the survey design is insufficient, which makes the question ambiguous, and secondly, the survey deals with a topic that is irrelevant for the respondent, expressed by U_t close to zero.

Finally, in the last type of situation, both content- and situation-related motivations are strong ($U_t > 0$ and $U_s > 0$). Further, the level of transparency and resulting categorization of the interview situation is high, so that the respondent can unambiguously forecast which outcome a certain response option will trigger (p_{1t} and p_{2s} both close to 1). Since the links between response options and their respective objectives are clear and take similar values, the subjective expected utility levels of both response options are high. As a result, the selection of a response option is arbitrary and subject to very small variations in the parameters of the situation. The basic equation for this case is

$$\begin{aligned} SEU(A_1) &= p_{1t}U_t + 0 \\ SEU(A_2) &= 0 + p_{2s}U_s. \end{aligned} \tag{3.5}$$

Since the selection of an option is now very sensitive to small changes in the relative expected utility levels, the response is highly prone to be affected by any (even marginal) characteristics of the interview situation. The existence of SDR is extremely hard, if not impossible, to prognosticate in this case. Interestingly, the subjective expected utility of the response that is not selected is also very high and it constitutes an opportunity cost of choosing the other response. This cost is responsible for a certain level of stress in the respondent when answering such questions. When both a well-defined true answer and a clear indication of which response is socially desirable exist (and differ, as is assumed above), the respondent is caught in the struggle of the two objectives, namely reporting the truth or yielding to the pressure of social norms and other situational factors. This is an explanation of why "sensitive questions" are so hard for respondents to answer. Both the intensity of a true value and the impact of social desirability concerns are very strong, which makes the selection of a response very burdensome (expressed by the opportunity cost of forgone utility of the neglected response option) and might explain the comparably high ratios of "don't know" or even missing answers to such questions.

Implications of the model

The above model and its implications serve well to emphasize several important aspects of how a good survey interview should be designed and conducted. When looking at the situation in type IV, the justification for many rules of good interview practice to be found in the relevant literature becomes obvious. For example, it is agreed upon that questions should be formulated as clearly as possible and that their content should be relevant for the respondents in the sample. By assuring these conditions, the value of U_t can be increased, which in turn increases the likelihood of getting valid responses. Yet, if only one of these conditions is met, for instance when the question is very well formulated but the respondent does not hold any latent true answer to this topic, the precise formulation is useless.[18] Further, it is common practice of professional survey companies to standardize the appearance and speech of their interviewers as much as possible in order to complicate a categorization of the interview situation by the respondents and thus avoid any influence of related social norms and situational factors on responses. In terms of the above model this corresponds to a situation characterized by low values of p_{2S}. Assurances of anonymity also decrease the value of p_{2s} in a similar way because the relationship between a certain response option and its impact on the social approval the respondent might receive from it (i.e. the utility level U_s) is much looser. If a response cannot be perceived by the public or by the interviewer there is no potential increase in social approval to be gained by responding what is allegedly socially desirable. Interestingly, the model also shows that assurances of anonymity – even if they are believed by the respondent – are useless if there is no sufficiently strongly rooted true answer. In this case the SEU levels of both response options would be equal (or close to) zero and the type I situation would be the result.

It can be stated that modern survey practices are able to avoid many sources that are able to foster the biasing of responses by social desirability concerns. In cases where situational influences are not present, the above rules for interview practice yield valid results. However, if such influences exist, the values of p_{2S} and U_S are no longer equal or close to zero. Imagine that in a situation with positive incentives for SDR a question is very well formulated to raise p_{1t} and to increase the likelihood of a valid response. Esser (1986) warns that such a clear formulation also defines the situational and social demands of the interview situation and in turn also increases the tendency to select the socially desirable response ($p_{2S}U_S$). If at the same time the tendency to select the true answer is close to zero, a simple lack of reliability due to the unclear question is turned into a systematic error caused by situational and social desirability. It is interesting to note this rather unexpected result, the intuition of which obviously makes sense: The striving for "perfect" question formulations as well as so-called probing (further explanations by the interviewer to make the respondent answer a question after initial hesitation) might under certain circumstances even aggravate the problem of social desirability because it also sharpens the definition of which response is most desirable. It is therefore important to assess the specific nature of these circumstances to prognosticate this type of situation. This is the main rationale of the three-factor model to be developed below.

18 Remember that one assumption of the model in this case was for U_t to exceed a certain minimal value.

This dilemma is a well-known problem in the CVM literature. When designing a contingent valuation questionnaire and the payment scenario and elicitation question in particular, the researcher must find a middle way between too precise and too vague a description of the payment mode. On the one hand the payment vehicle, a tax or fee for instance, must be specified to a sufficient degree to make it possible for the respondent to form a realistic idea of her WTP. On the other hand the better and more detailed both the project scenario and the payment vehicle are introduced, the clearer are associations with social norms that have to do with that specific scenario and payment mode. It is therefore possible that respondents state a zero WTP not because they do not value the proposed project but simply because they reject the (well-specified) payment mode.

The last implication of the rational choice model of response behavior concerns the concurrence of the true and the socially desirable response. Esser (1986) analyzes the case when the true response is identical to the socially desirable one for all four types. He concludes that in the type I and II situations the result would be unaltered, whereas for type III where a true answer was assumed to be non-existent in the first place, this case is not applicable anyway. The only interesting case is the type IV situation. If the socially desirable and the true response options are identical, the inconsistency in this type of situation in the basic model turns into a situation in which $SEU(A_1)$ by far exceeds $SEU(A_2)$ and the true answer is given. The reason is simply that the motivation of the respondent to answer truthfully is now not biased but rather reinforced by the incentive to state the socially desirable answer.

What can be learned from this model? Firstly, at many steps of the model it becomes apparent that the conditions for SDR to influence survey responses and thus threaten the validity of the elicited survey data are very complex and not as easily met as it appeared at first sight. Esser (1986) refers to Gove and Geerken (1977) who concluded that these complex conditions are responsible for the at most minimal influence of SDR on their survey results – however, at the time still lacking an explicit theoretical framework for such a claim. Concerning survey-based environmental valuation and especially CVM research, the fact that the conditions for the existence of SDR are rather hard to be met might be reflected in the limited amount of research in this field. Although SDR is referred to in reports of many CVM surveys there are only a few studies which systematically investigate this form of response bias. In addition, it follows from these considerations on the complex conditions that the mere application of SDR scales with a survey and the subsequent correction of the responses according to the SDR score obtained from that scale do not necessarily solve the measurement problem associated with SDR. Such a simple procedure is prone to neglect other factors of SDR and thus make erroneous predictions regarding its occurrence. Secondly, the model includes the case when SDR is not necessarily a bias from true answers but can under certain conditions reinforce the tendency to report the true answer. This, too, adds to the complexity of the task of prognosticating under which conditions SDR impairs the validity of survey results.

Thirdly, the above illustration shows that the influence of the interview situation and of social norms is especially strong when there is no true response grounded in the personal identity of the respondent. This might often be the case in survey-based environmental valuation studies where respondents are confronted with hypothetical market situations which might sometimes be entirely new to them. This characteristic of contingent valuation studies makes a thorough analysis of influences of social desirability effects within this method highly necessary. However, as indicated above, the mere administration of an SDR scale along with the CV survey is not necessarily sufficient to detect SDR in environmental valuation. In addition to that, other factors such as interviewer characteristics have to be taken into account.

Fourthly, several crucial features of the interview situation are covered by the above rational choice model. It provides an appropriate framework to consider gains and losses simultaneously. Further it covers the problem of respondents who have to make risky decisions (Tourangeau et al. 2000). This aspect is covered by the inclusion of the subjective probability levels p_{ij}. Eventually, the assessment of the situation as expressed by the individual values of U_t, U_s and p_{ij}, is subjective, i.e. they can vary from respondent to respondent. Therefore, if it is possible to assess the factors of the model empirically, it is possible to distinguish between respondents with and without incentives for SDR. This is the main idea of the empirical investigation of this study.

Finally, a word has to be said about the limitations of the rational choice approach to response behavior. Clearly, this approach conceives the respondent as fully rational. It is assumed that she both knows how to evaluate different response options according to rational choice theory and has information about all possible outcomes and how they are related to her response options. Of course, this concept is an idealization and does not cover certain more realistic behavioral patterns, such as habits and customs. If a respondent answers favorable to a certain set of questions simply because she usually does so, such a pattern of behavior is unlikely to be influenced by different degrees of anonymity of the interview situation or interviewers with different appearance. Nor does the model consider bounded rationality. Contrary to theoretical assumptions it has been found that respondents to CV surveys might employ non-rational heuristics to arrive at WTP statements (Frör 2008). In addition to that, impulsive and emotional reactions to question stimuli and situational demands are not covered by this model, either. In all these cases the interaction of the above factors cannot be expected to work as predicted by the rational choice model. However, stressing the behavioral impact of social norms does not conflict with the notion of a rational decision maker. Even an individual that evaluates courses of action in a fully rational manner follows what is prescribed by social norms as long as non-compliance results in utility losses (Mohr 1994). This is exactly the way that even the rational choice approach can integrate to a certain extent emotional and impulsive motivations. If negative emotions as a result of a negative evaluation by the interviewer or the environment are interpreted as future costs, they clearly have a motivational influence on current behavior. If the costs are expected to be very high and the probability that a certain response indeed causes these costs, the rational choice model predicts that such a response is not selected. In addition to that, the model in its completely rational form remains rather easy to handle and empirically applicable. This leads to the insight that this model is a mere heuristic in order to prognosticate the exact conditions for the occurrence of socially desirable response behavior. As Esser (1999) notes, sociologists are not that naïve to think that each respondent has such a rational choice model in mind when taking part in a survey interview. The model is not supposed to copy the decision process that is really going on in a respondent's head. What it is supposed to illustrate, however, is the interaction of different sources of influence that determine the final response.

Factors of the rational choice model

The above rational choice approach is able to take into account six types of factors potentially influencing response behavior. These are (1) the salience of the survey topic, (2) the sensitivity of question content, (3) need for social approval of the respondent, (4) her subjective rating of the desirability of the response options, (5) the degree of anonymity of the interview situation and (6) other interview and interviewer characteristics. In the following it will be scrutinized to which extent these factors are relevant in a contingent valuation survey.

The salience of the survey topic refers to the question whether the respondent perceives the environmental problem and understands both environmental project and payment mode. Further, this factor contains the degree to which an environmental problem and its mitigation as proposed in the CV scenario are relevant for the respondent's living conditions. Yet, a good CV survey has to employ diligent questionnaire design to make sure that each respondent has a sufficient level of understanding of the environmental project in order to make a WTP statement. Additionally, the survey sample should be drawn in a way that the population affected by the policy measure providing the environmental good is covered. If this is the case, an insufficient salience of the survey topic should not be a threat to the validity of the survey data. This factor should therefore be given for each respondent to a contingent valuation survey.

Due to increasingly severe environmental decline and the emergence of more salient environmental norms in recent decades the question about one's contribution to environmental protection should be sensitive i.e. subject to strong social norms (cf. section 3.2.4). In addition to that, stating a WTP for an environmental project can also be interpreted as the contribution to the private provision of a public good, a situation where free-riding would be the rational action (Olson 1965). Since there are clear-cut social norms against such free-riding behavior the question of contributing to the financing of public goods is definitely subject to social norms and in this sense a sensitive issue. This second factor, which might vary across respondents, is covered by the assessment of trait desirability of different response options. When respondents are asked how desirable it is to state a high, low or zero WTP for an environmental project this also shows how sensitive they regard this question. In other words, what is measured here is the degree to which a respondent perceives stating a certain answer to the WTP question to be governed by relevant social norms. Similarly, all remaining factors are potentially varying across respondents. This is definitely the case for need for social approval, which is a personality characteristic of the respondent. Likewise, the subjective rating of the desirability of the response options, referred to as trait desirability (including the aspect of the sensitivity of question content as explained above), might differ across respondents. That means even with the most sophisticated survey technique it is not possible to hold these factors constant across all individuals. Therefore, in a study investigating the influence of these factors on the occurrence of SDR they have to be assessed in addition to the original survey content. Finally, strict assurance of anonymity and standardization of interview conduction on the part of the interviewer are supposed to reduce the influence of the remaining factor, namely level of anonymity. However, while these requirements can objectively be met by means of considerate survey design and professional implementation, the subjective evaluation of the level of anonymity from the perspective of the respondent cannot as easily be controlled. Therefore, this factor also has to be assessed separately.

What becomes apparent in this discussion is the fact that if a contingent valuation survey is conducted perfectly according to the recommended way laid down for instance in the report of the NOAA Panel (Arrow et al. 1993), certain factors are already set to desirable values. The salience of question content is certainly such a factor. That means that their potentially biasing influence can be assumed to be deactivated. This increases the likelihood of the survey to yield valid data. However, as shown above the influence of another set of factors cannot be held constant even under perfect survey conditions. These are need for social approval, subjective trait desirability ratings, and the perceived level of, which have to be assessed separately. Subsequently, the influence of these factors on WTP statements and the form of their interaction have to be analyzed empirically. This result of the above rational choice approach to response behavior is the main rationale for the introduction of a three-factor model of social desirability which will be presented in the following subsection.

3.3.2. The three-factor model of desirable responding

The idea of the rational choice approach to modeling response behavior introduced in the last subsection serves as a means to integrate the two conceptualizations of SDR as response style and response set. SDR as response style, which is consistent across time and situations, can be associated with the interpretation of this concept as a personality characteristic. SDR as a response set on the contrary highlights the influence of situational factors on socially desirable behavior in surveys. A logical consequence of this duality is the idea that multiple factors – personal and situational – should be included in a comprehensive measure of incentives for socially desirable responding.

What is now needed is a theoretical model to specify the conditions for motivations to respond in a socially desirable manner, i.e. to integrate the factors that have already been identified to be relevant in the previous subsection. Such a model holding these three factors responsible for survey participants to respond in a socially desirable manner is developed by Stocké (2004, 2007). Based on the theory of rational choice, this model interprets the interview as a situation that confronts an agent with a choice of possible actions. The respondent as a rational decision-maker chooses the action (response), the expected results of which maximize her expected payoff. In such an interview situation this payoff consists of the social approval of the respondent by the interviewer. The extent of the expected approval can be interpreted as the overall incentives to engage in SDR. Before elaborating the idea of a non-compensatory interaction of the three factors, they will be introduced one by one.

Need for social approval

The first factor of the model is a respondent's need for social approval. This term, already introduced in subsection 3.2.1, was coined by Crowne and

Marlowe (1964) and refers to the importance a person attaches to the evaluative judgments of others. Such external judgments entail social approval when they are positive and social disapproval when they are negative. This is the way how social approval can be "supplied" by others (Brennan and Pettit 2004). These authors, who use the notion "esteem" synonymously with social approval, refer to the two sides of approval as the "positive asset of approbation and the negative liability of disapprobation". As one of the three basic desires in social life[19], individuals strive for accumulating positive esteem (or approval) and avoiding negative esteem, because it constitutes a liability or a cost. Further, individuals seek this asset of approbation in different ways and with different intensity and motivation simply because the importance of this asset across individuals may differ. Consequently, this is exactly what the concept of need for social approval covers – the importance that individuals attach to the positive asset of approbation. While some individuals are very sensitive to the evaluation of their appearance by others and thus modify their behavior in order to trigger positive evaluations, others do not care about what others think about them at all. So, what becomes clear at this point is the motivating function of social approval. Individuals with high need for approval are more willing to change their behavior to make sure others provide the amount of approval they need.

With respect to the survey interview, need for social approval describes a general propensity to give responses in a way to please the interviewer or the social environment in an effort to gain social approval. Correspondingly, starting from the early research on social desirability this individual disposition of the respondent is the major precondition for the existence of SDR (Crowne and Marlowe, 1960, 1964). Crowne and Marlowe (1960) are the first to distinguish between social desirability as describing an item characteristic (in this text referred to as trait desirability) and need for social approval as denoting a personality characteristic of the respondent. Stocké (2004) refers to this factor as the "inner precondition" for SDR, i.e. only respondents with a sufficient need for social approval are receptive for the "outside", i.e. the situational factors. Thus, this factor is indispensable for the existence of SDR because the motivating and incentive character of social approval in individuals is very strong (Brennan and Pettit 2004).

When it comes to the assessment of need for approval, following the long history of SDR research this factor can be measured by means of an SDR scale individually for each respondent. The development of different measurement scales has been outlined in section 3.2.2. These scales, such as the Marlowe-Crowne SD scale or the BIDR, yield a score that indicates the strength of an individual's need for social approval, i.e. of the individual's

19 The other two are the desire for property and the desire for power (Brennan and Pettit, 2004, p. 1).

potential to be biased due to the pressure of compliance with social norms. When assessing the need for social approval, yet one big assumption has to be made. Krosnick (1999, p. 48) points out that "the big assumption involved in this approach is that the tendency to answer one set of questions with a social desirability bias can effectively predict the extent of such bias in a single question". This implies that respondents who are found to bias their responses to a certain set of questions into the social desirable direction do this in the same manner with regard to any other question topic. Therefore, the criticism of this assumption leads Krosnick (1999) to further doubt that such an SDR scale is able to assess the complete extent of social desirability. In fact it is rather likely that situational factors such as the combination of interviewer and respondent characteristics as well as the specific question topic account for a portion of this bias, too. This is in accord with the basic idea of the three-factor model in this study.

Lack of anonymity

The above discussion of need for approval emphasizes that this phenomenon can only emerge through the interaction of at least two individuals. Consequently, what an individual does in order to gain social approval must potentially be perceived by another person or group of persons. That also means that the link between the identity of the individual and the action must be noticeable by another person, i.e. what is referred to above as sanctioning institution. Of course it is possible that people approve of their own behavior with nobody else noticing it and thus provide themselves with approbation. This form of self-esteem may be another incentive for a certain type of behavior, but what we are concerned with here is the approval or esteem that is to be gained from other individuals – or more generally – from the social environment. In a survey interview it is therefore necessary that some other person observes and evaluates a respondent's answers. If answers were stated under perfect anonymity, there would be no incentive to bias them towards some socially or culturally approved content because nobody except the respondent herself would be able to assign the resulting approval to her – in fact, there would be no outside approval. For need for social approval to have an influence on survey responses the perceived anonymity of the respondents must therefore not be complete. The situational influence of (less than perfect) anonymity is explicitly mentioned in Paulhus (1984, 1991).

Before the lack of anonymity can be incorporated into the three-factor model, a clearer definition of anonymity and a differentiation from confidentiality are necessary. Ong and Weiss (2000) make clear the difference between anonymity and confidentiality. Anonymity refers to a situation in which an individual's action cannot be monitored by others. This is practically achieved in a situation in which the researcher or interviewer do not know the identity of the respondent, so the perceivable responses cannot be linked to that identity. In contrast to this, the concept of confidentiality implies that although the researcher knows the respondent's identity, the former assures that "no traceable record of the participant's data will be disclosed" (Ong and Weiss 2000, p. 1694). While confidentiality is assured by most surveys, anonymity is much more difficult to create. The reason for this difficulty is the difference between the concepts of internal and external anonymity on the one hand and objective and subjective anonymity on the other hand. This distinction implies that under confidentiality both the interviewer and the researcher who actually works on the survey data know the respondent's identity, whereas under conditions of strict anonymity the respondent's identity is not disclosed to anybody, not even the researcher. An alternative denotation for these concepts that makes their difference clearer is internal and external anonymity. External anonymity, corresponding to confidentiality, is the assurance that survey data of a respondent are not disclosed to some outside public, whereas internal anonymity refers to strict anonymity in the above sense. Since confidentiality is usually assured in practical survey research, what can be varied by the researcher is the level of internal anonymity.[20] This is mostly done by assigning respondents to different treatment groups. When internal anonymity is assured, respondents usually complete a survey questionnaire in a self-administered way and put it into a sealed ballot box (cf. Alpizar et al. 2008b, Arrow et al. 1993). When such a procedure is applied not even the interviewer or experimenter is able to perceive the responses, i.e. link them to the respondent's identity. Consequently, the response cannot be traced back to the specific respondent in any way, and internal anonymity is achieved.

However, what could be objected to the above explications is the fact that the respondent does not necessarily believe the assurances of (internal and external) anonymity from the part of the interviewer or researcher. While an interview setting may be objectively and externally anonymous because the resulting data are indeed not disclosed to anybody except the researcher, the respondent may *perceive* the situation in a different way and have doubts about the actual anonymity of the interview (Baumeister 1982). This difference is referred to as the distinction between objective and sub-

20 Of course there are experiments that also test the influence of the lack of external anonymity on responses. This can for instance be done by telling respondents that after completing the survey interview (or other type of experiment) the answers will be discussed with other participants. However, such treatments are irrelevant for the case of survey-based environmental valuation and will thus not be considered any further.

jective (or perceived) anonymity and it points to the problem that assurances of anonymity have to be believed by respondents to actually influence response behavior. Therefore, it is rather the lack of perceived anonymity than of objective anonymity that constitutes the second factor in the model of response behavior. Consequently, models that want to test the influence of varying combinations of the three factors on a certain independent variable have to focus on subjective perceptions of anonymity rather than merely on different objective interview settings. The different types of concepts of anonymity are displayed in table 3.4. The distinction between objective and subjective anonymity is of importance when the research setting for the empirical analysis is specified in section 5.2.2.

Table 3.4: Different types of anonymity

	Anonymity / internal anonymity	**Confidentiality / external anonymity**
objective	objective anonymity (assured by self-administered survey using a voting box)	objective confidentiality (assured in the whole survey)
subjective (perceived)	subjective anonymity (assessed by question 40.1, appendix)	subjective confidentiality

Another aspect that becomes clear in this respect is that an environment of complete and subjectively believed anonymity is rather hard to establish in a survey interview, especially when it is conducted in person. For the model of response behavior this means that the second indispensable factor of the model, the *lack* of complete anonymity, is present most often except under very special circumstances. These circumstances include on the one hand the researcher intentionally making an effort to create an objectively and internally anonymous situation and the respondent believing this setting to actually be internally anonymous on the other hand. Only under such circumstances is the interview situation not public at all (not even towards the interviewer) and the incentives for SDR, i.e. the product of the three factors, are zero.

Trait desirability

The third factor of the model of response behavior – trait desirability – is an expression of the respondent's expectations about how an answer to a survey question will be judged by some outside audience (Stocké and Hunkler, 2007). Only when the respondent expects different response options to the same question to result in different evaluations as to the appropriateness of such an answer and to result in different levels of social approval, does she have an incentive to bias her answer in a certain direction. This factor indicates which items have “distortion potential” (Phillips and Clancy 1972).

Many traits, opinions, or intended behavior are especially sensitive issues and thus subject to social desirability as a result of the existence of social norms governing these topics. While talking about such topics, respondents might feel anxious about what kind of evaluation their answer triggers on the part of the interviewer, and consequently how they will appear in the eyes of the latter. In this context, trait desirability – sometimes also termed as social desirability beliefs – is an expression of a respondent’s expectations about how a certain answer concerning such traits, opinions, or intentions will be judged by some outside audience (Stocké and Hunkler 2007). Being confronted with a survey question, a respondent can usually choose from different response options. The precondition of incentives to bias the response is the existence of different expected evaluations of the answer options by the interviewer. In case all response options appear equally desirable, the respondent would not have any means to influence the picture of herself that she draws for the outside. Therefore, Stocké and Hunkler (2007, p. 314) refer to trait desirability as “the cognitive basis of creating a favorable impression in others or themselves”.

Since in a well conducted standardized interview, the interviewer should not show any sign of how she judges the respondent’s answers, the latter usually has to rely on her own beliefs regarding the desirability of certain traits. Due to the lack of information originating in the appearance of the interviewer, she therefore has to draw on general social norms. The assessment of trait desirability is thus an assessment of the strength and direction of social norms relevant to a certain survey topic. Since social norms are not necessarily perceived by all members of society, the individual level of norm perception has to be accounted for in the three-factor model. This is done by means of the trait desirability factor. Such social norms are sometimes activated and even reinforced by certain characteristics of the interviewer or the interview situation. So, even if interviews are conducted in a perfectly standardized manner, the characteristics of the interview setting, such as demographic information of both interviewer and respondent, or the time and location of the interview might serve as a basis upon which a respondent develops her trait desirability ratings (Stocké and Hunkler, 2004). Therefore, this factor must be assessed on an individual level in order to be able to distinguish groups that are characterized by different strength or direction of overall incentives for SDR. It is possible that the desirability or non-desirability of certain traits differs between subgroups within the survey sample. An example from the literature makes this point somewhat clearer. In a survey on sexual behavior, men have been shown to overreport the number of sex partners while women underreport that number, which is, however, only a false indicator of a correlation between gender and promiscuity (Tourangeau and Smith 1996). The reason for this pattern in the data is rather that the trait desirability with regard to the trait "number of sex partners" is different for men and women. While men feel that a high number is socially desirable, women perceive that they can gain social approval by stating a low number. Consequently, different groups distort their responses into different directions.

Concerning the elicitation question in a contingent valuation survey, trait desirability indicates the level of desirability of different WTP responses. Thus, trait desirability assesses for instance if a respondent perceives that stating a zero WTP for a certain environmental project is socially acceptable or highly undesirable or if stating an exceptionally high WTP is desirable or not. Especially when it comes to CVM surveys in different cultural and societal settings, it is not a matter of fact that a zero WTP is always regarded undesirable and a high WTP judged desirable. Further, the type of the environmental good to be valued is also likely to influence the trait desirability of respondents. It is conceivable that a respondent to a CV survey finds it unacceptable to state a zero WTP as contribution to a very urgent environmental problem but thinks that a zero WTP to another project that is rejected by public opinion is highly desirable. Especially, for the case of China, where modesty is an important factor, it is conceivable that extremely high WTP statements are rated rather undesirable than desirable. Therefore, in an effort to determine the preconditions for the occurrence of SDR in contingent valuation surveys, trait desirability ratings of the set of answers to the elicitation question have to be assessed and included into the three-factor model of SDR.

In sum, the trait desirability is zero if a respondent judges all possible answers to a question to be equally socially desirable. In such a situation there is no way for the respondent to gain social approval by deviating from her true answer, so overall incentives for SDR are zero. Only if the respondent regards one response option to be more or less desirable than the other(s) is the trait desirability factor non-zero.

The non-compensatory relationship of the three factors

The main proposition of the three-factor model of response behavior is that the above factors can only exert an influence on a certain dependent variable in a survey when they are all present simultaneously. Following Stocké (2004, 2007), these three factors are necessary for the existence of incentives to respond in a socially desirable way. That means that an SDR bias can only be expected in situations without complete anonymity, with sufficiently large differences in the perceived desirability of different answer options (trait desirability), and by a respondent with at least some need for social approval. The three factors are non-compensatory, since the lack of one of them makes the incentives for SDR vanish entirely.

To make this point somewhat clearer, the consequences of the lack of one or more factors can be considered. In order to study these cases the rational choice approach displayed above will be employed as means of illustration. Recall the framework of the rational choice approach and the type IV situation labeled "inconsistency" where there are both a strong true answer and strong situational effects. This situation is characterized by high values of U_t and U_s, so that

$$\begin{aligned} SEU(A_1) &= p_{1t}U_t + 0 \cdot U_s \\ SEU(A_2) &= 0 \cdot U_t + p_{2s}U_s \,. \end{aligned} \tag{3.6}$$

Assume further that $U_s > U_t$ because both need for social approval and trait desirability jointly drive up the potential utility that can be gained from giving the socially desirable response. At the same time the transparency of the question is clear so that p_{1t} and p_{2s} are both close to 1. In this situation the respondent would select the second response option (the socially desirable response) simply because it is assumed that $U_s > U_t$.

Employing this framework the consequences of a lack of each of the three factors for the decision problem of the respondent can be studied. First, imagine a respondent in an in-person interview who perceives one response option to be more desirable than all others but who has no need for social approval. Although trait desirability and lack of perfect anonymity are given, this respondent does not feel an incentive to bias her response because she does not strive for any social approval. The model assumes that a person without need for social approval does not care about her impression on other people. Therefore, despite the presence of an interviewer and the high desirability of one response option she will not respond in a socially desirable manner. Technically, the lack of need for approval decreases the level of U_s so that it is smaller than U_t. This will make the respondent select the first response option, i.e. stating the true answer, because the subjective expected utility of this option is now greater.

Now think about a respondent in an anonymous interview situation who has a certain need for social approval but perceives no trait desirability. This type of respondent basically seeks social approval and is therefore also willing to give a biased statement in the survey interview. However, since she does not know which response option is more desirable than the others, the action of responding to this question is no opportunity to present herself in a norm-compliant way. The mere lack of trait desirability deactivates overall incentives for SDR simply because the respondent does not know which response option is more desirable. In the rational choice framework this situation is characterized by both a lower value of U_s and by setting both p_{1s} and p_{2s} equal to 0.5. Firstly, the potential utility gain caused by answering in a socially desirable way decreases like in the previous situation when only need for social approval was lacking. Secondly, the respondent cannot discern anymore which response is socially desirable, so both responses are equally likely to trigger outcome U_s, the utility gain from answering in a socially desirable way.

Finally, it is possible that a respondent with a high need for approval judges one response option to be highly desirable, i.e. trait desirability is also non-zero. However, if the interview situation is completely anonymous, according to the model this respondent will not bias her response into the socially desirable direction. Although she knows how to satisfy her need for approval because it is clear to her which response option is the most desirable, there is no use in selecting this option. The rational respondent knows that nobody will ever perceive this response and thus it will have no impact on how she is evaluated by others (i.e. the interviewer). When the implications of the rational choice approach were displayed it was mentioned that perfect anonymity results in a very vague definition of the situation. Consequently, the respondent knows that her response cannot be evaluated by the interviewer and thus there is no connection between a certain response A_i and an outcome U_j – or more precisely, the connection is completely random. Therefore, like in the situation without trait desirability, both p_{1s} and p_{2s} are equal to 0.5. Modifying 3.6 accordingly, the subjective expected utility of giving the true response A_1 exceeds the utility value of the socially desirable response A_2 in this situation.

In this manner, it has been shown that the intuition behind the three-factor model can be illustrated by means of the rational choice approach to response behavior. It should be noted that this specification matches the situation of the elicitation question in a typical CV survey interview quite well. Although respondents are assumed to have a true WTP based on individual preferences, the fact that valuations of environmental goods or other types of public goods are quite unusual might make the influence of situational effects comparably strong. This idea is expressed by the assumption that $U_s > U_t$. Further, the three cases described above can be easily applied to the elicitation question in CVM. By means of this approach the study can investigate the exact constellation of boundary conditions for the occurrence of SDR as announced in the introduction. If all three factors of the model can be assessed empirically, it is possible to predict when a respondent reports her true WTP and when she deviates and states an allegedly socially desirable WTP amount. To this end, the next chapter uses these theoretical considerations to build a practical model to test the influence of incentives for SDR on WTP statements in contingent valuation surveys.

3.4. Summary

The purpose of this chapter was the introduction of the concept of socially desirable responding (SDR) and the development of a behavioral model incorporating different components of the concept. The chapter started by tracing advances in psychological research in this field and defining the concept of SDR. It became clear that the tendency to answer in a socially desirable way is both a characteristic of the respondent's personality and the content of the specific question. The former phenomenon is labeled need for social approval, whereas the latter is termed trait desirability. The personality characteristic of SDR can further be theoretically and empirically divided along two lines. Firstly, psychologists separate between impression management and self-deception and secondly, between enhancement and denial. The first distinction refers to the addressee of SDR. While impression management is a deliberate modification of one's responses in order to make a good impression in the face of others, self-deception is a distortion of answers that even the self believes to be true. It is argued that in surveys only the impression management dimension should be controlled for. The second distinction separates two strategies of gaining social approval. In this respect, enhancement is the claiming of exaggeratedly positive descriptions for the self, whereas denial refers to the tendency to overly reject negative self-descriptions. The connections between these strategies and the statement of WTP amounts in CV surveys were discussed. Based on findings with regard to prospect theory it is conjectured that the denial component exerts stronger behavioral influence and therefore distorts WTP statements more strongly. In addition to that, the difference of SDR and acquiescence and warm glow of giving was discussed in that section. While acquiescence is content independent by definition, SDR mostly appears for sensitive topics and has therefore a clear link to question content. The crucial difference between SDR and warm glow of giving is that the latter forms a legitimate part of a respondent's utility from the perspective of the welfare theoretical background of CVM, whereas the utility gain resulting from increased social approval does not. On top of that, the ability of warm glow to generate utility for the respondent when stating a positive WTP is not dependent on the presence of an interviewer. Unlike need for social approval, warm glow of giving makes the respondent feel better about herself after stating a positive WTP even when this happens with complete anonymity.

Subsequently, the sociological perspective on SDR focuses on the question which components actually make up this construct. The early studies to relate both need for social approval and trait desirability with certain psychological and sociological variables of interest were reviewed and findings were discussed. That makes evident the role that social norms play in determining what kind of behavior is actually desirable and what is undesirable. This discussion demonstrated that social norms are the basis for SDR. Consequently, it has to be scrutinized whether pro-environmental behavior, such as contributing to a public environmental good via contingent valuation surveys, is governed by social norms. That this is the case can easily be shown by discussing the "new environmental paradigm" and quoting empirical research on environmental attitudes. The conclusion of this section is that in today's society clear and sufficiently widely known social norms exist, which call for both pro-environmental mindset and behavior. However, employing the concept of environmentally desirable responding instead of SDR turned out to be still not possible in the present study, because that new concept is not yet methodologically sound, and an appropriate inventory for its measurement does not exist.

Since the empirical part of this study is based on a CV survey in Southwest China, the discussion of the role of social norms was extended in an intercultural dimension. Cultural differences between Chinese society and Western countries, where SDR research originates from, were identified. Overall, it was found that members of rather collectivistic societies such as the Chinese are more likely to engage in impression management than respondents from rather individualistic societies. Several studies that find Eastern subjects to score higher on measures of impression management than Western respondents were discussed. The existence of strong environmental norms and an emerging environmentalism can also be registered for the case of China. So, in conclusion, investigating the influence of SDR in a contingent valuation survey in China appears to be highly necessary.

Based on the above insights of the interplay of different components of the SDR phenomenon, in the second main part of this chapter Esser's (1986, 1991) rational choice approach of modeling response behavior was introduced. It is assumed that respondents form rational expectations about different outcomes resulting from a set of possible response options. This framework was used to theoretically explore the interaction of a set of personal and situational factors potentially responsible for the occurrence of SDR. Eventually, this analysis was able to identify three factors, which all have to be present to provide the rationally utility maximizing respondent with incentives for SDR. These factors are a general need for approval, trait desirability and a lack of anonymity of the interview situation. While the first two factors had been dealt with in the first sections of the chapter already, the concept of anonymity in the interview situation was discussed in detail here. The analysis distinguished between anonymity and confidentiality and objective and subjective anonymity. As factor of the SDR incentive model, subjective (perceived) anonymity should be employed. The crucial idea of this three-factor model is the fact that these factors are non-compensatory, i.e. the lack of only one of these factors makes overall SDR incentives vanish completely. Based on this conceptualization of SDR as multi-component phenomenon, the next chapter will relate this type of response bias and its components to WTP statements in contingent valuation surveys.

Chapter 4

The role of SDR in CVM

4.1. Outline of the chapter

In the precedent chapter, it was shown that strong social norms are at work in the field of environmental protection. As a consequence, questions about private contributions to the provision of environmental goods such as reforestation, clean air or biodiversity protection become normatively sensitive issues. Since such topics are increasingly governed by social norms which prescribe what one should or should not do, respondents who are sensitive to the influence of norms are more and more likely to perceive incentive to bias their answers. So, for the case of contingent valuation surveys, one of the main preconditions for the appearance of SDR is given: they deal with sensitive issues. Consistent with this finding, it was argued in the introductory chapter that social desirability is mentioned quite frequently as a response bias in the contingent valuation literature. It was also said, however, that although many studies touch this topic to some extent, except for Laughland et al. (1994) there is no survey that systematically relates the tendency to respond in a socially desirable manner to WTP statements. In order to provide a comprehensive investigation of the existence of SDR in contingent valuation, the third chapter of this study developed a behavioral model based on rational choice theory. This model identified personal and situational factors that constitute the SDR phenomenon and theoretically specified how these factors are related. It becomes clear that each factor is necessary for SDR incentives to work on the respondent. Consequently, the product of the three factors is what is referred to as SDR variable in the present chapter. After introducing contingent valuation in chapter 2 and the concept of socially desirable responding in chapter 3, the overall aim of this chapter is to develop the theoretical foundations of an empirical investigation of the influence of SDR on WTP statements in contingent valuation surveys. It is in this chapter that the concept of SDR is integrated into the CVM framework. To this end, section 4.2 provides a discussion of the importance of SDR in CVM. The main rationales for an investigation of this response bias in contingent valuation surveys are presented. Firstly, WTP statements in contingent valuation surveys are a form of reported behavior. Respondents indicate what they would do under certain circumstances. Both sociology and psychology find that in such situations SDR is very likely to distort survey responses. Secondly, the increasingly strong social norms with regard to environmental protection raise the likelihood that respondents in contingent valuation surveys bias their answers in a socially desirable direction. Subsequently, the empirical literature on social desirability in CVM is reviewed. It will become clear that this strand of literature is mainly confined to the detection of mode effects, whereas direct assessments of social desirability are almost completely missing.

When it comes to the specific form of influence of SDR on WTP statements for environmental goods, two basic types can be identified: There might be a direct influence of SDR incentives on the decision whether or not to state a positive WTP and on the specific WTP amount. In section 4.3, this relationship between a respondent's incentives to answer in a socially desirable manner and the WTP response is established. Looking at the whole sample of observations, this means that SDR is potentially biasing the distribution of WTP statements affecting both the shape of the distribution, i.e. the relative frequency of the different WTP amounts, and the resulting mean WTP. To this end, a two-step analysis is provided. In a first step it is investigated to what extent SDR is influencing the fraction of respondents selecting a positive WTP amount instead of stating zero. Subsequently, the effect of incentives for socially desirable responding on the selection of a specific WTP is studied. Different types of regression models will be introduced to control for these channels of influence of SDR on WTP responses. In addition to that, it is conceivable that the two components of need for social approval, namely enhancement and denial, exert a different behavioral influence on respondents. Therefore, this section will also look at the theoretical relationships of those different features of the SDR construct and derive research hypotheses to be tested in the empirical analysis in chapter 5.

4.2. Socially desirable responding and the CVM

There are several reasons that call for a systematic analysis of SDR and the conditions for its occurrence in applied environmental valuation. Contingent valuation is a survey-based method and survey literature has long been acknowledging the distorting influence of social desirability in surveys (Krosnick 1999). As mentioned above not only sociology but also other disciplines that rely on survey data admit the proneness of responses to survey questions to be biased as a result of the respondent's attempt to convey a positive self-image. These considerations also hold for the field of survey-based environmental valuation in general and the CVM in particular. Therefore, concern for SDR in contingent valuation surveys has been accompanying the methodological advances in this field of research from the early days of this method. Mitchell and Carson (1989) mention the possibility that respondents shape their answers to CV surveys in order to please the interviewer or the sponsoring institution. The latter phenomenon is referred to as "sponsoring bias" (Mitchell and Carson 1989, p. 238). The fact that these authors discuss social desirability together with compliance and interviewer bias already indicates the close relationship of these phenomena.

Most concern for SDR in sociology revolves around so-called surveys dealing with reported behavior. Since many types of behavior cannot be observed by the researcher, or could only be observed at high costs, behavioral patterns of individuals are assessed through their own reports. For example people are asked what they would do in a certain situation or how they usually act in daily life. This "shortcut" is one typical form of behavioral research in sociology and psychology (Phillips and Clancy 1972). Contingent valuation interviews share this crucial feature with those self-reports because the central question in CVM is the elicitation of the WTP of a respondent for a public project. Due to the hypothetical nature of that question, its response is hypothetical, too. The respondent indicates what she would be willing to pay to realize the project *contingent* on its realization at some future point in time. So, as a result of this common feature of self-reports in sociology and psychology on the one hand and CV interviews in environmental valuation on the other hand, the two methods are equally likely to be prone to evoke SDR. This is easy to understand because in both methods the researcher has to rely on the statements of the respondent in order to assess the variables of interest – reported or hypothetical behavior. The reported and hypothetical nature of the stated response in turn is the reason why the respondent can very effectively influence the picture she conveys to the interviewer or the outside world in general. To this end no change in actual behavior is necessary, but merely a modified statement of what one would do in a certain situation, for instance how much one would be willing to pay if the respecttive project were to be realized.

Another reason why SDR is an issue for the CVM is the fact that environmental protection is associated with widely known social norms as discussed in section 3.2.4. The report of the NOAA Panel mentions that preserving the environment is widely considered desirable (Arrow et al. 1993), which hints at the central role of social norms as precondition for the occurrence of SDR.[21] In this "era of environmental concern" (Mohr 1994), public awareness for problems of the environment such as destruction of ecosystems, air and water pollution, depletion of natural resources, or climate change has risen

21 This idea is the basis for the inclusion of the factor *trait desirability* into the three-factor model of SDR in the third chapter.

sharply in many countries. At the same time, environmental protection has become one of the main foci of government policy all over the world. As a result of the huge public attention for environmental problems in recent years and decades, it is increasingly likely that surveys that deal with environmental topics, such as survey-based environmental valuation, are influenced by social norms. If the majority of people hold pro-environmental views, the statement of indifferent or even negative attitudes towards environmental protection will most likely result in social disapproval. This kind of moral appearance that is at stake when talking about normatively charged topics works as a very powerful motivation to consider one's own self-presentation and even alter statements to avoid social disapproval.

Empirical research on SDR in contingent valuation

As indicated in the introductory chapter, social desirability is often mentioned to be a biasing factor in CV data, yet there have been very few attempts to systematically investigate this influence. The means of analyzing the role of SDR in contingent valuation most commonly applied in the literature so far is the variation of the level of anonymity – or put the other way around the level of "publicness" – of survey responses and the whole interview process. In order to reduce the likelihood of SDR to occur, the NOAA Panel suggests the use of a so-called "simulated ballot-box" (Arrow et al. 1993). This has led researchers to systematically compare WTP estimates of different survey modes (cf. section 2.2.1) in order to isolate the effect of a variation in "publicness", or rather in the degree of exposition of responses to the interviewer. This is because in the field of contingent valuation, most studies that investigate the impact of social desirability associate it very closely with the presence of an interviewer. Therefore, the bulk of studies that aim at this direction have compared WTP statements across different survey modes, such as mail, telephone, and in-person interviewing (e.g. Loomis and King 1994, Mannesto and Loomis 1991, Nielsen 2011). Two major methodological shortcomings that many of these studies suffer from are differing sampling frames and different response rates across the modes. That means that these studies are not reliably identifying the conditions of the modes, which are compared as being exclusively responsible for the different WTP estimates. Rather three potential sources of influence remain, namely non-response, coverage, and social desirability.[22] This holds for the studies in Mannesto and Loomis (1991) who find WTP from an in-person

22 As will be demonstrated below, it is not even clear whether or not the comparison of survey modes that only differ in the existence or non-existence of an interviewer is really evidence for socially desirable responding.

survey to be higher than from a mail survey, Loomis and King (1994) who discover WTP from a mail survey to be higher than from a telephone survey, and Nielsen (2011) who detects no difference of mean WTP from in-person and internet surveys. With difference in response rates of different modes as high as for instance 24 percent in a mail survey and 97 percent in an in-person survey in Mannesto and Loomis' (1991) study, it is obvious that these findings cannot be regarded as evidence for the impact of SDR on WTP statements.

This criticism is addressed by several more recent studies which explicitly hold the two factors sampling frame and response rate constant or at least approximately equal while comparing WTP statements across different modes (Ahlheim et al. 2010, Ethier et al. 2000, Leggett et al. 2003, Smith 2006, Whittaker et al. 1998). Additionally, these studies explicitly control for differences in demographic variables across different survey modes. Thus all remaining differences can be attributed to mode effects. Table 4.1 summarizes the results of all quoted studies that compare WTP estimates across different survey modes.

Table 4.1: Studies that compare WTP estimates across different survey modes

Study	Mean WTP estimates	Comment
Mannesto and Loomis (1991)	in-person > mail	Sampling frame and/or response rates across modes differ.
Loomis and King (1994)	phone < mail	
Nielsen (2011)	in-person = web-based	
Whittaker et al. (1998)	phone > mail	No significant differences in sampling frame and response rates across modes.
Ethier et al. (2000)	phone = mail	
Leggett et al. (2003)	in-person > self-administered	
Smith (2006)	in-person = phone	
Ahlheim et al. (2010)	in-person > mail (DC) in-person = mail (PC)	

In a survey to assess WTP for visiting a recreational park, Whittaker et al. (1998), in addition to holding constant sampling frame and response rate, also weigh responses by demographic variables that differ between the telephone and the mail sample. While these authors find mean WTP estimates in the telephone sample being significantly higher than in the mail sample, a study by Ethier et al. (2000) finds these two modes to yield the same WTP estimates for green electricity. Yet, the latter study detects significantly different responses to several non-WTP questions with obviously socially desirable content across the two modes. These authors conjecture that SDR does not affect WTP statements but only attitudinal questions.

Further evidence against a strong influence of SDR on WTP responses is reported in Smith (2006) who does not detect a difference in WTP estimates between an in-person and a telephone survey in a health economic context, either. However, these findings contrast the conclusion of Whittaker et al. (1998) who hold social desirability responsible for the significantly higher WTP statements in the telephone survey.

In response to the shortcomings of comparing data across survey modes Leggett et al. (2003) design a study that attempts to hold constant all characteristics of the survey by conducting two surveys at the same location and time. These authors compare WTP statements for user fees of a recreational park in the Southern United States elicited through either in-person or self-administered interviews. They find that WTP estimates of the in-person survey are significantly higher than such estimates of the self-administered survey and interpret these results as more reliable evidence for the existence of social desirability. Yet, this conclusion is dubious because what their findings really indicate is the following. Firstly, the level of anonymity represents a factor that is potentially biasing results in CVM surveys and secondly, that it might drive stated WTP alone, i.e. without interaction with other factors of SDR because these are not explicitly assessed and analyzed. Merely showing that WTP statements actively elicited by an interviewer are higher on average than such statements made on the questionnaire by respondents themselves does not necessarily prove the existence of SDR. Findings by Ahlheim et al. (2010) suggest that the form of the elicitation question, too, might influence the occurrence of such mode effects. In this study, WTP statements for the improvement of tap water quality in Thailand are found to differ between in-person and mail survey when the dichotomous choice (DC) format is applied but to be similar across these modes when the PC format is used. The authors can, however, only speculate whether this derives from the fact that DC responses are more prone to be influenced by yea-saying, i.e. social desirability. Further, by conducting two surveys – one before and one after revisions in the questionnaire based on results from so-called citizen expert group discussions – it can be shown that one reason for these differences between the in-person and mail survey is the self-selection bias associated with the latter survey mode. After the questionnaire has been modified according to input from local citizens, this biasing influence seems to have vanished. Thus, what these results portend is the fact that social desirability might not be the only factor being responsible for different WTP estimates across modes.

From a more general perspective, the CVM exercise resembles a voluntary contribution to the provision of a public good. Experimental economics provides some interesting insights as to the effect of anonymity on such contributions. While numerous laboratory experiments show that relaxation of the participants' anonymity increases voluntary private contributions to the provision of public goods (Andreoni and Petrie 2004, Rege and Telle 2004), several studies investigate the role of different degrees of "publicness" and thus also the effect of social desirability on such contributions in natural field experiments that resemble CVM settings more closely (Alpizar et al. 2008a, List et al. 2004). For instance List et al. (2004) conduct an experimental study in order to assess the role of different degrees of response perceptibility on actual and hypothetical contributions to a public good. They find that both actual and hypothetical contributions are highest when responses are perceptible by other participants of the experiment compared to settings when they can only be known by the experimenter or by nobody except the participant herself. The authors interpret the willingness to contribute more in the public setting as utility that participants receive from publicly advertising their goodwill. This utility must be separated from the "lump" value of the public good to be provided. This very much resembles the problem of SDR in contingent valuation where the additional WTP of a respondent influenced by social desirability concerns can analogously be interpreted as the value of the social approval she gets from this statement. Obviously, such an overstatement of WTP distorts the valuation of the good in question. Support for these findings is reported in Alpizar et al. (2008a) who are studying the effect of the degree of respondent anonymity and of the information of the contribution of others on the willingness to pay a voluntary entrance fee for a national park in Costa Rica. These authors find that social context defined as the degree of perceptibility of contribution statements by the experimenter is influencing actual and hypothetical contributions in the same way as in List et al. (2004). Although the focus of both studies is on the investigation of hypothetical bias, what is important is that decreasing anonymity increases WTP, and that social approval or esteem is likely to be the motivation for such behavior.

Apart from the experimental results regarding the relaxation of anonymity the above findings on mode effects in CVM are very inconsistent and indicate no clear tendency whether the use of in-person or telephone interviews results in higher or equal WTP estimates compared to mail or self-administered surveys. Further, the results in Ahlheim et al. (2010) show that it is far from clear that social desirability is the sole explanation for these mode effects, which is, however, the basic assumption of most of the work quoted above. Rather than conceptualizing differences in WTP estimates across survey modes as sufficient condition of the existence of SDR, it is likely to be in fact merely a necessary condition. If SDR is at work, survey modes that employ active interviewers, such as in-person and telephone surveys, can be expected to yield different WTP estimates than mail or self-administered surveys. However, if merely such a difference in results is reported it is not safe to attribute this exclusively to the influence of SDR, since other factors, such as elicitation format, self-selection bias, the specific appearance of the interviewer and the time and location of the interview might play a role, too.

Therefore, in order to assess the influence of social desirability in CVM interviews a more direct approach has to be employed. The only study that has ever attempted to directly measure the tendency to respond in a socially desirable manner and relate this to stated WTP is reported in Laughland et al. (1994). In this study, the Marlowe-Crowne SD scale is administered along with a self-administered CV questionnaire in a student sample. The hypothesis that respondents with higher need for social approval as measured by the Marlowe-Crowne SD scale generally have a significantly higher WTP for socially desirable goods, such as improved food safety and landscape preservation, is not supported by the data. This means that simply correlating a psychological SDR score with open-ended and dichotomous choice WTP data is not necessarily able to reveal any impact of SDR on contingent valuation statements. Although the authors acknowledge the existence of a more differentiated concept of social desirability consisting at least of need for approval and trait desirability, this conceptual multidimensionality is not taken into account in their empirical study. The reason for the weak effect of need for social approval might be the fact that the level of social desirability of the two goods to be valued is not explicitly assessed and included into the model. Thus, the failure of separately measuring if the good to be valued is indeed considered socially desirable (trait desirability) and relating this to the score of need for approval might be an explanation for the failure of finding a robust relationship between SDR and WTP statements in this study. These considerations are the basis of the development of the three-factor approach displayed in the previous chapter and tested in the empirical part of this study.

4.3. The effects of SDR on WTP statements

The influence of incentives for SDR on WTP statements manifests itself in a direct relationship between these two variables. It is conceivable that WTP statements are systematically affected by the SDR variable, i.e. by the factors that constitute this variable according to the three-factor model of socially desirable responding. In other words, it will be tested if incentives for SDR are a determinant of WTP statements.

At this point the main implications of the three-factor model for the statement of WTP in a contingent valuation survey must be investigated in greater detail. Section 3.3 introduces the three-factor model of overall incentives for SDR that includes both situational and personality characteristics. The first factor, need for social approval, constitutes a personality characteristic. The measurement scale employed in the survey assigns a need for approval score to each respondent with a high score indicating a relatively high need for approval and a low score a low level of approval seeking. In addition to this personality variable, the level of perceived anonymity in the interview situation and the trait desirability with respect to the specific question content are conditional on the interview situation, i.e. they are situational variables. In the case of the essential part of a contingent valuation interview, namely the elicitation of the WTP for a public project in the environmental sector, trait desirability refers to the perceived desirability of stating a high amount. Thus, this factor is positive only for those respondents who feel that it is socially desirable to contribute more to the environmental project in question than less. If the respondent perceives a high level of anonymity, this means that she does not consider the interview to be public and does not even believe the interviewer to be able to get to know her WTP statement. Therefore, only with a lack of perfect (perceived) anonymity does the respondent feel that her responses are perceived by the interviewer or another outside public.

The basic idea of a set of factors jointly determining the level of individual bias as conceptualized in the three-factor model can be found in several other studies that investigate survey bias. The sociological studies that first investigated the relationship between need for social approval and trait desirability have been discussed in detail in section 3.2.3 (Gove and Geerken 1977, Phillips and Clancy 1970, 1972). While the results in Phillips and Clancy (1972) indicate that need for social approval and trait desirability independently influence a variety of self-reported characteristics and patterns of behavior, Gove and Geerken (1977) do not find any systematic influence of the two factors on three different indicators of mental health. In addition to that, two more recent studies test the interaction of more than one constituting factor of SDR (Chen et al. 1997, Stocké 2004, 2007). Chen et al. (1997) identify an interaction effect between perceived desirability of positive and negative affectivity (i.e. trait desirability) and need for social approval as measured by the Marlowe-Crowne SD scale.[23] The data of this study show that the probability of a respondent endorsing an item of the two scales measuring positive and negative affectivity is closely related to the judged

23 In this context, positive affectivity is defined as "individuals' level of pleasurable engagement with their environment" (Chen et al. 1997, p. 184). In contrast to that, these authors refer to negative affectivity as an "aversive mood state" towards the environment. While high positive affectivity is associated with enthusiastic, active and energetic feelings, negative affectivity manifests itself in distress, anger, disgust, and nervousness.

desirability of this item. This relationship turned out to be much stronger for respondents with high need for social approval, i.e. the level of need for approval modifies the relationship of trait desirability and dependent variables. This is equal to an interaction effect of need for social approval and trait desirability. Stocké (2004a, 2007) tests the three-factor model as specified above with respect to attitudes of Germans towards foreigners. The results of this study support the hypothesis of the three-factor model, namely that there is only a significant influence of SDR on survey responses if all three factors of this construct are at work simultaneously. Although both need for approval and trait desirability have a significant and independent effect on attitudinal statements regarding foreigners, an interaction model of all three factors yields a significant interaction effect. It should be noted that this is the only study that practically integrates the lack-of-anonymity factor into the model. However, it is not assessed as perceived anonymity but simply as objective anonymity by means of comparing different interview treatments. Therefore, it is not clear to what extent respondents in the anonymous treatment actually believe the assurance of anonymity, and how strong the resulting influence is on response behavior. Like discussed in section 3.3.2 it would be more appropriate to employ lack of *perceived* anonymity as the third factor in the model.

In the only application of an SDR scale in a contingent valuation survey by Laughland et al. (1994) discussed above, a significant effect of need for social approval on WTP statements for improved food safety and landscape protection cannot be found. What is totally neglected in that study and might also be a reason for the failure to find significant impact of SDR on WTP statements is the influence of an interviewer because the survey is self-administered. That means that for each respondent the lack of anonymity factor equals zero (i.e. the situation is in fact anonymous), and according to the three-factor model in such a situation no influence of the other factors on the dependent variable can be expected. In an in-person survey results might have been different.

In sum, empirical evidence on the interaction of the different factors of SDR is highly inconclusive. While some studies find a viable interaction effect of two or all three factors for certain survey topics, results of other investigations show independent influence of the different factors. Presumably the specific topic of the survey, i.e. the dependent variable of the analytic model is crucial to the applicability of the three-factor model of SDR. Therefore, this study wants to scrutinize the applicability of this approach to survey-based environmental valuation. It is hypothesized that if all three factors need for social approval, trait desirability, and a lack of perfect anonymity are present, a respondent feels the urge to respond in a socially desirable way rather than entirely truthfully. However, this idea of conceptualizing SDR as the result of the simultaneous existence of three factors is new in the field of survey-based environmental valuation. Therefore, the appropriateness and plausibility of this model has to be scrutinized empirically.

This can be done in two steps. Firstly, it is conceivable that these incentives affect the decision of a respondent whether to state zero or a positive WTP. So as the first part of the analysis, the influence of SDR on this decision is investigated. In societies characterized by publicly promoted environmental concern, the statement of a zero WTP for a public environmental good might trigger social disapproval. As environmental conservation is beneficial to the whole society, citizens are likely to perceive that everybody should contribute to this effort (cf. section 3.2.4). Therefore, it can be expected that a good part of respondents perceive social norms that call for a contribution to the environmental project independent of the individual valuation of it. Clearly, such calls for a contribution can be expected to influence respondents with incentives for socially desirable responding more strongly. This means that the incentives for SDR also work as a motivation to state a positive WTP to avoid social disapproval regardless of these respondents actually valuing the environmental project or not. It can thus be hypothesized that the fraction of zero responses in a sample is influenced by the existence of SDR incentives. Consequently, the following hypothesis can be formulated.

Hypothesis 1: Respondents with overall incentives for SDR are significantly more likely to state a positive WTP than respondents without such incentives.

This hypothesis can be tested by employing a simple probit regression model with the likelihood to state a positive WTP as dependent variable. In addition to this regression model, the first part of this empirical analysis is simply to check whether there are more respondents selecting the first (0 RMB) or second (1-5 RMB) interval on the payment card when the SDR factors are present or not. To this end, histograms of the response frequencies of the different WTP amounts on the PC will be displayed. Since respondents with incentives for SDR are dependent on the evaluative judgement of their social environment, it can be expected that those who originally wanted to select a WTP of zero switch to the first positive interval to avoid social disapproval. From the point of view of these respondents the switch to the next highest PC interval might appear insignificant, especially because they might perceive the hypothetical nature of the elicitation question. However, this kind of misreporting of WTP statements will bias the estimation of mean WTP and therefore of the social value of the public project in question.

As a second step, the analysis investigates the effect of incentives for SDR on the specific WTP stated by a respondent. Since the trait desirability variable assesses whether respondents think that expressing a higher WTP is better, it can be expected that respondents with incentives for SDR systematically state higher WTP amounts. As above, the main idea is the non-compensating relationship of the three factors in the model. This means that it is expected that the biasing influence of SDR incentives only exists for those respondents who exhibit all of the three factors need for social approval, lack of perfect anonymity and trait desirability. Therefore, the following hypothesis will be tested:

Hypothesis 2: Respondents with overall incentives for SDR state a significantly higher WTP than respondents without such incentives.

If this hypothesis can be rejected it has to be investigated which of the single factors systematically influence WTP statements and whether they do it independently or jointly. To this end, the factors will also be included as a set of explanatory variables independently. The specific research design including the estimation model to test these hypotheses will be introduced below.

The influence of enhancement and denial

As is further documented in chapter 5, a modified version of the impression management subscale of the Balanced Inventory of Desirable Responding (BIDR) is employed to measure need for social approval in the empirical part of this study. One of the main advantages of the use of the BIDR is its capability of separately measuring the two components of need for approval, namely denial and enhancement. These concepts and their influence on WTP statements have already been introduced in section 3.2.2, and it is at this point that their dichotomy becomes relevant for the empirical analysis. The BIDR allows for the calculation of three different scores: an overall score of need for social approval, an enhancement score, and a denial score. It is very well conceivable that individuals score differently on the two subscales when they are following different strategies to gain social approval. In this respect it must consequently be investigated if the enhancement and denial components of social desirability exert a differing influence on mean WTP.

Is has been shown that the strategy of approval seeking is to some extent conditional on the cultural background of the individual (Lalwani et al. 2006, Lalwani et al. 2009). Although for the case of Western subjects several studies have presented evidence that the dichotomy of denial and enhancement cannot be detected empirically within the impression management dimension of SDR (Paulhus and Reid 1991), this is still fervently debated concerning Asian respondents (Li and Li 2008). Therefore, in the framework of this empirical analysis the relative strength of the enhancement and denial components to influence WTP statements will be tested.

A rationale for the expected stronger behavioral influence of denial can be found in prospect theory (cf. section 3.2.2). Within that framework, individuals value losses more strongly than equivalent gains (Kahneman and Tversky 1979). Thus, the fear of a loss has a stronger motivating influence on behavior than the prospect of an equivalent future gain. If this characteristic of the individual value function within the larger framework of prospect theory is correct, the behavioral influence of the denial component of SDR should be stronger than that of enhancement. It has been introduced earlier that the strategy referred to as enhancement is the conscious exaggeration of one's own positive qualities in order to receive approval from others, whereas denial refers to a defensive strategy in which the individual seeks to avoid dropping under a certain minimum level regarding her appearance in the eyes of others. So, indeed enhancement corresponds to the prospect of a positive change in social approval, whereas the denial concept refers to the fear of decreased approval by others.

The idea that denial influences the statement of WTP more than enhancement is further supported by the fact that the survey in the present study is conducted in the socio-cultural context of China. When it comes to rural China, it makes sense to assume that the more defensive denial strategy is of greater importance than the enhancement strategy. It has been reported that Chinese people are educated in a way not to stand out among a group of people. Liu et al. (2003, p. 292) quote an important Confucian teaching: "Tall trees catch more wind", which stresses modesty and warns people not to strive for individualistic goals. Such a mindset would result in much less enhancement of Chinese individuals that have a basic need for social approval compared with their Western counterparts. Empirically, the above expectation can be tested by the following hypothesis.

Hypothesis 3: In all the above models, the denial component of need for social approval has a stronger influence on WTP statements than the enhancement component.

This hypothesis can be tested by replacing the overall need for approval score in the three-factor model by the separate denial and enhancement scores in turn. That means that the subscores are both included in a model that investigates the main effects of the three factors of SDR and in interaction models.

Research design

After the main hypotheses for the empirical investigation have been formulated, the actual research design is to be introduced in greater detail. When modeling the three factors in an empirical application in a CVM study, one of them is continuous while the others are binary. Since the first factor, need for social approval, is measured by means of a social desirability scale, its output is a score and thus continuous. Following the tradition of decades of social desirability research outlined in sections 3.2.2 and 3.2.3, respondents can be classified as having any level of need for social approval. As introduced above, this is a general personality characteristic of the respondent which is assumed not to vary across situations, i.e. survey topics and settings. In the following, the need for approval variable for respondent *h* will be denoted N_h.

In this setting, perceived anonymity is modeled as a binary variable because it describes a certain state of the interview situation – the interview setting is either perceived as anonymous, i.e. the respondent feels that her answers cannot be linked to her in any way, or it is not. When the former is the case and the respondent perceives complete anonymity, the interview situation can be interpreted as non-public, which is modeled with the binary variable P_h. This variable takes the value 1 if the respondent does *not* feel that the interview situation is anonymous (i.e. it is somehow *public*) and zero if she perceives it to be anonymous. Coded in this way, the variable equals 1 if there is an incentive to respond in a socially desirable way and zero if there is no such incentive.

Eventually, the desirability of a certain answer option is assumed to be binary for the following reasons. The main variable of interest in CVM studies is of course the WTP response, so the trait desirability variable T_h should asses how socially desirable a certain answer is. Due to the numerousness of possible answers in the PC elicitation format[24] respondents are simply asked if they think that it is more desirable to state a high WTP than a low one. If this is the case, the variable equals 1. Yet, if respondents do not think that stating a higher WTP is more socially desirable, T_h is equal to zero. Respondents agreeing to this statement (i.e. having $T_h = 1$) are assumed to perceive a social norm that asks for a high contribution to the good to be valued. When it comes to stating their WTP for the environmental project in question they simply feel that stating the more the better. The question for trait desirability is thus a tool to assess to what extent a respondent perceives the social norm concerning the topic in question – the contribution to the provi-

24 In open-ended CVM the number of possible answers is infinite since any positive number is a potential answer. When the PC approach is employed, all intervals on the card are possible options, which are still quite numerous. Only when the DC elicitation format is applied could one think of another way of assessing trait desirability by just asking how desirable it is to accept / not to accept a certain bid.

sion of a public environmental good. The three SDR variables are summarized in table 4.2.

Table 4.2: Coding of the variables of the three-factor model of SDR

Variable name	Name of the factor	Range	Symbol
BIDR14	Need for social approval	[0; 14]	N_h
PUBLIC/EXPUB	Lack of anonymity or "Publicness"	0,1	P_h
TRAIT	Trait desirability	0,1	T_h

In the first model hypothesis 1 is tested. This is done by means of an ordinary probit regression model with the dummy variable *posWTP$_h$* as dependent variable. This variable is 1 for respondents with a positive WTP and zero when a respondent states a zero WTP. In addition to the usual set of demographic variables, the three SDR variables enter the regression model according to 4.1. In that equation, s_h is a j-dimensional vector of characteristics of household h as well as the whole interview setting. Accordingly, γ is a j-dimensional vector of coefficients (Haab and McConnell 2002, p. 26). It thus holds that

$$\gamma s_h = \sum_{j=1}^{J} \gamma_j s_{jh}. \tag{4.1}$$

This relationship is of importance in order to assess the influence of characteristics of the respondent or the interview procedure on WTP statements. It is the vector s_h that comprises all explanatory variables of the WTP estimation model, such as respondent's demographic and attitudinal variables as well as specific settings of the interview process. Consequently, the SDR variables have to be included in this manner, as well.

The second model refers to hypothesis 2. In order to test the influence of SDR on the specific WTP amount, the above factors have to be included as explanatory variables in an estimation model. This model for payment card CV as introduced in section 2.2.2 is basically a maximum likelihood procedure (cf. Cameron and Huppert 1989). The log likelihood function of the PC approach is specified in 2.24 for respondents $h = 1, \dots, H$. Similar to model 1, it can be extended to include more explanatory variables besides the boundaries of the selected PC interval according to 2.25. After setting up the basic models to find determinants of positive WTP and the specific WTP amount, respectively, the inclusion of the factors of SDR should be illustrated. The interpretation of the influence of the respective coefficients is the same in both models and will be discussed in the following.

The three-factor model of SDR gives clear instructions how the three factors are to be combined to yield the SDR variable that will be included into the model as additional explanatory variable. As a result of the non-compensatory nature of the relationship between the three factors they have to be multiplied. From an econometric perspective, the model appropriate for the inclusion of three mutually influencing variables is a fully specified interaction model (cf. Brambor et al. 2006, Kam and Franzese 2007). Thus, the factors enter the estimation equation both separately and multiplicatively connected. With this model in its fully specified form the vector of explanatory variables reads[25]

$$\begin{aligned} \gamma s_h = \sum_{j=1}^{J} \gamma_j s_{jh} + \delta_1 N_h + \delta_2 P_h + \delta_3 T_h + \delta_4 N_h P_h \\ + \delta_5 N_h T_h + \delta_6 P_h T_h + \delta_7 N_h P_h T_h. \end{aligned} \tag{4.2}$$

In this equation, N_h is the need for approval score, P_h the level of "publicness" and T_h the trait desirability rating of respondent h (cf. table 4.2). Assuming that N_h is continuous and both P_h and T_h are binary variables describing a certain state, the interpretation of the coefficients δ_1 to δ_7 is as follows. δ_1, δ_2, and δ_3 describe the influence of the respective factors of SDR on WTP if the two other factors are zero, respectively. For instance, if both need for approval N_h and trait desirability T_h are zero, δ_2 indicates the effect of the fact that the interview is not completely perceived to be anonymous. Coefficients δ_4, δ_5, and δ_6 describe the influence of an interaction of two factors on WTP when the respective third factor is zero. Coefficient δ_5 for example represents the effect of need for approval on WTP for respondents who perceive trait desirability but no lack of anonymity. That means that this coefficient describes the effect of a two-part interaction of need for approval and trait desirability when lack of anonymity is zero. The other two coefficients of this kind, δ_4 and δ_6, also indicate the impacts of such two-part interactions with the respective third factor being equal to zero. As hypothesized according to the three-factor model, these two-part interactions are not expected to be significantly different from zero.

The main coefficient of interest, however, is δ_7, the coefficient of the overall interaction term. If this coefficient is significantly positive, hypotheses 1 and 2, respectively, cannot be rejected. This means that there is a significantly positive influence of SDR when all three factors are non-zero.

25 Note that this equation indicates the general form of a regression model. Although it was mentioned that a probit model is employed to test hypothesis 1, the focus at this stage is on the form of inclusion of explanatory variables. Therefore, this general form is chosen.

Analogously, δ_1 to δ_6 are not expected to be significantly different from zero because these coefficients express the simultaneous influence of one or two SDR factors when the respective rest of the set of factors is zero. According to the three-factor model, in such situations there would be no influence of (such an incomplete form of) SDR on WTP statements.

As an alternative to the fully specified interaction model, a short version of that model will be applied, too. In general, interaction models with three interacting variables are unlikely to yield significant results because the presence of so many product terms computed of the same three factors leads to relatively high correlations between these additional explanatory variables. Therefore, the fact that the two situational factors are binary can be exploited and they can simply be multiplied to yield one new factor. So, after multiplying trait desirability T_h and lack of anonymity P_h, the new dummy variable PT_h is equal to one for respondents who do not perceive perfect anonymity and rate the desirability of stating higher WTP amounts higher than stating lower amounts. The new variable is equal to zero when either both or just one of the original variables are zero. It consists of the two situational components of incentives for SDR and is thus the situational precondition for the third factor, need for social approval, to be able to exert influence on WTP statements. This means that only in situations which are favorable to the influence of SDR incentives (i.e. without perfect anonymity *and* with trait desirability at the same time) can an influence of need for social approval be expected. Thus, this new situational dummy can be interpreted as a moderator of the influence of need for social approval on WTP statements. According to hypotheses 1 and 2, when the dummy is 1, need for approval potentially influences WTP, and when it equals zero there is no such influence. With this short interaction model, the basic character of the three factor model to integrate both personal and situational components of SDR is preserved. The alternative interaction model with need for social approval N_h and the product of trait desirability and lack of anonymity PT_h for respondent h has the form

$$\gamma s_h = \sum_{j=1}^{J} \gamma_j s_{jh} + \delta_1 N_h + \delta_2 PT_h + \delta_3 N_h PT_h. \tag{4.3}$$

Again, when the coefficient of the interaction term δ_3 is significantly different from zero, hypotheses 1 and 2, respectively, cannot be rejected. At the same time, the coefficients of the two constituent terms δ_1 and δ_2 should not be significant. These two interaction models constitute the way the additional social desirability variables will be included into the model to estimate determinants of WTP. In addition to this empirical test of the three-factor model, the main effects of the three factors will be tested. This will be done by including the all factors N_h, P_h and T_h independently. According to hypotheses 1 and 2, there should be no independent influence of any of the factors on the decision to state a positive WTP and on the specific WTP amount, respectively.

Model 3 tests the influence of the enhancement and denial components as expressed in hypothesis 3. To this end, the need for social approval score N_h is replaced in all models specified above in turn by a score of all enhancement items N_h^e of respondent h and a score of all denial items N_h^d, respectively. Apart from this, nothing else changes in the respective models. That is, first the model of WTP determinants according to 2.24 is calculated including in turn the fully specified interaction model, the short interaction model, and the main effects model for both enhancement and denial. In addition to all this, two more models are tested including both N_h^e and N_h^d simultaneously. This is firstly, the main effects model including both the enhancement score N_h^e and the denial score N_h^d as well as the other two factors P_h and T_h. Secondly, the last variation uses the two interaction terms that can be calculated with the enhancement and the denial score only, i.e. $N_h^e P_h T_h$ and $N_h^d P_h T_h$. In both of these models the relative influence of the enhancement and denial components can be compared directly.

4.4. Summary

This chapter integrated the concept of SDR as developed in chapter 3 into the framework of the CVM. Two main reasons can be found why concern for the occurrence of SDR in contingent valuation surveys is justified. Firstly, CVM is a survey-based technique that assesses statements about intended behavior, i.e. the WTP statement. If respondents only indicate what they would do under certain circumstances they have the chance to please the interviewer by simply modifying their verbal response without having to change actual behavior. Secondly, in today's societies pro-environmental behavior is heavily charged with social norms. If more and more people hold pro-environmental attitudes, the statement of indifferent or negative views regarding the contribution to the provision of environmental goods is associated with costs in the form of social disapproval. As a consequence, respondents anticipating such disapproval are likely to bias their responses in order to comply with the norms they perceive. Subsequently, some approaches of SDR research in contingent valuation were reviewed. Most of these empirical studies compare mean WTP estimates across survey modes and often find mode effects. Generally, surveys employing interviewers, such as in-person and telephone surveys, elicit higher WTP statements than mail or self-administered surveys, which do not rely on the active involvement of an interviewer. However, it is argued that this finding is rather a necessary than a sufficient condition of the existence of SDR. Instead, a more direct approach, such as the administration of a social desirability scale along with the CV survey and the inclusion of other factors of this response bias, has to be employed.

In the second part of the chapter, section 4.3 developed the research hypotheses and introduced the specific research design for the empirical study reported in chapter 5. That section dealt with the direct influence of SDR on WTP statements. The main assertion of the three-factor model of desirable responding is expressed in hypotheses 1 and 2: If all factors are present there is a significant influence of SDR on WTP statements. This can be tested by including the three factors into the regression model to identify the determinants of WTP responses as an interaction model. Different specifications of this model will be tested in the next chapter; these are a fully specified interaction model, a short interaction model and the main effects model which includes all factors independently. This analysis is done in two steps. Hypothesis 1 specified that there is an effect of incentives for SDR on the decision whether to state zero or a positive WTP amount. Individuals perceiving such incentives are expected to be more likely to give a positive WTP response. Similarly, hypothesis 2 states that the presence of all three factors biases the stated WTP amounts upwards. Respondents who feel the incentives to answer in a socially desirable manner are expected to state systematically higher WTP amounts than respondents without such incentives. The research design consisting of the different types of regression models apply to both steps of this analysis. The last aspect to be discussed in that section was the relative influence of the enhancement and denial components of need for social approval on WTP. Following the notion of loss aversion in prospect theory, the influence of the denial component on WTP is expected to be stronger. This expectation is expressed in hypothesis 3. Therefore, in all the above models the overall need for approval score is replaced by separate enhancement and denial scores to test their relative impact on WTP statements.

Chapter 5

Empirical application

So far, this study has developed a theoretical framework for the analysis of the impact of social desirability on WTP statements in contingent valuation surveys. In the previous chapter the theoretical links between SDR and the statement of WTP were discussed. After finding that SDR is a potential problem threatening the reliability and validity of WTP statements because of the strong influence of social norms in this field, the fundamental form of impact of SDR on such statements was discussed: direct influence of SDR on WTP statements in CVM. Based on these theoretical insights five research hypotheses were derived. Consequently, the main objective of this chapter is to empirically test whether these hypotheses can be rejected.

Therefore, this chapter presents the empirical application of a practical contingent valuation survey to determine the social value of a future land-use scenario that fosters the conservation of biodiversity through reforestation in a nature reserve area in Southwest China. This survey serves as the framework for testing the hypotheses derived in the previous chapter. The impact of socially desirable responding on WTP responses to a valuation survey can thus be empirically investigated. To this end, appropriate methods of measurement have to be developed that allow for an assessment of the factors of the models devised above. Basically, this will be questions and question inventories to measure the three factors of SDR. These question inventories have to be developed and their reliability and validity has to be documented. Only if these new questions reliably assess what is specified in the three constructs of need for social approval, incomplete anonymity and trait desirability, can the resulting data be used as input into empirical models that test the above research hypotheses. Therefore, the present chapter consists of five sections. Section 5.1 introduces the study area, its historical background and environmental problem and portrays the research project providing the framework for this study. Thereafter, section 5.2 reports on the development of appropriate question inventories to assess the different factors of SDR. This part will take some room because it includes a discussion of shortcomings of existing question inventories, details on the adaption process of questions for this study and extensive evidence of the reliability and validity of the questions eventually employed in the survey. The next two sections report data from the valuation survey. Section 5.3 provides some overall results of the contingent valuation study, and section 5.4 provides an extensive analysis of the impact of SDR on WTP statements in that survey. A variety of models is tested including the influence of social desirability on the fraction of zero responses and the amount of stated WTP. After these four main sections, major results are summed up and discussed in section 5.5.

5.1. Deforestation and rubber monocultures in Xishuangbanna, SW China

The Sino-German research cooperation "Rural development through land use diversification: actor-based strategies and integrative technologies for agricultural landscapes in the Southwestern Chinese highlands" constitutes the framework of the following empirical study.[26] The cooperation's duration was from 2007 to 2010 and it was jointly funded by the German Federal Ministry of Education and Research (BMBF) and the Ministry of Science and Technology (MOST) of the People's Republic of China. While the cooperation comprised numerous universities and research institutions in both countries, major partners were University of Hohenheim on the German side and Xishuangbanna Tropical Botanical Garden (Chinese Academy of Sciences) on the Chinese side. Main research site was the Naban River Watershed National Nature Reserve in Xishuangbanna Prefecture in the southern part of Yunnan Province, China. As part of this research cooperation, the subproject ECON A "Employing direct and participatory valuation methods for supporting allocative decisions in environmental policy" conducted a contingent valuation study in Jinghong, the capital city of Xishuangbanna Prefecture. This subproject was jointly led by Prof. Dr. Michael Ahlheim and Dr. Oliver Frör of the University of Hohenheim. The following section will briefly provide information on the background of the LILAC project and further introduce the CVM survey, its specific content and then turn to the operationalization of a measurement tool of incentives for socially desirable responding.

26 The short-name reads "Living Landscapes – China" (LILAC). In the following, the research cooperation will be referred to as LILAC project.

5.1.1. Study area, the environmental problem and the LILAC project

Xishuangbanna Dai Autonomous Prefecture is located at the southernmost edge of Yunnan Province in Southwest China, bordering Laos and Myanmar. The prefecture lies at the northern edge of tropical Southeast Asia in the transition zone between tropics and subtropics. Therefore, its climate is affected both by warm air-streams and monsoon coming from the Indian Ocean and cooler subtropical winds from continental parts of inner China (Li et al. 2007). This is the basis for the division of the year into two seasons, a rainy season from May to October and a dry season from November to April.

The nature of this transition zone between tropics and subtropics is also the reason for a diverse mixture of plant and animal species both from tropical and moderate origin (Cao and Zhang 1997). Therefore, Xishuangbanna is the region with the highest biodiversity in the whole of China (Li et al. 2007), a diversity hotspot in species-rich Yunnan Province, which in China is often referred to as "Kingdom of Plants". While it only accounts for 0.2% of the land area of the PRC, Xishuangbanna is home to 25% of all plant species in the country (Xu 2006). The topography of the region is mountainous with about 95% of the area being covered with mountains and hills (Li et al. 2007). The Mekong River (*Lancang Jiang* in Chinese) runs through the prefecture from north to south on its way from the Tibetan Plateau towards the lower regions in Southeast Asia. The prefecture hosts about 20 tributaries to the Mekong River which form a complex system of watersheds. One of these tributaries is the Nanban River Watershed where the main research site of the LILAC-project is located.

Due to its proximity to Southeast Asia the region is characterized by a high degree of ethnic diversity, which is reflected in its status within the Chinese administrative system as an Autonomous Prefecture of the Dai people. The prefecture's population divides roughly into one third Han Chinese, the major ethnic group in the People's Republic, one third Dai, and another third consisting of another 12 ethnic minorities including for instance Akha (*Hani* in Chinese), Bulang, Yi, and Jinuo. With the prefecture being mostly rural the only major city is Jinghong, the prefectural capital. The population in urban Jinghong amounts to approximately 100,000 people. Roughly half of them are Han Chinese (Jinghong 2008).

Major economic sectors are tourism, border trade, and agriculture, i.e. mainly rubber cultivation. They are responsible for the comparatively good economic performance and rapid development of Xishuangbanna compared to most other prefectures in Yunnan and the province as a whole (Eng 1998). Widely known for its ecological and ethnic diversity, Xishuangbanna is a major tourist destination in Yunnan and the whole of China. Basis for this fast development of the tourism industry during the last two decades were huge marketing efforts to portray Xishuangbanna as an "exotic land" within the Chinese territory (Eng 1998) as well as the construction of an airport in 1990 and a new highway to Kunming, the provincial capital. The second main economic sector, domestic and international trade, has been developed after initiation of the policy of reform and opening up in 1979 and especially since the 1990s. After political tensions between China and its southern neighbors Vietnam and Laos eased in the late 1980s the central government set out to internationalize the economy of Yunnan Province in an attempt to decrease the growing imbalance compared to the fast developing coastal provinces (Eng 1998).

When it comes to the third main sector of economic activity in the prefecture, commercial farming, the major cash crop in the region today is rubber (*Hevea brasiliensis*), which constitutes more than half of the output value from agriculture (Eng 1998). Rubber trees are not a native species of the region and were introduced to Xishuangbanna only in the 1950s. Traditional land-use patterns before the founding of the PRC in 1949 included paddy rice and vegetable growing in the valley bottoms and several plains in the region mostly by the Dai. Other ethnicities mainly settled in the uplands and practiced shifting cultivation or were hunters and gatherers. After the new Chinese state was established, the first state rubber farms were set up in the mid-1950s, and rubber was exclusively cultivated by these socialist production units. In the early 1980s the introduction of the household-responsibility system marked the starting point for a rapid expansion of rubber cultivation outside these farms, which on their part were not allowed to expand plantations anymore after 1995 (Sturgeon 2010). This development, which further accelerated throughout the 1990s into the new century, happened in several waves. The driving forces of the expansion were the state's policy to make small-scale farmers plant rubber to meet the rising domestic demand, as well as to raise (mostly indigenous) farmers' incomes (Sturgeon 2010). Since in China rubber plantations officially count as forest, the planting of rubber trees was also regarded as a countermeasure to deforestation in recent years. Yet, this further development of the rubber industry is the main reason for the tremendous decline in natural forest area in the region on plots below 1000 meters above sea-level. In regions above this threshold, it is mainly the cultivation of tea and also bamboo that lead to large-scale deforestation. Today, the continuous expansion of rubber cultivation is primarily driven by the high domestic demand for natural rubber associated with the rapid development of China's automobile production (Li et al. 2007).

The planting of rubber trees in monocultures is at the root of several environmental problems, the consequences of which are becoming more and more apparent in the region today. Most prominently, the replacement of natural forests and traditional shifting agricultural land by both large-scale and small-scale rubber plantations leads to a huge loss of biodiversity (Ziegler et al. 2009). Moreover, the existence of these monocultures threatens the whole hydrological system of the area. This includes the increased run-off of precipitation in the monocultures, which reduces rainwater infiltration (Ziegler et al. 2009), and the increased use of pesticides and chemical fertilizers in the plantations, which endangers water quality in local rivers and streams. The clearing of forest on sloped land further leads to soil erosion, increasing also the risk of landslides (Ziegler et al. 2009). Overall, it appears that the economic benefits of rubber cultivation which are obvious in the region, are bought at an ever increasing environmental and ecological price.

Against the background of such rapid changes in land-use towards more rubber cultivation and the associated detrimental environmental effects, especially the loss of biodiversity, the LILAC project was devised. It is a research cooperation consisting of a consortium of several German and Chinese universities and research institutions. The German side is represented by the University of Hohenheim, while the main Chinese project partner is the Xishuangbanna Tropical Botanical Garden of the Chinese Academy of Sciences.

In recent years, attempts of biodiversity conservation mostly focused on the interaction of man and nature and on how the latter can be protected from the further. Yet, such a clear separation of areas for "protection" and "utilization" of landscapes and natural resources often does not lead to the desired outcome, i.e. the effective protection of biological diversity. Therefore new concepts such as the "Man and the Biosphere" program of the United Nations Educational, Scientific and Cultural Organization (UNESCO) explicitly regard human economic activity as part of the natural environment. So far, such new concepts have not been applied to highly sensitive cultural landscapes such as Xishuangbanna. For such landscapes, tools that allow for an impact assessment and evaluation of alternative land-use policies in collaboration with local decision-makers do not exist yet (LILAC 2007). This is the void that the LILAC project wants to fill. The objective of this interdisciplinary research cooperation is the analysis of land-use changes, the identification of main drivers of these changes and the development of an interdisciplinary decision support tool to calculate and visualize future land-use scenarios.

The study area of this research cooperation is the Naban River Watershed National Nature Reserve (NRWNNR), a nature reserve area at the southern bank of the Mekong River about 25 kilometers northwest of the prefectural capital Jinghong. The NRWNNR was established in 1991 and is also managed according to the UNESCO concept "Man and the biosphere". The area of the nature reserve amounts to 266 square kilometers and covers mainly the catchment of the Naban River and in its eastern part a mountain slope directly adjacent to the Mekong River. The ethnic and cultural diversity of Xishuangbanna can also be found in the NRWNNR, which is inhabited by 5538 people distributed among 32 villages (figures as of 2002). Agriculture is the main source of income of the villagers with main products being corn and potatoes for self-consumption as well as peanuts, tobacco, sunflowers, vegetables, and tea as cash crops. Yet, similar to the development in the whole prefecture, also in the NRWNNR rubber cultivation has been expanded rapidly in recent years and is becoming one of the main income sources (LILAC 2007). Since rubber trees can also be planted on steep slopes, plots that were formerly considered to be inappropriate for agricultural use and thus remained natural forests can now be cultivated and can generate income for the farmers.

Several subprojects from the fields of ecology, agricultural science, economics, and sociology are assessing the main factors and causes for the recent changes in land-use in the NRWNNR. As introduced above these changes mainly constitute a transition towards more cultivation of rubber trees. The data collected in the field are then to be integrated into a land-use cover change (LUCC) model based on geographical information systems (GIS). The objective of the LUCC model is to allow for calculations of future land-use scenarios under the conditions of different land management strategies applied today. This makes it possible to evaluate alternative land-use policies and provide a decision-support tool for local policy-makers. In particular, the impact of decisions that affect land-use changes on socio-cultural, economic, and ecological factors can be visualized, evaluated, and compared (LILAC 2007).

5.1.2. The subproject ECON A: A CVM survey in Jinghong

In order to develop a method to evaluate land-use policies and to assess their social value, the subproject ECON A of the LILAC project deals with the adaption of the contingent valuation method (CVM) to the socioeconomic and cultural background of Southwest China. As introduced above, the CVM is a technique for the valuation of public goods, such as governmental policy measures in the environmental, traffic or health sector. Especially for the case of land-use policy, many effects are beneficial for the society as a whole, which makes it difficult to quantify them. Therefore, the subproject has both an empirical and a methodological objective.

Regarding the methodology, the subproject aims at the development of a generalizable technique for the support of allocative decisions by government in the environmental sector. Therefore, the possibility of applying the CVM in China, an emerging economy characterized by insufficiently developed markets and people's lack of experience in dealing with market prices, is to be analyzed. This means in particular that the CVM, which is obviously very sensitive to cultural and socioeconomic differences due to its survey-based nature, should be adapted to the special socio-cultural background of the research area (LILAC 2007). With the employment of so-called citizen expert groups (CEGs) the subproject takes a participatory approach at the adaption of the CVM to local conditions. Individuals, who have already been interviewed during the pretest of the survey and showed an interest in the environmental problem under investigation, are invited to join several waves of focus group discussions. Crucial about this approach is the fact that the same group of participants convenes repeatedly, which is believed to raise participants' motivation and level of information and is likely to produce more meaningful results (Ahlheim et al. 2010). This is the defining characteristic of CEGs compared to focus groups. During these CEG discussion meetings the researchers introduce the overall idea of the project, the scientific background of the method, and the questionnaire to the participants who comment on these issues and ideally make suggestions for improvements as they accompany the whole process of the survey. Since these citizens are residents of the respective study area they are likely to possess valuable information on issues such as clear question wording, sensitive topics, resentments, or taboos in that society.

In addition to that, field experiments are employed to identify factors in the design of the questionnaire, the scenario and the interview situation that systematically distort WTP statements. To this end, several alternative versions of the questionnaire were designed in which certain features were modified. For example, a subsample of respondents is being confronted with a different payment scenario, while the interview process for other subsamples is slightly modified. The objective of these experiments is to check if and to what extent such methodological modifications influence respondents' answers to CVM surveys and especially their WTP statements. Since these field experiments are not related to the overall objective of this study, they will not be introduced in further detail.

The empirical objective of the subproject is the assessment of the social value of a more sustainable land-use scenario for the Nabanhe Nature Reserve. As introduced above, the rapid expansion of rubber cultivation produces a wide range of detrimental effects, also in a nature reserve area like the NRWNNR. During the pretest stage of the survey, the perceptions of residents of Jinghong are assessed as to how large-scale rubber cultivation influences the environmental situation and living conditions in the city. The perceptions of most respondents reflect the scientific insights into this problem and are largely consistent with the consequences that scientists find. Obviously (1) the destruction of forest is the consequence of rubber cultivation that comes to the mind of most people. Since the forest is home to many plant and animal species, its destruction in turn leads to (2) a loss of those species. Many respondents appear to be very aware that tropical rainforest is one of the distinctive characteristics of Xishuangbanna Prefecture and that for this reason it is worth being preserved. Further, rubber plantations are perceived to facilitate (3) soil erosion and the occurrence of several hydrological problems. These are (4) the drying up of rivers and streams in the region and (5) a drier climate in general as well as (6) the intensive use of pesticides and chemical fertilizers in the plantations, which endangers water quality in local rivers and the groundwater. Finally, rubber processing is known to result in (7) severe air and water pollution. These results of in-depth interviews with residents of urban Jinghong as well as with local authorities show that rubber cultivation in the region does create negative external effects, which can be felt by the urban population.

Therefore, the subproject conducts a CVM survey in urban Jinghong to assess the social value of a hypothetical reforestation project in the NRWNNR, which would lead to an abatement of the above mentioned negative consequences. The scenario is specified following the "Sloping Land Conversion Program" (Bennett 2008), sometimes also called "Green for Grain" or following the direct translation from Chinese referred to as "Return Farmland into Forest" program (*tui geng huan lin*). This national reforestation program initiated in 1999 was planned according to the concept of "payment for environmental services" and is widely known among the population of rural China. Farmers that retire cropland according to a national plan and reforest it, receive a subsidy over a period of several years. For the case of rubber in the NRWNNR, the hypothetical scenario designed for this CVM survey is called "Return Rubber into Forest" program to make clear the analogy to the existing program. Respondents to the survey are informed about the high degree of biodiversity in the NRWNNR and the threat that the fast spreading of rubber cultivation also in that area poses to it. They are further informed that government authorities are planning to initiate a program to convert rubber plantations back into forest. That program would lead to an array of positive consequences, such as a partial restoration of the original forest cover, the reestablishment of habitat for many plant and animal species, an improvement of water quality, and a reduction of pesticide residues in agricultural food products and the whole natural environment. Finally the implementation of such a reforestation program would contribute to the conservation of the environmental heritage of Xishuangbanna for future generations. It should be noted that the value of the environmental improvements resulting from the implementation of this program can also be interpreted as the social cost of rubber cultivation in the NRWNNR. It has been mentioned that the detrimental effects are negative externalities, the costs of which have to be (at least partially) borne by the survey population in urban Jinghong. Therefore, by having people value the benefits from the abatement of the above mentioned negative consequences of rubber cultivation this study is assessing its external cost to society.

The urban population of Jinghong was selected as research target because factors such as household income, level of education, professional background, and ethnicity were expected to have a greater variance in an urban setting than in the villages of the NRWNNR. In addition to that, the farmers residing inside the NRWNNR profit from rubber cultivation to different degrees, which makes it extremely difficult to have them value a land-use scenario which will initiate containment or even renaturation of rubber plantations. Among the urban population, however, only a minority of people possesses rubber trees themselves and thus does not profit directly from their cultivation. That means that by merely surveying the population of the city of Jinghong proper, possible distorting income effects for households whose rubber plantations would be subject to the reforestation can be avoided.

The main survey was conducted from June to August 2009 with a total number of 2,021 interviews including ten split samples (one control group and nine alternative treatments). To conduct such a large number of in-person interviews 15 interviewers were recruited from the local population. Since Jinghong does not have a university, the usual practice of recruiting students to conduct the CVM interviews could not be used. Instead interviewers were recruited with the help of the Municipal and Prefectural job centers. Interviewers received an introduction to the background, objectives and methodology of the survey as well as two-day practical training before independently conducting survey interviews.

The sampling procedure is based on population data made available by the local government. For 11 out of the 14 districts of Jinghong the respective district administrations provided complete lists of all housing units including number of residents for their jurisdictions. Regarding the three districts, which consist of suburbanized villages where such lists are not available, maps were drawn for each village indicating the location of each house. While drawing the maps, the number of residents of each house was recorded. This procedure resulted in a list of all addresses (housing units in the 11 urban districts and single- and multi-family houses in the suburban villages) in urban Jinghong with the respective number of residents. From this registry a random sample of desired size can be drawn. During the conduction of the survey, interviewers could then be sent to each household by specifying the address and the number of the household within this unit.

5.1.3. The research design

The questionnaire of the contingent valuation survey that constitutes the background of the analysis of the effect of socially desirable responding on WTP statements consists of five parts. To begin with, the respondents are confronted with (1) some warm-up questions about their knowledge and perception of rubber cultivation in Xishuangbanna and the environmental consequences associated with it. After that (2) the project scenario is introduced. Respondents are provided with an explanation of the basic features of the hypothetical reforestation program, and a colored brochure with a map of the NRWNNR and several pictures of rubber plantations and natural forest is displayed. Subsequently (3) the payment mode is explained and the respondent is asked how much he or she is willing to contribute to this program. Both project and payment scenarios are reproduced in box 5.1. After that the interview continues with (4) attitudinal questions on the proposed program, environmental protection in general, satisfaction with different aspects of life, and consumption of media. The interview is concluded by (5) a set of demographic questions such as age, level of education and household income. The whole questionnaire can be found in section 8.1.1 of the appendix.

In the third part of the interview right after the project scenario is presented the method of payment is specified (payment scenario). Respondents are informed that a fund will be founded for the realization of the reforestation program and that all citizens of Jinghong will have to contribute (cf. box 5.1). During the design phase of the survey questionnaire, Jinghong residents taking part in the CEG discussion meetings suggested that a payment every three months would be most plausible. Respondents are then asked to indicate on a payment card displayed in the questionnaire in the appendix how much they are willing to pay every three months during the next five years to contribute to the "Return Rubber into Forest" program. In the payment scenario no details are given on how the money would be used and how exactly the reforestation would be administered. Although for instance Ziegler et al. (2009) mention two strategies to slow down the expansion of rubber monocultures, namely the payment of upland farmers to give up rubber and the development of more sustainable agricultural techniques such as intercropping, this information was not provided. During the pretest phase it turned out that especially the mentioning of compensation payments to farmers who would be forced to give up existing rubber plantations caused many respondents to protest against the scenario. This finding was supported by the results of the CEG meetings, in which participants indicated that specific details about the use of the collected funds would not be necessary since this would only distract respondents.

Project scenario:

A rubber conversion program for the NRWNNR

The NRWNNR has always been a so-called biodiversity hotspot where many endangered plants and animals exist, which are already completely extinct in many other places. This variety of plants and animals is jeopardized by the fast spreading plantation of rubber trees. As a consequence of the ecological damages that might result from rubber cultivation in the NRWNNR, government authorities as well as scientists are thinking about a program to convert rubber plantations in the NRWNNR back into forest. This program will be called "Return Rubber Into Forest". This program will partly restore the original forest area in the NRWNNR and thereby create habitats for rare plants and animals so that the NRWNNR can resume its original function as an important biodiversity preservation area for whole China.

(Interviewer: hand over booklet to interviewees, one minute break)

Preserving biodiversity in NRWNNR means an important contribution to the survival of these rare species which might be useful for medicine and as inputs in many production processes in the future. If these plants and animals will be extinct, our children and grandchildren will never have the chance to see them and to benefit from their existence, i.e. as important ingredients for medicine.

The "Return Rubber Into Forest" program would further lead to an increase in the overall forest area as compared to today and to a better water quality in the Naban, Mandian and Mekong rivers. For example, there would be less pesticide contamination in the water, since less pesticides would be brought out to the fields. As a consequence less pesticide residues would be in the whole ecosystem and, therefore, fruits and vegetables would be less contaminated. The danger ensuing from agricultural products to human health would be reduced.

All in all, the "Return Rubber Into Forest" program would be an important contribution for the conservation of the environmental heritage of Xishuangbanna.

Payment scenario:

The "Rubber into Forest" program will be organized by the NRWNNR under the guidance of higher levels of government. In order to finance this environmental protection program a fund will be founded to which all citizens of Jinghong will have to contribute. This fund will be organized by the relevant government departments. The money in this fund will be used exclusively for the "Rubber into Forest" program.

Considering the benefits of this program for all people in this region and for you personally, we would like to ask you to mark in the following list how much at most your household would be willing to contribute every three months to this fund for the next five years in order to get the "Rubber into Forest" program realized:

- payment card -

Box 5.1: Project and payment scenario

It was mentioned before that field experiments are employed as a means to adapt the CVM to the socio-cultural background of Southwest China. At this point of the discussion, that field experiments that bears immediate relevance for the analysis of the impact of SDR in CVM should be introduced. In all but one treatment (including the basic treatment) the whole interview is conducted in-person, with the interviewer reading out the items and recording the respondent's verbal answers on the questionnaire. Alternatively, one subsample is asked to answer certain questions by writing the responses on a detached sheet of paper without the interviewer seeing it and subsequently putting it into a sealed ballot box. These questions are the rating of the different features of the proposed program (question 12), the overall rating on a 10-point scale (question 13) and – most importantly – the elicitation question (question 14). The two questions directly in front of the WTP elicitation question are to be answered in the same way in order to make respondents fully understand this alternative way of responding when it finally comes to the WTP question. This is very important because – unlike applications in the literature – in the anonymous setting not the whole questionnaire but only its most crucial questions are to be answered with the ballot box. Therefore, not only the elicitation question but two more questions directly previous to it are to be answered on a detached sheet of paper. Referring back to the definition of anonymity in a survey interview, this modified response situation is anonymous because there is no link between the WTP response and the respondent's identity from the perspective of the interviewer. In contrast to the standard procedure, the use of the sealed ballot box is designed so that such a link cannot even be constructed by the interviewer. All other split sample experiments do not bear any importance for the present study and will thus not be introduced in detail here. Yet, the data analysis makes use of the whole data set including all split samples. In order to control for the effect of these slightly modified interview settings dummy variables will be employed in the regression models.

5.1.4. Caveats for survey research in China

The emergence and existence of environmental norms in China is outlined in section 3.2.4. It is argued that the discrepancy between a considerable prevalence of environmental norms in Chinese society and the low level of pro-environmental behavior provide extremely favorable conditions for the existence of SDR in environmental surveys. In addition to that, other more general societal influences may exacerbate the impact of this type of response bias. Eventually, doing survey research in China might go along with certain culture-specific problems, especially when survey instruments are used without careful scrutiny and due modification.

When it comes to the political and historical background of the study, Chinese society is now in a state of post-totalitarianism (Ren 2009). While in the totalitarian era before the 1980s the coercive force of government successfully penetrated people's way of thinking by actively disseminating propaganda and at the same time mercilessly punishing dissent, individuals in the post-totalitarian state do not believe all propaganda anymore. Instead, people hold two attitudes, one being their private attitude and the other being the socially approved one. Of these two opinions the socially approved one is in line with the dominant ideology and is also termed the "mythological level" of opinion because it is publicly promoted but people do not believe in it (Shlapentokh 1985). Opinions of the mythological level, which are often highly desirable and utopian and thus not realistic, are merely uttered in order to conform to social pressure in authoritarian political systems. In pre-reform China "holding the correct view" was extremely important because failure to do so was likely to be punished by denial of privileges and during the Cultural Revolution (1966-1976) even exile or death (Adler et al. 1989). In contrast, private attitudes and opinions really affect behavior but cannot be made public in such a system. This two-level approach of opinions in authoritarian systems explains the discrepancy between environmental attitudes and behavior among Chinese people reported above because Chinese society is currently in a post-totalitarian state. The influence of government authorities and society on everyday life of Chinese citizens has been reduced sharply compared to the pre-reform era with the power of propaganda and coercion being ever weaker. In today's China, there is room for uttering differing opinions and for living out more individual lifestyles like never before in the history of the PRC. However, the habits, reflexes and perceived norms of the authoritarian era die away only gradually and certainly still influence behavior in the public space, such as responding to surveys dealing with environmental protection. It can be observed in many different situations that people obviously do not utter their true opinions but merely reproduce publicly accepted or even required points of view. Shlapentokh (1985) even holds that the discrepancy between the two levels of opinion is distinct in systems with only mild repression compared to both heavy repression and full freedom of speech. After more than 30 years of reform and opening up, China today can be classified as exactly such a society with mild repression. This potential bias in survey interviews on politically important topics such as environmental protection is a form of socially desirable responding. Respondents perceive supporting the dominant public ideology as desirable because doing so will result in social approval, or more precisely in the prevention of social disapproval in the form of political persecution and repression. As a consequence, the influence of SDR on survey responses can be expected to be comparably strong in this society, especially in inner and rural parts of the country where the influence of former authoritarian rule recedes even more slowly.

On a more methodological field, it is conceivable – and there is also limited empirical evidence – that certain tools of survey design usually employed in Western surveys do not work in the same way in China (Roy et al. 2001). Furthermore, these authors doubt that evidence about anchoring effects, which is derived from studies in Western countries, also applies to Chinese respondents. The use of 5- or 7-point Likert scales for instance might work differently for Chinese respondents. On this type of rating scales they tend to select more options in the middle, thus answering more moderately than their Western counterparts. Avoiding extreme answers reflects the valuation of modesty and eschewal to stand out in Chinese culture. Roy et al. (2001) point to the fact that in certain situations Chinese language does not allow for such subtle semantic differentiation to sufficiently name each out of 5 or 7 Likert-type response options. Similarly, finding matching antonyms might be harder in Chinese than in most Western languages. Consequently, when employing such instruments in China, response scales must not only be translated but also discussed with representatives of the survey population as well as pretested. If the wording is implausible or even unintelligible to respondents, modifications are necessary. The rationales and process of item modification for the application in the present study is reported in the subsequent section.

5.2. Measurement of the relevant variables

While section 3.3 displayed the theoretical basis for the three-factor model to account for incentives for socially desirable responding, this subsection introduces the empirical tools to actually measure the different factors. As introduced below, several existing measures for the three factors were found in the literature. None of them completely matches the requirements of a face to face survey in rural China, so the question inventories had to be modified and pretested. The original measures, the selection process, including reasons for selection as well as the final questions, are presented in the following subsections.

5.2.1. Measuring need for social approval

After more than half a decade of intensive research in the field of social desirability, the researcher today has the choice between several measurement scales with the most prominent being the Marlowe-Crowne Social Desirability Scale and the Balanced Inventory of Desirable Responding (BIDR) as introduced in section 3.2.2. The following study employs a modified version of the impression management subscale of the BIDR. The reason for selecting the BIDR is its ability to separately measure the two dimensions of need for approval, namely impression management and self-deception, whereas the Marlowe-Crowne Scale lacks this ability. Further, the BIDR consists of the same number of socially desirable and socially undesirable statements, which makes it possible to separately assess the respondents' tendency to overly deny negative characteristics on the one hand and to falsely claim positive ones on the other. This ability to separate between the enhancement and denial components will be important for testing hypothesis 3, which states that denial exerts a stronger motivational influence than enhancement.

In this study, only the IM subscale is employed for the following reason. When it comes to contingent valuation, Laughland et al. (1994) argue that the self-deception dimension should not be controlled for. The CVM researcher controlling for SDR is interested in detecting statements of WTP that do not represent true economic preferences for the respective environmental good. These statements either have to be deleted from the data set or at least to be corrected. If, however, a respondent engages in self-deception regarding the valuation task, i.e. she deceives herself about her own true valuation, the economic meaning of the statement is not impaired, since information that the respondent herself regards to be true is a valid factor influencing her utility. Therefore, self-deception is regarded as a legitimate factor of her true WTP and should thus not be corrected. As a consequence, merely the IM dimension of need for approval – the conscious and potentially incorrect presentation of something towards the outside – is to be measured.

The original version of the IM subscale of the BIDR consists of 20 items which describe general patterns of behavior (cf. figure 5.1). Respondents to this inventory are asked to indicate on a 5-point Likert scale how much they associate a certain statement with themselves. When employing this approach, an individual need for approval score can be calculated as follows. For each respondent, only the extreme answers into the socially desirable direction are counted, i.e. the *not true* options for the 10 denial items (the odd items) and the *very true* options for the 10 enhancement items (the even items). The basic logic of this score is that only respondents who state *extreme* confidence in possessing (not possessing) a positive (negative) characteristic are likely to make this statement out of a social desirability motivation. Respondents stating some moderate response option ("2", "3", or "4") might actually be responding truthfully and might not just be exaggerating.

Instructions: Read each statement, and circle the number that best describes you, from *Not True* to *Very True* about you.		Not true (1)	(2)	(3)	(4)	Very true (5)
1	I sometimes tell lies if I have to.	○	○	○	○	○
2	I never cover up my mistakes.	○	○	○	○	○
3	There have been occasions when I have taken advantage of someone.	○	○	○	○	○
4	I never swear.	○	○	○	○	○
5	I sometimes try to get even rather than forgive and forget.	○	○	○	○	○
6	I always obey laws, even if I'm unlikely to get caught.	○	○	○	○	○
7	I have said something bad about a friend behind his or her back.	○	○	○	○	○
8	When I hear people talking privately, I avoid listening.	○	○	○	○	○
9	I have received too much change from a salesperson without telling him or her.	○	○	○	○	○
10	I always declare everything at customs.	○	○	○	○	○
11	When I was young, I sometimes stole things.	○	○	○	○	○
12	I have never dropped litter on the street.	○	○	○	○	○
13	I sometimes drive faster than the speed limit.	○	○	○	○	○
14	I never read sexy books or magazines.	○	○	○	○	○
15	I have done things that I don't tell other people about.	○	○	○	○	○
16	I never take things that don't belong to me.	○	○	○	○	○
17	I have taken sick-leave from work or school even though I wasn't really sick.	○	○	○	○	○
18	I have never damaged a library book or store merchandise without reporting it.	○	○	○	○	○
19	I have some pretty awful habits.	○	○	○	○	○
20	I don't gossip about other people's business.	○	○	○	○	○

Figure 5.1: The original version of the IM subscale of the BIDR (cf. Paulhus 1998)

Since the 20 items in the inventory represent behavior that is either socially desirable – i.e. requested by social norms – but almost not existent in society in such a pure form (the even items), or socially undesirable but very common (the odd items), extreme answers are very likely to be deliberate exaggerations of a respondent's self-presentation. Summing up these extreme answers yields an individual need for approval score, ranging from 0 to 20 with a high score indicating a high need for social approval.[27]

Before scrutinizing if and in what way the above inventory has to be modified for an application in an environmental valuation survey in rural China, two aspects of its inner logic have to be discussed in a critical manner. In addition to the condition that the items must describe either socially desirable or undesirable behavior, a second condition applies to them which requires truthful responses to be very unlikely (Hartmann 1991). The enhancement items in this scale represent patterns of behavior which are socially desirable but very uncommon for the vast majority of respondents. Analogously, the content of the denial items is very widely observed behavior which is yet socially undesirable. Since these statements about the common and uncommon nature of the behavioral patterns are mere assumptions, the researcher applying this scale can obviously never completely rule out the case of a respondent who gives an extreme response which is actually true. In this case the response would falsely be counted as evidence for approval seeking. It is also obvious that the scale measures need for social approval the more accurately the fewer of these cases exist. If the scale only consisted of one item, it would be very sensitive to this problem. So this is the reason for the scale to include 20 items that describe characteristics or patterns of behavior.

The rationale behind this is that even if a respondent happens to entirely possess the quality described in one of the items and her extreme response is consequently falsely taken as indicator of approval seeking, it is very unlikely that the same applies with regard to the remaining items. Therefore, the fact that the scale comprises of many items makes sure that the very unlikely cases of a respondent actually possessing (or not possessing at all) the described characteristics do not impair the measurement quality of the scale. Even when this problem is acknowledged, a high score resulting from this scale is still a clear indication of a respondent who seeks social approval, whereas a low score implies the opposite. As a result, respondents overly claiming the desirable patterns of behavior and completely denying the

27 This procedure is referred to as *dichotomous scoring*. An alternative, the so-called *continuous scoring*, first reverses the scores of the denial items and then simply adds up the score associated with each answer, thereby also counting moderate responses. For the differences between dichotomous and continuous scoring see (Stöber et al. 2002).

undesirable ones can be regarded as having a comparably high need for social approval. They seek for this approval by conveying a picture of themselves that is in accordance with social norms in an exaggerated manner.

Further, another type of criticism that can be brought forward against this inventory is the assumption that respondents do not realize that extreme responses are very unlikely to be truthful. It was mentioned that the main criterion for selecting items for the BIDR is that they describe socially desirable but highly uncommon or socially undesirable but very common behavior. However, if a respondent realizes this pattern, there is no reason for her to state the extreme response anymore because by claiming this response she runs the risk of embarrassing herself in front of the interviewer. Consequently, the question arises why the respondent – like the researcher – should not be able to realize that an extreme response is very unlikely to be truthful. If the researcher intentionally employs items, which are either socially desirable but very uncommon or socially undesirable but very common, this pattern might as well be discovered by the respondent.[28] If this is true, then stating an extreme response is not necessarily an indicator for need for social approval but rather for the respondent's naivety or even foolishness. In such a situation only respondents who do not realize that extreme responses are most likely a rather ridiculous exaggeration would state such responses. As a result, what could be measured by means of this set of items is not only the tendency to seek social approval but also the degree of naivety and/or foolishness of the respondent, which potentially impairs the validity of the inventory. Surprisingly, this problem has apparently not been addressed in the relevant literature so far. Obviously, items for which stating an extreme response potentially embarrasses the respondent should not be included in such an inventory because this problem constitutes an important shortcoming of this approach for measuring need for social approval. Attention to this fact is paid during the modification process reported below.

Rationale for and process of scale modification

Since it was demonstrated that cultural and social norms lie at the root of socially desirable responding and thus determine its occurrence and strength, it is apparent that this phenomenon is very sensitive to cultural differences (Middleton and Jones 2000). The original version of the BIDR was developed

28 Note that the respondent is not informed about the purpose of these questions, i.e. she does not know that her level of social desirability is to be assessed. This reduces the probability that a respondent realizes that stating an extreme response might not be credible. Consequently, this objection might in fact turn out to be less important for the applicability of this inventory than suspected.

for middle-class respondents in Western societies, so certain patterns of behavior described in the inventory might not be applicable outside of this group of respondents. Certain activities might not exist at all or at least not be so prominent and common in other societies (Hartmann 1991). This is especially true for the case of China, where both the cultural background and the political system differ significantly from Western countries. Despite its popularity among Western researchers, the BIDR has but a short history of application in China. In addition to that most studies employing this scale in China were conducted in urban settings and used student samples (Bai et al. 2004, Guo et al. 2006, Li and Li 2008). It seems that the BIDR has not yet been applied in the inner and more rural parts of China. Although there exists a Chinese version (Wang et al. 1999), which has been employed by the researchers quoted above, this version is not considered to be appropriate in the context of a rural small-sized town in the Southwestern border region with high ethnic and linguistic diversity. Roy et al. (2001) point to the problem of intra-country differences in language, which is especially virulent for the case of China. Expressions that have a fixed meaning in standard Mandarin might have a second and conceivably completely different meaning in a regional dialect, of which there are plenty in China.[29] Therefore, certain steps were performed to adapt the Chinese version of the scale to local circumstances. This process, which is displayed in detail below, included in-depth interviews about the social and moral norms governing the behavior described by each of the items, deletion and linguistic modification of inappropriate and difficult items, and rekeying of items where necessary.[30] Switzer et al. (1999) provide criteria under which circumstances an existing inventory can be modified. Besides discussing cultural, historical, and political differences among study samples, these authors focus on the appropriateness of an existing inventory in a new environment. Two of several conceivable justifications for a modification include the fact that the "original measure is too long for the current research purpose" and that an "original item is unclear or not relevant to the current population" (Switzer et al. 1999, p. 405). These guidelines have to be kept in mind when the modification process is discussed in the following.

As a first step, the 20 items of the subscale in the original translation (Wang et al. 1999) were discussed with Chinese individuals in the survey area. By going through the items one by one in in-depth discussions with these individuals, valuable insights into this matter could be gained. This

29 For instance, the expression *chui niu* pejoratively meaning "to boast off" in standard Mandarin is usually used in the neutral meaning of "having a chat" in Yunnan Province, where the inventory is to be applied.

30 Throughout the description, reference is made to the English translation of the Chinese scale (Wang et al. 1999) which is actually employed in the survey.

approach has two objectives. Firstly, it has to be ascertained that the behavioral patterns described in the items are applicable to the members of the study population (Switzer et al. 1999). Secondly, the in-depth discussions aim at scrutinizing the existence of social and moral norms that refer to the behavior described by the items in rural China. As the basic idea for constructing this inventory is to find socially desirable but quite uncommon as well as socially undesirable but quite common patterns of behavior, a sufficient degree of desirability of the behavioral pattern described in each item perceived by the respondent has to be ensured (Hartmann 1991). As Stricker (1963) notes, social desirability operates for those items, the behavior of which is most clearly associated to widely-perceived social norms. This means that only the reporting of behavior, for which clear norms about what is desirable and what is not desirable exist, is likely to be biased into such a direction. Thus, the reason for this process of deleting several items is to ascertain that only items are included in the measurement scale, the behavior of which is meaningful to the study population and in which the norms are sufficiently clear-cut in this part of China.

At this stage, deletion is preferred to modification of problematic items because the BIDR constitutes a fixed question inventory with rich evidence of its reliability and validity (Li and Bagger 2007, Paulhus 1991). If, however, certain items within such a scale are obviously impossible to employ with the relevant sample of respondents, the exclusion of these items is less prone to result in measurement error than their deliberate modification without proper evaluation of the characteristics of the modified scale (Switzer et al. 1999). Such a procedure has been frequently used in the literature on social desirability in China. Guo et al. (2006) delete three out of the 40 items of the complete BIDR and also modify several items for a study in Northeast China. Further, the results of a factor-analysis reported in Li and Li (2008) make these authors delete 10 of the 40 BIDR items, among them items 2, 5, 8, and 11 of the IM subscale. Regarding the Marlowe-Crowne SD scale, a deletion of single items is conducted by Liu et al. (2003).

For the case of a rural town in Southwest China characterized by a high degree of ethnic diversity, this step resulted in the deletion of items 1, 5, 10, 13, 15, and 19 (refer to figure 5.1 above). The behavioral patterns described in the statements, their appropriateness or inappropriateness as well as the degree to which the items are understandable to the local population were discussed in-depth with *N*=9 citizens (referred to as 'judges' below). Stress was laid on scrutinizing whether or not a norm referring to an item exists and if it is sufficiently clear to the general population. This means that subjects were both asked to indicate to what extent they themselves perceive a certain norm and in how far they judge the general population to hold a similar view on that matter. Specific reasons for the deletion of these six items are the following. The norm governing the first item, which would read "do not tell lies", undoubtedly exists in Xishuangbanna, but the additional "if I have to" confuses the situation. It is this additional specification of the situation that might serve as an excuse to regard lying as morally acceptable. Further, several judges asked for an explanation of what exactly this addition means. While lying in general is regarded as morally bad behavior, certain circumstances may allow a lie. As, however, these circumstances are not described in sufficient detail in the item, the existence of this rather confusing specification led to the decision to delete this item. The social norm referring to item 5 would read "Try not to get even but forgive and forget instead". Several judges mentioned that this norm does not exist in that form in China, and that especially in a rural areas revenge is not considered as bad. Acknowledging the fact that this norm is of Christian (or at least Western religious) origin and that Christianity does have a merely negligible influence on Chinese culture, this assumption appears to be plausible.

Travelling abroad is still very uncommon for people in rural China. The same holds for owning a car and driving. Consequently, items 10 and 13 were dropped, since both actions (passing customs and driving one's own car) are not relevant for the large majority of respondents in Xishuangbanna. Additionally, traffic rules such as speed limits are still not as much respected in rural areas as in urban China or industrialized countries. Therefore, violating this rule is likely not to be regarded as socially undesirable behavior, which, too, renders this item not applicable. The majority of judges criticized that item 15 is not specific enough and offers too much room for interpretation. While in the Western context this ambiguity is the purpose of this statement, Chinese subjects were unable to judge whether such behavior was socially desirable without further specification of such "things".

Moreover, it is part of Chinese culture, which values modesty, to remain silent about one's own good deeds (Liu et al. 2003). Therefore, the implication that "things that I don't tell other people about" are necessarily bad things does not hold in China, where the relationship is more likely to be the other way round. In a similar way, item 19 was criticized for its impreciseness. The majority of judges found it hard to tell whether the reporting of bad habits is socially desirable or not without further specification. In addition to that, it was mentioned that naturally everybody has some bad habits and that this is nothing to be ashamed of. This in turn means, that there is no social pressure that makes respondents bias their answer towards stating that they do *not* have any bad habits. Therefore, the total denial of this item cannot be considered to indicate need for social approval, yet a majority of Chinese people rather frankly admit having bad habits.

After deleting the above six items, the wording of some of the remaining statements had to be modified in order to guarantee that they are understood by all respondents of the survey. The expression "I am a person that..." was added to four negatively keyed statements (2, 4, 12, and 20) in order to create affirmative main clauses and thus to make the statements easier for respondents to understand. During the pretesting phase of the survey a fraction of respondents showed difficulties in judging negative statements on a wrong-true-scale. Therefore, this modification was chosen to reduce this confusion.

old	new	**Now we would like you to answer some general questions regarding yourself. How true are the following statements regarding yourself?**	Completely wrong (1)	Predominantly wrong (2)	Partly wrong, partly true (3)	Predominantly true (4)	Completely true (5)
2	1	I am a person that doesn't cover up mistakes.	○	○	○	○	○
3	2	There have been occasions when I have taken advantage of someone.	○	○	○	○	○
4	3	I am a person that doesn't swear.	○	○	○	○	○
6	4	I obey laws, even if I'm unlikely to get caught.	○	○	○	○	○
7	5	In the past I have said something bad about a friend behind his or her back.	○	○	○	○	○
8	6	When I hear people talking privately, I cannot help listening.	○	○	○	○	○
9	7	It may happen that I receive too much change from a salesperson without telling him or her.	○	○	○	○	○
11	8	When I was young, I tended to steal things.	○	○	○	○	○
12	9	I am a person that never drops litter on the street.	○	○	○	○	○
14	10	I take pleasure in reading sexy books or magazines.	○	○	○	○	○
16	11	I would never take things that don't belong to me.	○	○	○	○	○
17	12	I have taken sick-leave from work or school even though I wasn't really sick.	○	○	○	○	○
18	13	If I damage merchandise in the supermarket I definitely report it to the staff.	○	○	○	○	○
20	14	I am a person that doesn't gossip about other people's business.	○	○	○	○	○

Figure 5.2: The final short version of the BIDR to measure need for approval. Note the new numbering of the items from 1 to 14

Some descriptions of past behavior (e.g. "I have received too much change from a salesperson without telling him or her.") and categorical statements (e.g. "I never take things that don't belong to me.") were changed into general statements of behavior (e.g. "It may happen that I receive too much change from a salesperson without telling him or her." or "I would never take things that don't belong to me."). Applying strict logic, the answer to the former type of items can only be *yes* or *no*, because a fact of the past or a categorical statement (containing expressions such as "always" or "never") can only be true or false. Further, this renders the moderate answer options in between void of any meaning. A careful test-taker should therefore deny all of these statements and only agree to more moderate statements. So, in order to avoid this inconsistency and to render the moderate answer options on the 5-point Likert scale meaningful, items 9, 11, 16 were changed into more general statements. Like indicated above, these modifications also served to reduce the risk of merely assessing the naivety and foolishness of respondents who fail to realize that extreme answers are very unlikely to be truthful.

In addition to that, four items were slightly reworded, the direction of three of them also changed. The double negation in item 18 was changed into an affirmative sentence because it was likely to lead to confusion. The new item wording reads "If I damage merchandise in the supermarket I definitely report it to the staff". Items 8 and 14 were rekeyed from enhancement into denial items by rewriting it as "When I hear people talking privately, I cannot help listening" and "I take pleasure in reading sexy books or magazines", respectively. In contrast to the old wording when a *completely true* represented a socially desirable response, now the *completely wrong* option indicates need for approval. These modifications yield the final scale consisting of 14 items, 7 of which are enhancement items and 7 are denial items. Finally, the wording of the response options on the 5-point Likert scale was modified. Instead of ranging from not true to very true with the middle categories lacking any verbal expression, the range *completely wrong – predominantly wrong – partly wrong, partly true – predominantly true – completely true* is employed. While these options are identical regarding their content it is believed that the fact that each option bears a verbal expression facilitates the selection of the response. The final scale is displayed in figure 5.2.

How are the items perceived? Does an extreme response really constitute exaggeration?

After modifying the original impression management subscale of the BIDR, some further notes on the principles of its operation, evidence for its validity, and potential shortcomings of its application have to be discussed. In order to support certain arguments in this discussion, reference is made to the responses to the modified inventory in the survey. Out of 1979 valid questionnaires, 1668 respondents completed all 14 items of the modified BIDR scale. Distributions of responses for all items are displayed in table 5.1. Only for those 1668 respondents who have answered to all 14 items can a need for approval score ranging from 0 to 14 be calculated, so this is the sample relevant for the analyses below. Note that there is a self-selection bias because respondents who complete all 14 BIDR items and those who do not differ significantly in several characteristics. The 1668 respondents who complete the inventory are younger, have a higher household income and a higher level of education. While this restrains the representativeness of the following analyses for the whole population in the study area, it does not impair the validity of the results regarding SDR.

Table 5.1: Relative response frequency for each item. Except for rounding errors, percentages sum up to 100% for each row. Note the new numbering of the items which is henceforth the reference for the analysis.

	N=1,668	Completely wrong	Predominantly wrong	Party wrong, partly true	Predominantly true	Completely true
1	I am a person that doesn't cover up mistakes.	2.5%	14.2%	14.3%	36.8%	32.3%
2	There have been occasions when I have taken advantage of someone.	31.1%	21.3%	19.5%	23.4%	4.7%
3	I am a person that doesn't swear.	10.2%	8.4%	8.3%	21.9%	51.1%
4	I obey laws, even if I'm unlikely to get caught.	1.0%	2.5%	4.3%	16.9%	75.4%
5	I may have said something bad about a friend behind his or her back.	29.6%	19.4%	22.9%	22.2%	5.8%
6	When I hear people talking privately, I cannot help listening.	39.0%	20.8%	15.0%	16.7%	8.6%
7	It may happen that I receive too much change from a salesperson without telling him or her.	65.2%	16.0%	8.9%	6.8%	3.1%
8	When I was young, I tended to steal things.	53.8%	11.5%	11.3%	15.6%	7.7%
9	I am a person that never drops litter on the street.	3.4%	7.4%	12.8%	22.0%	54.4%
10	I take pleasure in reading sexy books or magazines.	71.1%	15.0%	7.4%	3.5%	2.2%
11	I would never take things that don't belong to me.	2.6%	2.6%	4.4%	15.8%	74.5%
12	I have taken sick-leave from work or school even though I wasn't really sick.	48.7%	11.0%	11.9%	16.9%	11.5%
13	If I damage merchandise in the supermarket I definitely report it to the staff.	2.3%	3.4%	5.9%	17.8%	70.5%
14	I am a person that doesn't gossip about other people's business.	1.3%	2.6%	7.4%	21.6%	67.0%

For the modified scale to reliably measure need for social approval, extreme answers out of the range of options must represent exaggerated claims of behavior or character dispositions. This means that out of a set of different strategies to gain social approval from the perspective of the respondent, this measurement scale is merely tapping a subset of strategies, namely the exaggerated and thus untruthful claim or denial of behavioral characteristics. These strategies represent the traditional concept of social desirability and approval seeking in the literature as introduced in section 3.2.2. Referring back to one of the initial definitions of SDR as a tendency of the respondent to make himself look good in the eyes of the interviewer (Paulhus 1991), other strategies seem possible to attain this goal. For instance, it is conceivable that a respondent tries to please the interviewer and fulfill perceived social standards by intentionally stating a moderate response because she thinks the interviewer can be impressed by modesty and social conformity. This respondent might want to improve her social status by intentionally presenting a picture of herself as an average citizen lacking any outstanding characteristics. When the dichotomous scoring procedure is applied with the modified BIDR, such alleged expressions of need for social approval will go undetected. In addition, if such behavior really constitutes a form of approval seeking it cannot be distinguished from the basic type described above.

Further, in today's society certain respondents might seek social approval or social status by purposefully giving a response that explicitly contradicts prevalent norms and standards. A respondent could for instance react to the item "I never read sexy books or magazines" by stating "completely wrong" just to show that she is aware of the social norm governing this behavior but is not afraid to infringe it. She might even be proud not to conform to the norm and attempt to boast off with this to gain social approval. This might be another conceivable strategy of approval seeking. With the usual scoring procedure such "rebel responses" are not interpreted by this measurement tool as indicators of approval seeking and will thus go undetected, too. Yet, unlike moderate responses these "rebel responses" can more easily be quantified in the survey data, which is done below.

Clearly, these two strategies differ substantially from the traditional notion of need for social approval, which according to the literature can be gained exclusively by overly supporting socially desirable items and completely rejecting socially undesirable ones. These tendencies can undoubtedly be measured by means of the scale developed above. When looking at the other two strategies to convey to the interviewer a positive self-description, this obviously goes beyond the traditional conceptualization of social desirability and approval seeking. So, at this point the question arises if these two strategies are really consistent with the concept of SDR and social approval seeking and can be considered an integral part of it. If they are, the present scale is not able to measure the whole extent of that concept, which would significantly impair its content validity.

The difficulty of determining whether or not the statement of moderate and "rebel" responses is consistent with the concept of need for approval is the varying definition of this concept in the relevant literature. Although according to many authors social approval can be gained through emphasis of socially desirable characteristics and minimization of socially undesirable ones (Millham and Jacobson 1978), social desirability was merely defined as "the tendency to give positive self-descriptions" (Paulhus 2002, p. 49) or "the tendency to give answers that make the respondent look good" (Paulhus 1991, p. 17). At the same time Phillips and Clancy (1972, p. 923) refer to social desirability "as a response determinant [that] refers to the tendency of people to deny socially undesirable traits or qualities and to admit to socially desirable ones". Paulhus' definitions leave the strategy of giving such a "positive self-description" and to obtain a positive feedback open to the respondent, i.e. it is at the respondent's discretion what she considers as "positive self-description" and "looking good". According to these somewhat broader definitions all of the three strategies of approval seeking introduced above would count as SDR. The character disposition of a basic need for social approval can manifest itself in overly norm compliant response behavior, in moderate response behavior and even in deliberate negation of normatively approved responses. Yet, it seems plausible that exaggerated compliance with social norms, i.e. the overly reporting of desirable and the absolute rejection of undesirable items, is by far the most important strategy of approval seeking because the respondent has no – or at most very limited – information on the social background and judgement criteria of the interviewer. In this case, she must refer to social norms as to what kinds of statements will most likely result in social approval and which will not.

According to the other, somewhat narrower definitions by DeMaio, Millham and Jacobson and Phillips and Clancy, the reporting of neither moderate nor "rebel" responses is consistent with social desirability and need for approval. A respondent stating moderate responses to the modified version of the BIDR is not trying to convey a picture of herself as overly complying with social norms. Moreover, her statements are also likely to be true because she does not give any extreme responses. At least, the researcher does not have any means of verifying the truthfulness of the answers. Similarly a "rebel respondent" is not presenting herself as overly complying with social norms, either. The idea of "rebel responses" is just the very opposite of norm compliance. Table 5.2 summarizes the relationship between the different strategies of approval seeking and the differing conceptualizations of need for social approval and social desirability just introduced.

Table 5.2: Different strategies of approval seeking from the perspective of different definitions of social desirability and approval seeking.

Strategy	Narrow definitions	Broad definitions
	Social approval can be gained through the emphasis of socially desirable characteristics and the minimization of undesirable ones. (Millham and Jacobson 1978) "Social desirability [...] refers to the tendency of people to deny socially undesirable traits or qualities and to admit to socially desirable ones." (Phillips and Clancy 1972, p. 923)	Social desirability is the "tendency to give answers that make the respondent look good". (Paulhus 1991, p. 17) Social desirability is the "tendency to give positive self-descriptions" (Paulhus 2002, p. 49)
Desirable responding	*consistent*	*consistent*
Moderate responding	*not consistent*	*consistent*
"Rebel" responding	*not consistent*	*consistent*

When employed together with a contingent survey, the implications of the three different strategies of approval seeking for the statements WTP have to be studied. Firstly, in a society increasingly calling for everybody's commitment to environmental protection, a person overly claiming desirable characteristics and denying undesirable ones can be expected to overstate her WTP to support an environmental project in order to impress the interviewer. Such a respondent will try to impress the interviewer with the extent of her concern for environmental protection out of a strong need for social approval. This is the main hypothesis of the empirical analysis below. Secondly, a "rebel respondent" by definition wants to act contrary to what is demanded by social norms and standards. That is, in a society where environmental concern is the social norm, such a respondent can be expected to refuse to contribute to any environmental protection effort even if – or better especially when – she personally deems it desirable for society. For the case of the WTP for an environmental project this implies the statement of a zero WTP or at least a WTP that is biased downwards with respect to the respondent's true WTP. The objective of such a "rebel respondent" is the demonstration that she is aware of the social norm (i.e. "Everybody should take responsibility and contribute to environmental protection efforts.") but does not care to comply with it. That is, she knows that environmental protection and everybody's contribution to it are highly desirable but prefers to impress the interviewer by stating just the opposite. Note that for this kind of response behavior to occur it is not important whether or not the interviewer can be impressed by such a "rebel response" but merely that the respondents believes it to be impressive. Thirdly, the effect on the WTP of the type of respondent that wants to convey a favorable picture of herself by giving moderate responses is unclear. If such a respondent has a true WTP that she deems is within the socially desirable range she has no incentive to alter her response and will state her true WTP. If, however, from her perspective her true WTP is extreme, i.e. too low or too high, she might bias it towards the socially desirable range in order to appear positively in the eyes of the interviewer. As was demonstrated, all of the three different strategies of approval seeking potentially exert influence on WTP statements, with the traditional strategy of compliance with social norms being the major source of influence.

Regarding practical measurement, the question arises if the modified BIDR can assess and differentiate between these types of approval seeking. Obviously the scale cannot distinguish between moderate responses which are actually true and those which are made out of an approval seeking motivation. Thus, the scale fails to identify the latter type of respondent. Given the weak theoretical connection between stating moderate responses and having a tendency to give socially desirable responses, this shortcoming of the scale seems acceptable. It can thus be concluded that according to the conceptualization of SDR applied in this study giving moderate responses does not represent a strategy to give socially desirable responses.

"Rebel responses" on the other hand are comparably easy to identify empirically. Since these responses similar to the socially desirable and undesirable responses, are extreme statements on the response scale, they are very likely to be not entirely true. Therefore an extreme response in the opposite direction of what is socially desirable can be counted as a "rebel response" as long as the respondent fully understands the question. If this is not the case, however, i.e. if a respondent does not adequately understand the keying of an item, she might intend to state the socially desirable response but indeed falsely give the opposite response. Of course this type of measurement error should be reduced by careful item design and pretesting, but since it cannot be reduced to zero probably not all responses opposite to what is required by social norms represent truly intentional "rebel responses". Looking at the results of the survey displayed in table 5.2, one can see that the fraction of "rebel responses" to each item is comparably low, for some items even negligible. These responses are the "completely true" responses to items 2, 5, 6, 7, 8, 10, and 12 and the "completely wrong" statements with respect to items 1, 3, 4, 9, 11, 13, and 14. This finding supports the idea that respondents who want to look good in the eyes of the interviewer by means of this strategy represent a minority of all possible types of respondents. Merely for the items “I am a person that doesn’t swear” and “I have taken sick-leave from work or school even though I wasn’t really sick” the fraction or “rebel responses” exceeds 10%. Moreover, similar to the BIDR score a score of rebel responses can be calculated. This score is a sum of all “completely wrong” responses for each enhancement item and of all “completely true” responses for all denial items given by one respondent. The right-hand side of figure 5.3 displays the distribution of the rebel score among all respondents who completed the modified BIDR (*N*=1668). What can be seen in that figure is that the number of respondents giving more than one “rebel response” is very low. Virtually there is no respondent giving more than five “rebel responses”. This indicates that there is no such type of respondent as a “rebel respondent” who consistently wants to violate social norms and gain social approval by this. Rather it appears that the statement of “rebel responses” is a mere accidental phenomenon potentially resulting from lack of understanding of a fraction of respondents.

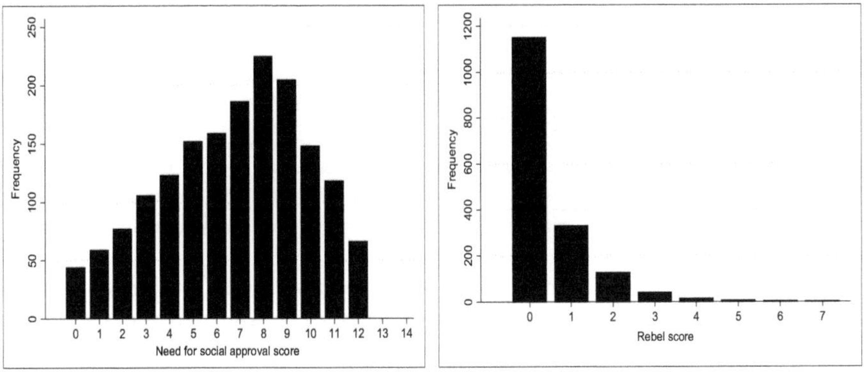

Figure 5.3: Distribution of BIDR scores and rebel scores (N=1668)

The above analysis demonstrates that only if the broad conceptualization of approval seeking is applied can moderate and “rebel” responding be regarded as a possible strategy to gain social approval. If, however, the more specific definition of social desirability and approval seeking as claim of desirable and denial of undesirable characteristics is applied, the statement of neither moderate nor “rebel” responses is consistent with the concept. In this case the modified BIDR is a valid measure of such need for social approval and thus social desirability. Summing up, both from the theoretical and the empirical measurement perspective the importance of moderate and “rebel” responses appears to be small compared to the traditional strategy of approval seeking by overly norm compliance.

Evidence of the scale's reliability and validity

After scrutinizing the theoretical and conceptual foundations of the modified IM subscale of the BIDR, its reliability and validity has to be assessed. Reliability in this respect is the extent to which the items of this inventory actually measure a single underlying construct, which is also referred to as "internal-consistency reliability" (Switzer et al. 1999). This criterion is an estimate how strongly the set of items in an inventory are interrelated or hang together. The indicator of internal consistency usually applied in the literature is Cronbach's alpha. For the modified IM subscale of the BIDR it is .695 with *N*=1,668. According to Switzer et al. (1999), alpha coefficients ranging from .50 to .80 indicate a sufficient degree of internal consistency. Additional indicators of a scale's reliability are split-half correlations, which assess the degree of correlation between two arbitrary halves of a scale. When the 14 items are split up into first and second half, the correlation between these halves is *r=0.480* and significant at the 5%-level. For splitting up the even and the odd items, the correlation is *r=0.542* and equally significant. These results indicate a sufficiently high correlation between two versions of the scale, which implies that it assesses the construct of need for approval reliably (Switzer et al. 1999).

When it comes to the assessment of the validity of the item inventory, three forms can be distinguished, namely criterion validity, construct validity and content validity. Criterion validity assesses the correlation of a measure with one or several established instruments that assess the same concept. For the case of a measure for need for social approval to be employed with a study sample in rural Southwest China, such an established measure does not exist. As a consequence, criterion validity cannot be formally assessed in the present context.

This situation is different for the case of construct validity. This concept assesses to what extent the construct that the inventory intends to measure is in fact measured. Evidence for construct validity can be gained by conducting a factor analysis and check if the inventory can successfully distinguish between different factors which should theoretically be included in it. Table 5.3 displays the results of a principal component factor analysis. The analysis is limited to two factors. What can be seen from the table is that most of the items clearly load on the expected factor even though the loadings between 0.5 and 0.7 are comparatively low for such an analysis. Merely for two enhancement items (6 and 10) and one denial item (3) are the loadings even below 0.5. So, although not in a perfectly clear way, the factor analysis succeeds in separating the two theoretical components enhancement and denial in this scale. This result adds to the evidence of construct validity of the modified version of the IM subscale of the BIDR.

Table 5.3: Results of a principal component factor analysis with quartimax rotation of the 14 remaining items of the modified version of the BIDR

	Items	Component DEN	ENH
5	I may have said something bad about a friend behind his or her back.	0.688	0.091
2	There have been occasions when I have taken advantage of someone.	0.678	0.116
8	When I was young, I tended to steal things.	0.528	0.034
12	I have taken sick-leave from work or school even though I wasn't really sick.	0.521	-0.003
7	It may happen that I receive too much change from a salesperson without telling him or her.	0.514	0.159
6	When I hear people talking privately, I cannot help listening.	0.476	0.081
10	I take pleasure in reading sexy books or magazines.	0.372	0.190
14	I am a person that doesn't gossip about other people's business.	0.201	0.629
4	I obey laws, even if I'm unlikely to get caught.	0.139	0.585
13	If I damage merchandise in the supermarket I definitely report it to the staff.	0.200	0.567
11	I would never take things that don't belong to me.	0.207	0.549
1	I am a person that doesn't cover up mistakes.	0.017	0.535
9	I am a person that never drops litter on the street.	0.026	0.531
3	I am a person that doesn't swear.	-0.020	0.461

Further, the different resulting BIDR scores for different subgroups of respondents can be compared with similar results in the literature. The distribution of BIDR score values in the overall sample is displayed in figure 5.3 above. While potentially respondents can reach any score in the range from zero to 14, there are no respondents scoring 13 or 14. The most frequent score out of $N=1668$ respondents who completed all items of this scale is 8, whereas the median score is 7. The overall mean score is 6.75. A significant difference in BIDR scores of male and female respondents can be detected in the data. While the mean score for male respondents is 6.31, it is 7.12 for female subjects. Applying a t-test this difference is significant at the 1%-level of confidence. This finding is frequently reported in the literature (Becker and Cherny 1994, Paulhus 1991). Additionally, the correlation between the BIDR score and respondent age is $r=0.342$ ($p=0.000$) indicating that older respondents have a higher need for social approval. This result, too, has already been found in other studies employing the BIDR (Winkler et al. 2006).

Finally, content validity indicates if the items in an inventory cover the whole theoretical construct. Some aspects of this type of validity were touched above when the influence of moderate and so-called "rebel" responses was discussed. It is concluded that the 14 items sufficiently cover the tendency of respondents to both overly claim good behavioral patterns and absolutely reject bad ones. It was also demonstrated that neither the existence of moderate responses nor giving "rebel" responses substantially impairs content validity. In this respect, further evidence of the fact that extreme responses really constitute exaggerated compliance to social norms and a departure from reality was gained through another round of 19 evaluation interviews regarding only the modified 14-item scale. Respondents to these in-depth interviews conducted after the main survey was completed were confronted with the scale, on which the respective socially desirable answers were already marked. In a first step, the respective social norm governing the behavior described in each item was introduced to the respondents. It was asked if the described behavior could be judged morally bad (for denial items) or good (for enhancement items). This question intended to check whether the denial items really represent undesirable and the enhancement items desirable statements from the point of view of the survey population. In other words, the existence of the social norms associated with the patterns of behavior is tested. Results to this question are displayed in table 5.4.

It can be seen that with respect to all items except numbers 3, 6, and 10 the huge majority of respondents perceive the relevant social norm. For some items such as "When I was young, I tended to steal things" even all respondents unanimously agree that such behavior is morally bad and undesirable. Consequently, the social norms related to the items with such a high fraction of "yes" responses obviously exist and are sufficiently clear within the survey population. Therefore, the first requirement of an item of this kind of social desirability scale, i.e. the pervasion of a social norm, is mostly fulfilled. Merely the social norms related to three items are not so very clear. For the case of the denial item "I take pleasure in reading sexy books or magazines" only 66.7% of the respondents think that there is a social norm prohibiting such behavior. Comments by several respondents indicate that reading such books and magazines belongs to the private sphere of people and would therefore not be subject to social norms. The behavior described in the item "When I hear people talking privately I cannot help listening" is only considered morally bad by 55.6% of the respondents. Some people explained this with the fact that often it is not possible to close one's ears and that therefore one is forced to overhear conversations by others.

Table 5.4: Stylized results of 19 in-depth interviews for the assessment of content validity of the modified version of the IM subscale of the BIDR

	Is this behavior desirable/undesirable? Does the respective norm exist?	N	% of valid Yes	% of valid No
1	I am a person that doesn't cover up mistakes.	17	94.1	5.9
2	There have been occasions when I have taken advantage of someone.	18	94.4	5.6
3	I am a person that doesn't swear.	16	13.3	86.7
4	I obey laws, even if I'm unlikely to get caught.	18	94.4	5.6
5	I may have said something bad about a friend behind his or her back.	18	88.9	11.1
6	When I hear people talking privately, I cannot help listening.	18	55.6	44.4
7	It may happen that I receive too much change from a salesperson without telling him or her.	18	88.9	11.1
8	When I was young, I tended to steal things.	18	100.0	0.0
9	I am a person that never drops litter on the street.	18	100.0	0.0
10	I take pleasure in reading sexy books or magazines.	18	66.7	33.3
11	I would never take things that don't belong to me.	17	94.1	5.9
12	I have taken sick-leave from work or school even though I wasn't really sick.	18	88.9	11.1
13	If I damage merchandise in the supermarket I definitely report it to the staff.	18	100.0	0.0
14	I am a person that doesn't gossip about other people's business.	18	88.9	11.1

Regarding the item "I am a person that doesn't swear" the fraction of respondents perceiveing a social norm that prohibits this behavior is even only 13.3%. The reason for this might be a translation error. While the English version of this item refers to swearing in terms of cursing and saying four-letter words, the Chinese translation interpreted the "swear" as taking an oath. It is very obvious that there is no social norm prohibiting taking an oath, so in the following analysis this item has to be treated with caution.

In a second step respondents in these additional evaluation interviews were asked if they believed such an extreme answer to be true. It was explained that during a household survey the following set of items had been used already and that the majority of respondents had stated the marked response to the respective items (the respective socially desirable response). Then reference was made to "the average citizen of Jinghong" and whether the respondent judges the extreme and socially desirable response to be credible or not. Answers to this question are summarized in table 5.5.

Table 5.5: Stylized results of 19 in-depth interviews for the assessment of content validity of the modified version of the IM subscale of the BIDR

	Do you personally believe this extreme statement?	**N**	**% of valid Yes**	**% of valid No**
1	I am a person that doesn't cover up mistakes.	17	17.6	82.4
2	There have been occasions when I have taken advantage of someone.	18	5.6	94.4
3	I am a person that doesn't swear.	16	56.3	43.8
4	I obey laws, even if I'm unlikely to get caught.	18	16.7	83.3
5	I may have said something bad about a friend behind his or her back.	18	16.7	83.3
6	When I hear people talking privately, I cannot help listening.	15	40.0	60.0
7	It may happen that I receive too much change from a salesperson without telling him or her.	17	35.3	64.7
8	When I was young, I tended to steal things.	17	5.9	94.1
9	I am a person that never drops litter on the street.	18	38.9	61.1
10	I take pleasure in reading sexy books or magazines.	17	17.6	82.4
11	I would never take things that don't belong to me.	18	27.8	72.2
12	I have taken sick-leave from work or school even though I wasn't really sick.	18	22.2	77.8
13	If I damage merchandise in the supermarket I definitely report it to the staff.	16	31.3	68.8
14	I am a person that doesn't gossip about other people's business.	16	12.5	87.5

By and large these figures show that for most items the overwhelming majority of respondents do not believe the respective socially desirable response (i.e. "completely true" for enhancement items and "completely wrong" for denial items) to be truthful. Several respondents explained that the response options "completely wrong" and "completely true" are too categorical to be true. One female respondent even commented on each item saying that it [the response of the majority of interviewees] *should* be "predominately wrong" or "predominately true", respectively. These results are a clear indication that extreme responses indeed constitute a departure from reality and are exaggerated. They also confirm the basic idea of the construction of this scale, i.e. the inclusion of behavioral patterns which are very desirable but uncommon and behavior which is very undesirable but common. The fact that for most respondents to these in-depth interviews the extreme answers could not be true indicates that enhancement items are indeed very uncommon and the behavior described in denial items very common. However, as for the previous question about the existence of the relevant social norms, the item "I am a person that doesn't swear" stands out. More than half of the respondents believe the respective socially desirable response ("Completely true") to be credible. This again is a result of the translation error in that taking an oath is not considered morally bad behavior, so an extreme statement such as "completely true" is found to be credible. Indeed it is quite likely that most respondents to the main survey have never taken an official oath. So, again this item has to be treated with caution.

Remaining problems with the scale's application

Despite the above evidence for the reliability and validity of the modified BIDR scale several problems related to its practical use remain. Firstly, it could be argued that SDR is likely to be at work when respondents complete the questions to measure this very phenomenon. If a respondent with a pronounced need for social approval responds to this set of questions, she will be likely to select significantly more extreme responses than the average respondent without need for social approval. This fact derives from the basic logic of the scale, which aims at detecting excessive claims of desirable characteristics and overly strong denials of undesirable ones that both constitute a departure from reality. Consequently, SDR is not a threat to the validity of this question inventory.

Another type of feedback effects, which admittedly poses a threat to the validity of this scale, is the existence of interviewer effects. If it is the case that the identity and characteristics of an interviewer significantly influence the likelihood of stating a socially desirable response rather than a moderate response, such effects are at work. In an attempt to detect interviewer effects in the social desirability scale, an OLS regression of the BIDR score as dependent variable is conducted. Independent variables are a set of demographic variables of both the respondent and the interviewer. The result as displayed in table 5.6 shows that level of need for social approval as measured by the modified IM subscale of the BIDR is only influenced significantly by the interviewer's gender (*imale*). Male interviewers elicit systematically lower BIDR scores than their female counterparts. This finding constitutes a slight impairment of the reliability of the modified scale because the resulting need for approval score of a respondent depends on whether the interview is conducted by a male or female interviewer. However, such problems apparently come with the use of this scale in a direct interview.[31] Neither the fact that the interviewer is Han Chinese (*ihan*) nor the interviewer's age (*iage*) influences the BIDR score. So, on the whole only one out of three interviewer characteristics, which were tested in the model, turned out to be systematically influencing the BIDR score.

31 Originally, the BIDR had been designed for the paper-and-pencil format. However, some surveys have made use of this instrument in in-person interviews, such as Winkler et al. (2006).

Table 5.6: OLS regression of the BIDR score

N=1,495	Coefficient	Std. error
CONSTANT	2.390***	(0.623)
FEMALE	1.148***	(0.150)
AGE	0.096***	(0.009)
MARRIED	0.526***	(0.171)
WORKER	-0.499***	(0.187)
OFFICIAL	0.535	(0.392)
SELF-EMPLOY	-0.202	(0.191)
HHSIZE	0.001	(0.055)
TIMEBN	-0.014**	(0.006)
RUBBER	0.008	(0.205)
EDU	-0.081	(0.068)
INCOME	0.000	(0.000)
ihan	-0.255	(0.175)
iage	-0.008	(0.011)
imale	-0.591***	(0.181)

In contrast to this, the significant effects of characteristics of the respondent, such as gender (*FEMALE*), age (*AGE*), marital status (*MARRIED*), or the time spent in the region so far (*TIMEBN*), are not a problem at all, since they only reflect that different kinds of people differ in their need for social approval. Especially the persistently positive influence of respondent's gender reflects the results from the group analysis above that women score higher on the BIDR than men.

Thirdly, applying strict semantic logic the moderate response options on the 5-point Likert scale ("2", "3", and "4") lack any meaning with respect to some items. For instance item 4 "I obey laws, even if I am unlikely to get caught" could logically only be answered with "yes" or "no" – a person either does this or not. Yet, the results for this item as displayed in table 5.1 show that almost one quarter of the respondents select a moderate response option to this item. Obviously many respondents do not answer this item with strict semantic logic but base their response on a somewhat freer interpretation of the item content. The problem here is that the application of the inventory rests on the assumption that respondents in fact interpret the five response options as different degrees of the accuracy of the statement with respect to themselves. Thus, a precondition for the inventory to yield valid and meaningful results is that respondents do not apply strict semantic logic when responding to these items but rather construe them in a quite free manner. In other words, it is assumed that respondents interpret the scale as increasing or decreasing intensities of the content of the respective item. Since it is very likely that this interpretation is dependent on individual characteristics of the respondent, which differ among respondents and cannot be controlled for by the researcher, the above assumption is problematic. The problem is further aggravated by the fact that the applicability of a 5-point response scale with two extreme and three moderate response options differs with different items. While it is somewhat problematic with respect to items that could logically only be answered with "yes" or "no", such as items 2, 4, or 12, the content of several other items appears to match better with a graded response scale. Consequently, the problems of meaningful moderate response to several items as well as the naivety of giving an extreme response persist to some degree even in the modified inventory. Also among these 14 items there are several that are logically difficult to answer on a 5-point response scale. Therefore, the assumption must be made that respondents interpret the response options as indicating the degree to which such statements apply to them. The problems that come with this assumption have been discussed above and remain an important shortcoming of this inventory.

Finally, the 5-point Likert scale itself might be hard to understand for some respondents in the target population in a small rural town in Southwest China. Especially those respondents with merely a low level of education might have trouble specifying if they consider an item as "predominantly true" or "completely true". Therefore they might simply choose the extreme answer, but not out of an approval seeking motive but simply because the other response options do not bear any meaning for them. Rather than employing the whole range of response options to express the intensity of their answer these respondents merely think in binary yes/no or true/wrong categories. For instance a respondent wants to convey the message that the statement "I am a person that doesn't swear" is basically true about her in most situations. According to the strict logic of the scale the response option "predominantly true" would be appropriate here. Yet due to a lack of understanding the rather subtle difference between "predominantly true" and "completely true", i.e. especially of the categorical nature of the extreme option, this respondent selects the latter. The result of such a reduced thinking process would be a need for approval score that is artificially biased upwards due to the many extreme answers a respondent has given. These extreme responses, which are counted by the scale as indicators of approval seeking are in fact only truthful statements of a somewhat smaller intensity.

In sum, the evidence for the reliability and validity of the modified inventory to assess need for social approval appears to be sufficient to assure meaningful assessment of the construct. It has been shown that the set of items is internally consistent and it actually measures need for social approval. Besides the statistical evidence, especially the results of the ex post in-depth interviews, support this conclusion. On the other hand, several important shortcomings of this approach persist, which potentially reduce the accuracy of measurement, i.e. the reliability of the inventory. It should be noted that these shortcomings are not a result of the application of the inventory in a new environment, but that they accompany this approach of measuring need for social approval by means of self-report questionnaire inventories in general. Regarding the subsequent analysis of the impact of the three-factor model of SDR on WTP statements, the modified scale is used to calculate a score which enters the model as the variable *BIDR14*.

5.2.2. Measuring anonymity

The second ingredient of the three-factor model as introduced in section 3.3 is the lack of sufficient anonymity perceived by the respondent. Following the differentiation of different concepts of anonymity in section 3.3.2, this aspect can be assessed in several ways. In that section it is argued that only perceived internal and external anonymity can actually influence response behavior. That is, as a first step, an objectively anonymous interview setting has to be created. In a second step, it has to be assessed whether or not the respondent believes these assurances of external and internal anonymity. Only if the respondent holds such a belief, does anonymity or confidentiality exist and exert influence on response behavior. Like demonstrated above, the mere modification of objective anonymity does not influence response behavior as long as it is not perceived and believed by the respondent. Therefore, the more important step is the assessment of anonymity perceptions. This assessment is a difficult undertaking because it has to be assessed by the same person that is (at least partly) responsible for this feeling of anonymity – the interviewer. In a way, the interviewer is asking for an evaluation of the conduction of her own interview because it is the interviewer who assures the respondent that all answers given will be treated confidentially. Nevertheless, this variable has to be measured, so appropriate questions have to be found. In the following, both the specific settings to create objective anonymity and the question to assess the subjective perception of it are introduced.

Many surveys vary the level of objective response anonymity by administering different interview techniques in different split samples (e.g. Alpizar et al. 2008b, Leggett et al. 2003). This study employs a similar approach by using a ballot box. This methodological modification described in section 5.1 is designed in order to raise the level of anonymity the respondent feels when she is answering the WTP question. Since the ballot box is sealed with a clearly visible lock, it is conveyed to the respondent that the interviewer, i.e. the direct opponent during the interview process, is unable to perceive the answers to these three questions.

40.1	How likely do you believe it is that your responses can be traced back to you when all questionnaires will be evaluated?	O Impossible O It is possible O I am certain

Figure 5.4: The question to assess perceived external anonymity

Having modified the level of objective anonymity, what is the important factor for the respondent is rather the question whether she perceives the situation as anonymous or not. Therefore, in a second step of the modification it has to be assessed whether the respondent perceives the circumstances of answering the WTP question as anonymous in the sense that nobody – not even the interviewer – can ever get to know the response. This is done by means of question 40.1 in the questionnaire (cf. figure 5.4). This question yields the binary variable *PUBLIC* which is 1 when the respondent states "It is possible" or "I am certain" and zero when she states "Impossible". This means that only if the respondent deems it impossible that her responses can be traced back to her, does she perceive the situation to be completely anonymous. In this case the variable *PUBLIC* is equal to zero. This type of anonymity also refers to the interviewer who, in the standard face to face setting, knows the respondent's WTP statement and could thus easily find the respondent again. However, in the ballot box setting a respondent with *PUBLIC* equal to zero is interpreted as feeling that the interview situation when answering the WTP question is externally and internally anonymous. This question is utilized for computing the variable *PUBLIC* for respondents in the ballot box split sample only. For all other split samples which are administered without the use of such a box, perceived anonymity is low, i.e. the response is perceptible by the interviewer. Regarding question 40.1 that means it is assumed that in all other split samples every respondent answers "I am certain" and that therefore the value of the variable *PUBLIC* is fixed at 1. So, according to this definition this variable is only allowed to vary in the ballot box split sample. Since the interviewer is at least partly responsible for the level of anonymity perceived by the respondent, this question should better not be asked by the interviewer who conducts the main part of the survey interview. Therefore, when the ballot box procedure is employed the interview is conducted by two interviewers. One of them is doing the main part of the CVM interview and then leaves the room. This is when the second interviewer takes over, goes through the SDR related questions and finishes the interview. By employing this procedure the respondent is given the opportunity to express her perception of the anonymity not towards the interviewer who conducted the main part of the interview but to another person. Response frequencies of this question are displayed on the left-hand side of table 5.7.

Table 5.7: Distribution of the variables PUBLIC and EXPUB

PUBLIC		EXPUB	
Value	**N**	**Value**	**N**
0: No lack of anonymity	32	0: No lack of anonymity	302
1: Lack of anonymity	1,629	1: Lack of anonymity	1,359
TOTAL	1,661	TOTAL	1,661

In addition to this, an alternative anonymity variable referred to as *EXPUB* is calculated. This alternative variable displays the actual results of the perceived anonymity question (question 40.1) for all splits, i.e. it does not assume that there is a lack of anonymity for all respondents outside the ballot box treatment (treatments 1 to 9). This modification of the anonymity variable from *PUBLIC* to *EXPUB* makes sense for two reasons. Firstly, the number of respondents without lack of anonymity in the ballot box treatment is only 32 out of 1661. Since in this setting, the vast majority of respondents are assigned a value of 1 for *PUBLIC*, the three-factor model practically turns into a two-factor model consisting only of need for social approval and trait desirability. In contrast to that, the variation of *EXPUB* is higher with 302 out of 1661 respondents believing that their answers on the questionnaire cannot be traced back to them after the survey (cf. the right-hand side of table 5.7). Employing this variable as the anonymity factor instead, the overall model becomes a real three-factor model. Secondly, *EXPUB* really assesses the level of external anonymity perceived by the respondents without any modifications in the level of objective anonymity. The subjective believe of a respondent to what extent her answers are visible to some outward audience (of the institution implementing the survey) and can be linked to her identity is the real motivational factor of response behavior. *EXPUB* is therefore only calculated for cases in the treatments 1 to 9 because the level of objective anonymity in these treatments is comparable. This is not the case for the ballot box treatment in subsample 10, which is excluded for that part of the analysis. The empirical analysis of the influence of the three-factor model of SDR on WTP responses reported below starts with *PUBLIC* as anonymity variable but also tests the effect of *EXPUB*. As a consequence of the greater plausibility and better performance of the latter, *EXPUB* is being applied as anonymity variable in the course of the further empirical analysis.

5.2.3. Measuring trait desirability

As introduced above, trait desirability is the judgement of a respondent which answer options to a specific question are socially desirable and which are not. This is why the measurement of this variable is necessarily related to the specific topic of a survey questionnaire, i.e. trait desirability is contingent on a specific question. Therefore it can only be assessed with respect to the question, the relationship of which with SDR is to be investigated. It has been mentioned above that only if there is a perceived difference in the social desirability level of two or more response options (traits), is a response potentially influenced by SDR. If all response options were judged by a certain respondent to be equally socially desirable, there would be no way to gain social approval from her perspective by selecting any other than the true option, simply because she cannot tell which one achieves the objective to gain social approval. Consequently, as hypothesized by the three-factor model in such a situation there are no incentives for SDR. Put more generally, the assessment of trait desirability is an exploration of the social norms relevant to a specific item topic. Social norms define which kinds of behavior or personality characteristics are desirable and which are not. Therefore, social norms also determine the desirability difference between response options. An assessment of the desirability of certain options thus equals an assessment of the relevant norm.

Several approaches to measure trait desirability can be found in the existing literature on social desirability (Edwards 1957, Stocké and Hunkler 2007). The classical approach of Edwards (1957) consists of having a group of judges rate the desirability of certain traits. According to this approach, the judges simply indicate if a certain personality characteristic that forms the content of a survey question is desirable or not from their own point of view. Alternatively, Stocké and Hunkler (2007) provide an overview of three widely used measures to assess trait desirability and their theoretical preconditions, namely the one-point measure, the simple difference scores and the domain-specific difference scores. All these methods have respondents rate the desirability of one or more possible points on the range of response options. The one-point measure – similar to Edward's approach – just has the respondents rate the desirability of one extreme end of the range of answer options assuming that the other end is rated neutrally and that the level of desirability between the two extremes increases or decreases monotonically. In contrast to that, the simple difference scores approach makes respondents rate the desirability of both end points of the range of responses (e.g. "completely true" and "completely wrong") and calculates their difference. In this case, only one assumption has to be made, namely the monotonicity of the desirability level for answer options between the two extreme options. This approach does not assume that one of the two extreme answers on the range of response options is evaluated neutrally with respect to its social desirability. Finally, the domain-specific difference scores approach assesses respondents' desirability ratings for the two extreme and the middle option of the response range in order to test if the monotonicity assumption really holds. It is by means of this approach that non-monotonic desirability profiles can be detected. A short example can illustrate this case. Imagine the survey question "How satisfied are you with the work of the current government?" with the five response options ranging from "very dissatisfied" to "very satisfied". The one-point measure would simply rate the desirability of responding "very satisfied" and assume that the other extreme is neutral, i.e. neither desirable nor undesirable. The simple difference scores calculate the difference in the level of desirability of the two extremes of the response scale. Yet for the domain-specific difference scores, it is possible that respondents rate the option "very unsatisfied" and "very satisfied" both to be equally socially undesirable but the middle option "neither unsatisfied nor satisfied" as being highly socially desirable. This is an example for a non-monotonic desirability profile because the level of desirability does not increase or decrease monotonically over the range of possible answers. However, the shortcoming of all these methods is that no matter for how many points on the response scale a desirability rating is assessed, the researcher can never be sure that the desirability level between two rated options is monotonically increasing or decreasing, respectively. Thus, for the case of a WTP question in a contingent valuation survey none of the above approaches appears to be suitable. This is because the range of possible answers to this question is limited only on one side (zero) but open on the other (an arbitrarily large WTP). Therefore, a simple rating of the desirability of arbitrarily chosen points on the range of response options (in this case WTP amounts) is not feasible. Since it does not make sense to have the respondents rate the desirability of specific amounts on the payment card, the domain-specific difference scores do not work, either. Which amounts should be selected for a desirability rating and what about the level of desirability of the amounts in between? Therefore, in the current study a new question format for eliciting the degree of social desirability of different response options to the WTP question is developed. Respondents are simply asked if they think that the desirability of the monetary contribution increases with its amount or not (cf. figure 5.5). This approach assumes that if a respondent thinks that higher WTP is more desirable, there is an incentive to bias her statement upwards. Since the true WTP of a certain respondent is not known to the researcher, this question format does not make reference to an absolute WTP amount. Therefore, this question should appeal to all respondents regardless of the amount of their true WTP.

38.2	When it comes to contributing to the Return Rubber into Forest program, do you think the more the better?	1 ○ Yes 0 ○ No

Figure 5.5: Assessing trait desirability with respect to the elicitation question

The responses to question 38.2 as displayed in figure 5.5 yield a variable called *TRAIT*, which equals 1 if a respondent answers "yes" and zero if the answer is "no". Respondents thinking that a contribution is the better the higher its amount judge higher WTP statements to be more desirable than lower ones. So these respondents perceive a potential to gain social approval by biasing their WTP statement upwards compared to their true WTP. Consequently, *TRAIT* equals 1 which means that the trait desirability factor of the model of socially desirable response behavior with respect to the WTP question is present for these respondents. Table 5.8 gives the survey results to this question. About four tenth of respondents answering this question perceive a higher WTP to be more desirable.

Table 5.8: Results of the trait desirability question

	TRAIT Value	**N**
"When it comes to contributing to the RRIF program, do you think the more the better?"		
	0: No	991
	1: Yes	668
	TOTAL	1,659

Two things should be noted at this point. Firstly, this question format also assumes social desirability of the WTP to increase monotonically with its amount. However, it is conceivable that after increasing over the range of comparably small WTP amounts, the level of desirability stagnates or even decreases for WTP amounts high on the payment card. Applying the present question format, such a pattern cannot be identified. A question that is able to also elicit a non-monotonic desirability function must make some reference to the absolute level of WTP in order to determine the point where the shape of the function changes. However, the advantage of the question type in figure 5.5 is that it is independent of absolute WTP and therefore independent of the specific household income of the respondent. This independence is not possible if a potential non-monotonic trait desirability function is to be detected. So, considering the tradeoff of independence of respondent characteristics and absolute true WTP amount on the one hand and ability to detect a negative relationship between WTP amount and social desirability on the other, the present question clearly favors the former objective. Secondly, the question does not explicitly specify if the desirability of a higher WTP should be judged from the perspective of the respondent or from society. Clearly, social desirability is a reflection of social norms, and it was demonstrated above that norms are part of a social system rather than of individuals. Yet, for social norms to influence behavior they have to be perceived by an individual. So, the existence of a social norm in society is reflected in its perception by the individual respondent. If a respondent thinks that contributing the more the better, it means that from her point of view there is a norm that asks for a contribution as high as possible. What is important about this is the perception of the norm. Whether this norm is actually shared by all members of society or whether the respective respondent holds the same view does not matter. Therefore, question 38.2 is employed in that very open format.

5.2.4. Calculation of the SDR variable

As a result of the empirical setup just introduced, two out of the three factors of the model of SDR are binary coded on 0 or 1, namely *EXPUB* (*PUBLIC*) and *TRAIT*, while the need for social approval score *BIDR14* can take values between 0 and 14. All three variables are positive when partial incentive for socially desirable responding is present and zero when it is not. So, this coding reproduces the relationship within the three-factor model of SDR, according to which each factor only affects WTP statements if the respective other two factors are present, as well. In other words this means that the three factors are non-compensatory, i.e. only if all factors are present is there incentive for SDR. This situation can be modeled by means of a multiplicative relationship between the factors.

$$SDR = BIDR14 \cdot EXPUB \cdot TRAIT \tag{5.1}$$

Overall incentives for socially desirable responding (*SDR*) are the product of the need for social approval score (*BIDR14*), the variable indicating lack of anonymity (*EXPUB*)[32], and trait desirability (*TRAIT*). This new variable can assume values in the range from 0 to 14, but with a spike on zero. This spike is the consequence of the multiplicative relationship of the three factors. Respondents with a strictly positive need for approval score but without one of the other factors are assigned an *SDR* value of zero according to 5.1. To put it another way, only one factor equaling zero is already sufficient to level that

32 Alternatively the variable *PUBLIC* is employed to indicate lack of anonymity (cf. section 5.2.2).

respondent's value of *SDR*. In the following section the *SDR* term is included in the regression equations to identify determinants of WTP statements as additional interaction term. Two types of interaction models were discussed and specified in section 4.3.

Before these interaction models are employed, it is necessary to look at the relationships between the three factors in further detail. Table 5.9 displays correlation coefficients between the factors based on the data of the contingent valuation survey in Jinghong. It becomes apparent that the factors are not completely independent of each other. The need for social approval score, for instance, is positively correlated with both *EXPUB* and *TRAIT*. This means that respondents with high need for social approval as measured by means of the modified BIDR are more likely to find a higher WTP socially desirable than respondents with low need for approval. This result does not come unexpected since respondents who perceive the desirability of a certain trait (e.g. a high WTP) should at least have a basic need for approval in order to be able to feel that desirability in the first place. A respondent that does not and did never care about the impression that she makes on others (i.e. has no need for social approval) will have problems to tell whether a certain statement or character trait is desirable. Therefore, it is quite plausible that these two characteristics – need for social approval and the belief that a certain statement is socially desirable – go hand in hand to a certain extent.

Table 5.9: Correlations between the variables of the three-factor model of SDR

	BIDR14	PUBLIC	EXPUB	TRAIT
BIDR14	1	0.027	0.088	0.111
p-value		0.270	0.000	0.000
PUBLIC	0.027	1	0.297	0.008
p-value	0.270		0.000	0.740
EXPUB	0.088	0.297	1	0.055
p-value	0.000	0.000		0.027
TRAIT	0.111	0.008	0.055	1
p-value	0.000	0.740	0.027	

This slightly positive relationship between need for approval and trait desirability has been frequently found in the respective literature (Chen et al. 1997, Stocké and Hunkler 2007). That finding also means that respondents scoring high on the BIDR are more likely to perceive a lack of anonymity of the interview. This result is also plausible because respondents with a higher need for social approval might be more cautious about where and by whom their statements are perceived. Conversely, individuals with a comparably low need for approval tend not to care so much about where their information is passed on to simply because they are not so anxious about how it is perceived.

The variable *PUBLIC* only shows significant correlation with *EXPUB*, the alternative anonymity variable but not to the other two factors. This is a consequence of its low variance. Remember that *PUBLIC* was assumed to be 1 for all splits except the ballot box split. Therefore, the majority of models in the subsequent subsection will be run employing *EXPUB* instead of *PUBLIC*.

When it comes to the fully specified interaction models of SDR, the positive correlation is a potential problem for these models because the three factors, the product of each pair wise combination and the product of all three factors (*SDR*) are included as additional explanatory variables. If the correlations between these seven components are too high, collinearity is a problem and the regression model is no longer able to separate the influence of the different variables. This would result in high standard errors and consequently low *p*-values of the regression coefficients. However, correlation coefficients between the three factors of less than 0.15 are still sufficiently low so that collinearity is not expected to impair the regression models.

5.3. General results of the contingent valuation survey

In this section, the empirical results of the CVM survey will be displayed. This will be done in several steps. To begin with, some descriptive statistics of important demographic variables of the sample population will be displayed, which will be followed by a discussion of results of willingness to pay. This is an analysis of the determinants of WTP. After this the next section will then proceed to the core part of this analysis, the test of the relationship between SDR and WTP statements. The hypotheses developed in section 4.3 will be tested one by one and conclusions will be drawn.

5.3.1. Demographic characteristics of the sample population

Out of the 2,021 returned questionnaires 42 were completed by respondents below the age of 18 or lacking age statement. Discarding these questionnaires results in a sample of 1979 valid cases, which form the basis for the subsequent analysis. 53% of all respondents are female, which reflects the gender ratio in the 2007 Statistical Yearbook of Jinghong Municipality (Jinghong 2008). Among all respondents, 68.2% have children with the number of children per household reaching from 1 up to 6. The average number of children among households that have at least one child is 1.4. Table 5.10 displays means and standard deviations of several additional demographic variables. Age of respondents ranged from 18 to 84 years with a mean of 36 years. The average household consists of slightly more than three people with household size ranging from 1 up to 16 members. However, most households (99.7%) do not have more than 8 members. The surprisingly small average household size for a developing country is the result of the one-child-policy in the People's Republic of China and the inclusion of migrant households in the sample. Migrant laborers mostly move to Xishuangbanna without their family but take up their fixed abode there. Since they permanently reside in the survey area they should be included in the relevant survey population. Average monthly household income in the sample amounts to 2,838 RMB.[33] This figure is slightly higher than the average household income for urban Jinghong as reported in the 2007 Statistical Yearbook, which is at 2,700 RMB (Jinghong 2008). Acknowledging that the survey was conducted in mid-2009, this difference is likely to reflect a normal rise in income as a consequence of fast economic development in China.

Table 5.10: Sample mean values for certain demographic variables

Variable	Mean	Standard deviation
Age	36.35	12.12
Household size	3.24	1.46
Monthly income (in RMB)	2,838.13	2,779.41

In figure 5.6 histograms of certain categorical demographic variables are produced. As introduced above, one characteristic of Xishuangbanna Prefecture is its ethnic diversity. This is reflected in the ethnic composition of the survey sample. Almost two thirds of the respondents are Han Chinese, the major ethnic group in the PRC. This exceeds the share of Han population officially registered in that area by about 15 percentage points (Jinghong 2008). Accordingly, the fractions of all other minorities are lower in the sample than in the official government statistics. At first glance, this seems to be a flaw in the sampling procedure, yet this phenomenon can be explained by extensive uncontrolled migration of mostly Han Chinese into the study area. Most of these migrants are not registered and thus not accounted for in the official statistics. Since the sampling procedure is based on the situation of the

33 At an exchange rate of 9.6 RMB / Euro in June 2009 this is equal to 296 Euros.

actual rather than the registered resident population, the representativeness of the sample is maintained.

Regarding marital status, approximately two thirds of respondents are married and 26% are not married. Only small fractions of respondents account for the remaining categories. When it comes to the level of education, most respondents have attended middle school and either graduated from junior high or senior high. While there is still a significant fraction of college graduates and people with a bachelor degree, higher academic degrees are virtually not represented. This reflects the comparably low level of education of Yunnan Province compared to the rest of China and the fact that Jinghong does not have a university. The distribution of occupation of respondents is similarly reasonable for the survey area with workers, employees of state units and self-employed representing the most frequent categories.

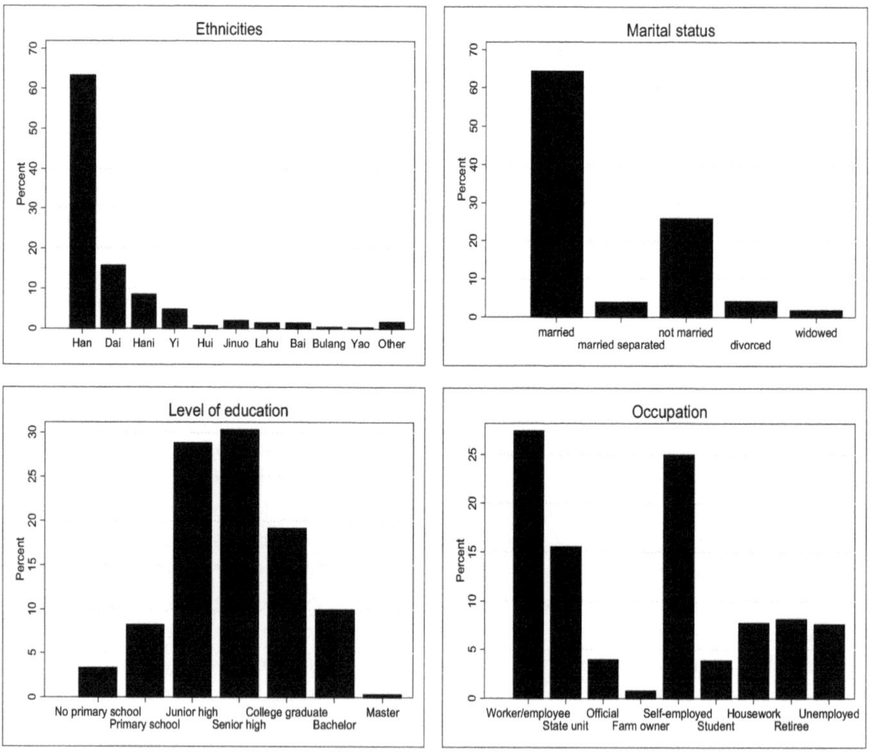

Figure 5.6: Relative frequency of some categorical demographic variables

5.3.2. Overall determinants of WTP

The contingent valuation survey reported here aims at the assessment of the willingness to pay of a representative sample of the resident population of Jinghong for a land-use scenario including reforestation of rubber plantations in a nature reserve area in the vicinity of the city. WTP statements refer to a municipal fee per household to be paid every three months. Out of 1979 valid questionnaires, 1946 respondents actually answered the WTP question, i.e. a fraction of 98.3%.

In order to check the plausibility of the WTP statements obtained in a CV survey the determinants of such statements have to be identified. That means it has to be assessed which characteristics of a certain respondent explain the WTP that she has actually stated in the survey interview. As discussed above, strong criticism against the CVM arises from the fact that responses are hypothetical and that their truthfulness cannot be verified. However, by developing and testing assumptions how specific respondent characteristics influence WTP statements the plausibility of responses can at least be verified to a certain extent. This test of the relationships of WTP statements and other explanatory variables, the validity of which is warranted to a greater extent, adds to the construct validity of contingent valuation data.

This analysis is done by extending the above probit model and including a set of potentially influencing explanatory variables. In addition to nine dummy variables controlling the influence of the different treatments (variables *T2* to *T10*)[34], several socio-demographic variables are included. In the following, these variables as listed in the regression output in table 5.11 are introduced and the respective expectations of the signs of their coefficients are discussed. As most basic demographic variables, respondents' sex (*FEMALE)* and age (*AGE)* are expected to systematically influence WTP. Further, married respondents as indicated by *MARRIED* are hypothesized to have a higher household WTP. This is the result of the fact that a married respondent is member of a household with more people enjoying the benefits of the environmental project in question. The same logic should hold for the variable that actually assesses the number of people in the household, *HHSIZE.* Regarding the occupation of the respondent, out of all categories of the respective question, dummies for three prominent and rather frequent occupations are included. These are *WORKER*, *OFFICIAL*, and *SELF-EMPLOY.* It is believed that these three types of occupation represent prototypes within Chinese society and that in contrast to workers and self-em-

34 These dummy variables will be included in all subsequent regression models, but their influence will not be further discussed in the framework of this study.

ployed people, officials might identify themselves most strongly with the state and therefore state a higher WTP. The coefficient of *OFFICIAL* is therefore expected to be positive.

Table 5.11: Determinants of willingness to pay, output of probit regression model

Model 1: Demographic characteristics		
N=1718	Coefficient	Std. error
CONSTANT	0.60***	(0.22)
BID	-18.74***	(0.22)
T2	-13.04	(97.71)
T3	-279.13**	(141.28)
T4	62.13	(95.65)
T5	-191.33	(124.86)
T6	-38.19	(103.25)
T7	-233.36*	(122.09)
T8	-6.85	(103.26)
T9	-116.00	(106.67)
T10	-64.25	(104.06)
FEMALE	-37.16	(55.21)
AGE	-6.57**	(3.00)
MARRIED	-150.85**	(64.98)
WORKER	-88.29	(66.31)
OFFICIAL	8.55	(138.49)
SELF-EMPLOY	-123.92	(75.73)
HHSIZE	-2.02	(19.24)
TIMEBN	0.96	(2.12)
RUBBER	108.64	(70.78)
EDU	127.62***	(24.09)
INCOME	0.04***	(0.01)

Next, it is assumed that people that have been staying in the region for a long time are more familiar with the environmental problems associated with expanding rubber cultivation. Additionally, since such people are more likely to identify themselves with the region and its geographical and environmental features, it is believed that this fact makes them more sensitive to the issue of biodiversity loss resulting from expanding rubber cultivation. Consequently, *TIMEBN*, the time they have lived in the region measured in years, should have a positive effect on WTP. On the other hand, the fact that a household owns rubber trees and thus actively profits from this expanding sector should result in weaker support for the proposed reforestation project. The variable *RUBBER* indicating whether a household owns rubber trees is therefore expected to exert a negative influence on

WTP. Finally, more educated people and households with a higher income are hypothesized to state systematically higher WTP. Therefore, the coefficients of both *EDU* and *INCOME* can be expected to be positive.

Looking at the results of the regression model as presented in table 5.11 the following determinants can be identified. To begin with, the variable *BID* representing the lower and upper limits of the interval on the PC that a respondent chooses has a significantly negative impact on WTP statements. This finding is plausible because the higher the interval on the payment card the less likely it is that a respondent chooses it.

When it comes to the demographic variables, the coefficients of both *AGE* and *MARRIED* are significantly negative. That means that older respondents and respondents who are married have a systematically lower WTP than younger and unmarried participants, respectively. Participatory approaches to evaluate government policies like CVM that ask for private contributions to the provision of public goods are still very uncommon in China today and were not employed at all in the pre-reform era before 1979. Instead, elderly people are rather used to simply following government directives and might not be used to evaluate government policy schemes, which results in the negative impact of respondent age. The negative influence of *MARRIED* is somewhat surprising, but can be explained by that fact that married people have to support their spouse or even a whole family, which tightens their budget constraint. As a consequence, the WTP of a married respondent for such an environmental project decreases.

As expected, the coefficients of both the level of education (*EDU*) of the respondent and the household income (*INCOME*) are positive and highly significant. This makes sense because better educated people usually have a higher level of awareness of environmental problems and perceive future problems in a much clearer way. As a result, their WTP to support projects to mitigate such problems is comparably high. Finally, households with a high income systematically have a higher WTP. The fact that this very basic relationship holds in the elicited data is an indicator of its plausibility.

Most of the remaining demographic variables, although not significantly influencing WTP statements, still point into the expected directions. Looking at the different categories of occupation, out of the list of response options three prominent and frequently selected options are included as dummy variables. The coefficient of *OFFICIAL* is positive, whereas the coefficients of *WORKER* and *SELF-EMPLOY* are both negative. Although these differences are not significant, government officials tend to have a higher WTP compared to the rest of the sample and workers and self-employed people a lower WTP. The positive sign of the coefficient of *OFFICIAL* makes sense because civil servants are more likely to endorse government policies. This can result from a stronger affinity to the state or merely from the perceived duty to support governmental positions even in this type of household surveys. Similar to the negative effect of *MARRIED*, the number people in the household (*HHSIZE*) also has a negative but not significant coefficient. In the same way contrary to what is hypothesized, the fact that a household owns rubber trees (*RUBBER*) has a positive coefficient. This is likely to result from the fact that owners of rubber plantations have a higher household income and therefore also a higher WTP to pay. Eventually, although the coefficient of the number of years a household has been living in Xishuangbanna Prefecture (*TIMEBN*) has a positive coefficient as expected, it is not significant.

Overall, the elicited WTP data appear plausible. Several essential relationships between demographic data of the household and respective WTP statements can be detected. Up to this point, no contrary results can be found that raise doubts as to the validity of these survey data. Yet, what has so far not been considered is the potential influence of situational factors on the responses given in this survey. Despite the seemingly plausible results above, it is still possible that such factors and SDR in particular systematically distort WTP statements. Therefore, in the following section this type of influence on the present data is studied.

5.4. Analysis of the relationship of SDR and WTP

The main objective of this study is the assessment of the influence of socially desirable responding on WTP statements in a contingent valuation survey. To this end, a three-factor model of desirable responding is developed in section 3.3 holding the interplay of need for social approval, incomplete anonymity of the interview situation and the relative desirability of one response option responsible for the occurrence of this response bias. It is hypothesized that only if all three factors are present, is there an influence of SDR resulting in biased WTP statements. The instruments to empirically assess these factors, introduced in section 5.2, consequently yield three variables. The analysis of the influence of these variables on WTP statements and on two types of response bias constitutes the content of this section.

The investigation is performed in two steps. Firstly, the interaction of the three factors will be included into the probit regression model of the decision whether to state a positive WTP as additional explanatory variables. In a similar way the model, which is used above in order to identify determinants of the specific WTP amount, is simply extended by the three-factor model of desirable responding. These two approaches serve as tests of the adequacy of the three-factor model. Subsequently, the differing influence of the enhancement and denial components in this model is investigated. To this end, the need for social approval factor in the above models is substituted by an enhancement and a denial score in turn. Employing this approach, hypothesis 3 can be tested.

Influence of SDR on the fraction of zero responses

The main statement of the three-factor model of desirable responding is expressed by hypotheses 1 and 2: When the three factors need for social approval, lack of anonymity, and trait desirability are at work simultaneously an influence of SDR on WTP can be expected. In order to test hypothesis 1, the influence of SDR on a very prominent feature of the distribution of WTP responses – the fraction of zero responses – is investigated. This is done in two steps. Firstly, the effect of each of the three factors on the shape of the WTP distribution is studied graphically in order to get a rough impression of the relative frequency of the different PC intervals. Secondly, determinants of the decision whether to state a positive or zero WTP are identified by means of a probit regression model. In this model, the different settings of the interaction of the three factors are included like specified above.

The aim of the first step of this analysis is to investigate the effect that different constellations of the three-factor model have on the form of the distribution of the WTP statements. Figures 5.7 (a) to (c) display the resulting histograms of WTP responses. An overall characteristic that all six histograms share is the fact that lower PC intervals have the highest response frequencies and that these frequencies decrease the higher the intervals. At the same time, this shape is disrupted for the case of the intervals "46-55 RMB" and "81-110 RMB", which show some local peaks. This might be the result of the amounts of 50 RMB and 100 RMB included in these intervals, which are selected more frequently than amounts such as 30 or 70 RMB. This finding reflects the fact that when respondents are selecting an amount on a payment card they are likely to be attracted by anchors in the form of "round amounts". Both characteristics of the distributions – the slanting shape and peaks on the intervals including 50 and 100 RMB – are plausible.

The first histogram in 5.7 (*a*) shows the distribution of WTP statements of respondents with a need for approval score lower than the sample median of 7 on the left-hand side, whereas on the right-hand side the WTP distribution for respondents with that score equal to or greater than 7 is reported. In other words these tables compare the relative frequency of WTP statements for respondents with relatively low and high need for social approval. While for the below-median respondents "0 RMB" is the most frequent answer followed by "1-5 RMB", this setting is reversed for the high need for approval respondents in the right-hand side histogram.

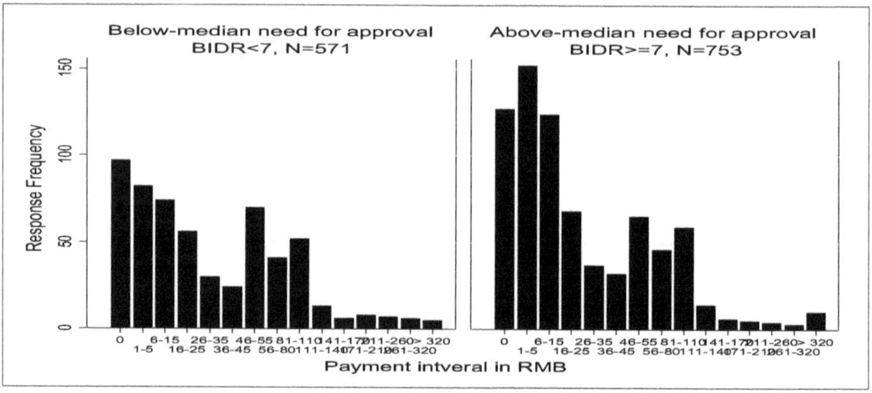

Figure 5.7 (a): Distribution of WTP responses grouped by need for social approval

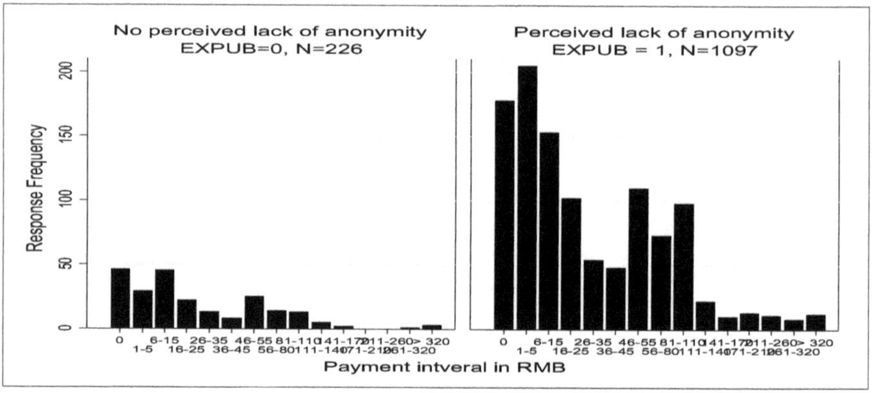

Figure 5.7 (b): Distribution of WTP responses grouped by perceived lack of ext. anonymity

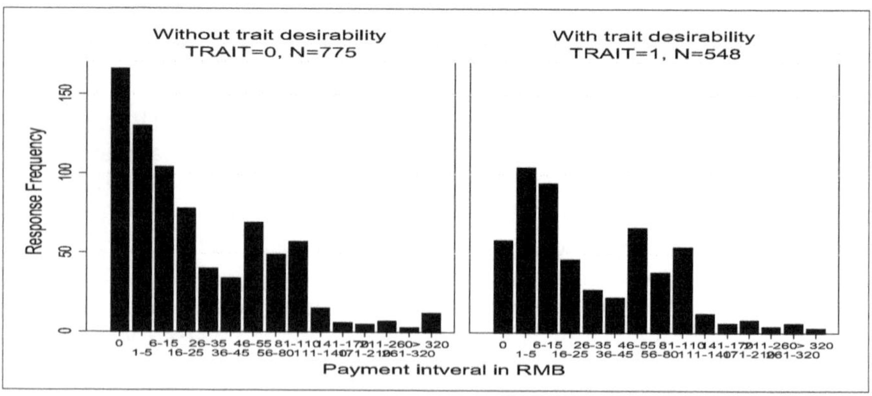

Figure 5.7 (c): Distribution of WTP responses grouped by trait desirability

The same pattern can be observed, if respondents are divided by the anonymity and the trait desirability variables, respectively. The left-hand side of histogram 5.7 (*b*) reports the WTP distribution of respondents without lack of anonymity, i.e. for respondents who do not think that their answers can be traced back to them (*EXPUB*=0). Except for the pronounced peak on the "6-15 RMB" interval, the distribution exhibits the plausible slanting shape. For the case of respondents who do not perceive external anonymity (*EXPUB*=1) in the right-hand side of this histogram the most frequent answer is the second interval. This pattern can also be found in histogram 5.7 (*c*), which displays the WTP distributions for respondents without and with trait desirability. For all three factors the WTP distributions have the normal slanting shape when the factor is absent and have "1-5 RMB" as peak when the respective factor is present. This finding is most pronounced for trait desirability, where the number of zero responses is roughly only half of the number of "1-5 RMB" responses when *TRAIT*=1. Apparently, the three SDR factors make part of the respondents switch from stating zero WTP to a positive interval.

Before looking at the regression results in detail, the variation of the lack-of-anonymity variable (*PUBLIC*) should be scrutinized more closely. By definition, this variable is equal to 1 in all except the ballot box treatments, because all of these interviews are conducted completely in-person (cf. section 5.2.2). That means the interviewer perceives all of the respondent's answers, so there is a substantial lack of anonymity and *PUBLIC* is set equal to 1. Only in the ballot box treatment is *PUBLIC* actually displaying the responses to the perceived anonymity question. As shown in table 5.7, merely 32 out of 176 respondents with a valid response to this question in this split sample perceive the statement of a WTP to be completely anonymous. Compared to the group of *N*=1661 valid responses to this question, this fraction might be too small to result in sufficient variation. In order to overcome this potential flaw the following procedure is applied. The anonymity variable *PUBLIC* is replaced by the variable *EXPUB*. This modification makes sense regarding the content of the variable, because the wording of the question is as follows: "How likely do you believe it is that your responses can be traced back to you when all questionnaires will be evaluated?". This question rather aims at an assessment of perceived *external* anonymity (therefore its name *EXPUB* referring to external "publicness"). Since for all treatments external anonymity is given but not necessarily believed by the respondent, alternatively applying this variable to all split samples is plausible. However, when this modification is implemented the cases of the ballot box treatment have to be excluded because they cannot be compared to the rest of the data. In this treatment, the level of objective anonymity is deliberately modified by the researcher by employing the ballot box, which is not the case for all other treatments. Therefore, it is likely that this ballot box modification also influences the respondents' perception of the level of external anonymity as assessed by question 40.1. As a consequence, the analysis will employ the reduced samples consisting of treatments 1 to 10 (and employing *PUBLIC*) and alternatively including only treatments 1 to 9 (and using *EXPUB* instead). The deletion of respondents confronted with the ballot box treatment leaves an alternative sample of *N*=1783 valid respondents. 1751 of them have answered the WTP elicitation question. Similar to the overall sample, this is a comparatively high response rate of 98.2%.

Table 5.12 displays the results of the probit regression model with the decision to state a positive WTP (*posWTP*) as independent variable. Several of the demographic variables are significant. Female respondents are more likely to give a positive WTP response (*FEMALE*), and the variables level of education (*EDU*), and household income (*INCOME*) exert a significantly positive influence, as well. Larger households (*HHSIZE*) are significantly more likely to state a zero WTP. Finally, the variable *SELF-EMPLOY* is significantly positive. That means that self-employed respondents have a higher likelihood of stating a positive WTP amount.

Now three different settings of explanatory variables are compared. When only the main effects are included as additional explanatory variables in the left-hand column, the coefficients of both lack of anonymity (*PUBLIC*) and trait desirability (*TRAIT*) are significantly positive. Those respondents who do not perceive the situation as anonymous and who think that contributing the more the better are more likely to actually state a positive WTP amount regardless of the need for approval factor. This result is contrary to hypothesis 1, which did not predict an independent influence of any of the factors.

Yet, like introduced in section 4.3, the appropriate model to test the existence of mutually influencing effects of the three factors on WTP responses is the fully specified interaction model, the results of which are displayed in the second column of table 5.12. This model includes the three main effects, the three two-part products of the factors and the overall interaction term. However, only the coefficient of *PUBLIC* is significantly different from zero. In this model, too, respondents who think that stating a higher WTP is desirable have a higher probability of stating a positive WTP regardless of the two remaining factors. Most importantly, in this model the interaction term is not significant, which indicates that the interplay of the three factors does not systematically affects the decision to state a positive WTP. Consequently, on the basis of this result hypothesis 1 would have to be rejected.

Table 5.12: The three-factor model of desirable responding. Probit model of positive WTP, including split samples 1-10

Dep. variable: *posWTP* N=1470	Main effects model Coeff.	Std.error	Full interaction model Coeff.	Std.error	Short interaction model Coeff.	Std.error
CONSTANT	-0.61	(0.44)	-1.41*	(0.84)	0.13	(0.33)
T2	-0.11	(0.18)	-0.11	(0.18)	-0.11	(0.18)
T3	-0.05	(0.18)	-0.05	(0.18)	-0.05	(0.18)
T4	-0.14	(0.18)	-0.13	(0.18)	-0.13	(0.18)
T5	0.08	(0.19)	0.08	(0.19)	0.08	(0.19)
T6	0.20	(0.19)	0.21	(0.19)	0.21	(0.19)
T7	0.03	(0.18)	0.04	(0.18)	0.04	(0.18)
T8	0.25	(0.19)	0.25	(0.19)	0.25	(0.19)
T9	-0.17	(0.18)	-0.16	(0.18)	-0.16	(0.18)
T10	0.15	(0.20)	0.16	(0.20)	0.00	(0.18)
FEMALE	0.25***	(0.09)	0.25***	(0.09)	0.24***	(0.09)
AGE	-0.01	(0.00)	-0.01	(0.00)	-0.01	(0.00)
MARRIED	0.08	(0.10)	0.07	(0.10)	0.08	(0.10)
WORKER	0.00	(0.10)	0.00	(0.10)	-0.01	(0.10)
OFFICIAL	-0.02	(0.22)	-0.03	(0.22)	-0.03	(0.22)
SELF-EMPLOY	0.32***	(0.11)	0.33***	(0.11)	0.30***	(0.11)
HHSIZE	-0.07**	(0.03)	-0.07**	(0.03)	-0.07**	(0.03)
TIMEBN	0.00	(0.00)	0.00	(0.00)	0.00	(0.00)
RUBBER	0.20	(0.12)	0.20	(0.12)	0.19	(0.12)
EDU	0.10***	(0.04)	0.10***	(0.04)	0.10***	(0.04)
INCOME	0.00	(0.00)	0.00	(0.00)	0.00	(0.00)
BIDR14	0.00	(0.01)	0.15	(0.12)	0.01	(0.02)
PUBLIC	0.78***	(0.29)	1.53**	(0.77)		
TRAIT	0.48***	(0.09)	-0.03	(1.54)		
BIDR14*PUBLIC			-0.15	(0.12)		
BIDR14*TRAIT			0.02	(0.24)		
EXPUB*TRAIT			0.61	(1.56)	0.63***	(0.22)
INTERACTION			-0.03	(0.24)	-0.02	(0.03)

A problem with interaction models consisting of three factors is that on the whole seven extra variables have to be added to the regression model. Since four of them are products of different constellations of the three constituent variables, correlations between these product terms can be rather high. Therefore, the model might have problems to separate the influences of each of these terms and the regression table might look like the one of the center column in table 5.12 featuring very large standard errors of the coefficient estimates. In order to circumvent this problem, two of the three constituent variables can be multiplied to create one new variable, which then enters a two-part interaction model with the third constituent variable. In this case, with two binary (*PUBLIC* and *TRAIT*) and one continuous (*BIDR14*) variables, it would be most appropriate to merge the two binary variables into a new binary factor. So the two variables lack of complete anonymity and trait desirability are multiplied and yield one new variable simply referred to as *PUBLIC*TRAIT* in table 5.12. The new variable is equal to 1 for respondents without complete anonymity who find that contributing the more the better, i.e. who think that stating a high WTP is socially desirable. For all other three combinations of the two variables lack of anonymity and trait desirability the newly created variable is zero. This modification results in an interaction model consisting of two constituent terms (*BIDR14* and *PUBLIC*TRAIT*) and one interaction term, which is easier to handle than a model with three interacting variables. This procedure increases the likelihood of getting interpretable results because the number of highly correlated variables in the model is reduced.

The results of this short interaction model are displayed in the right-hand column of table 5.12. In this setting, too, the coefficient of the interaction effect is not significant. Merely variable *PUBLIC*TRAIT* positively influences the amount of stated WTP, i.e. respondents who perceive both a lack of anonymity and trait desirability state a systematically higher WTP than respondents who perceive one or none of these factors. This result is independent of the respective need for social approval. Overall, these findings support doubts about the adequacy of the three-factor model with respect to this dependent variable.

The results of the alternative decision model of positive WTP employing only splits 1 to 9 are displayed in table 5.13. Note that perceived lack of anonymity is assessed by the variable *EXPUB*. The demographic variables yield the same pattern of significance compared to table 5.12 except for the fact that the ownership of rubber tress (*RUBBER*) also has a significantly positive impact on the decision to state a positive WTP. Looking at the main effects model in the left-hand column, only trait desirability (TRAIT) has a significantly positive impact. This result confirms the significantly lower fraction of zero responses among those respondents with *TRAIT*=1 (cf. figure 5.7). Yet, in this model need for social approval and lack of anonymity do not have any independent effect at all. These results reflect the graphical findings in figure 5.7. While the difference of the fraction of zero responses between absence and presence of the respective factor is very large for trait desirability (figures 5.7 c), it is comparatively small for the other two factors. As a consequence, the strong independent influence of *TRAIT* results in its coefficient being positive and significantly different from zero

Table 5.13: The three-factor model of desirable responding. Probit model of positive WTP, including split samples 1-9

Dep. variable: *posWTP* N=1323	**Main effects model** Coeff.	Std. error	**Full interaction model** Coeff.	Std. error	**Short interaction model** Coeff.	Std. error
CONSTANT	0.06	(0.35)	0.64	(0.43)	0.18	(0.34)
T2	-0.12	(0.18)	-0.12	(0.18)	-0.12	(0.18)
T3	-0.04	(0.18)	-0.03	(0.18)	-0.02	(0.18)
T4	-0.14	(0.18)	-0.14	(0.18)	-0.16	(0.18)
T5	0.08	(0.19)	0.05	(0.19)	0.08	(0.19)
T6	0.20	(0.19)	0.21	(0.19)	0.21	(0.19)
T7	0.05	(0.18)	0.03	(0.18)	0.05	(0.18)
T8	0.25	(0.19)	0.21	(0.19)	0.24	(0.19)
T9	-0.17	(0.18)	-0.18	(0.18)	-0.17	(0.18)
FEMALE	0.28***	(0.09)	0.28***	(0.09)	0.28***	(0.09)
AGE	-0.01	(0.01)	-0.01	(0.01)	-0.01	(0.01)
MARRIED	0.11	(0.10)	0.10	(0.10)	0.10	(0.10)
WORKER	0.03	(0.11)	0.02	(0.11)	0.04	(0.11)
OFFICIAL	0.11	(0.24)	0.10	(0.24)	0.13	(0.24)
SELF-EMPLOY	0.32***	(0.12)	0.31***	(0.12)	0.33***	(0.12)
HHSIZE	-0.08**	(0.03)	-0.07**	(0.03)	-0.08**	(0.03)
TIMEBN	0.00	(0.00)	0.00	(0.00)	0.00	(0.00)
RUBBER	0.23*	(0.13)	0.23*	(0.14)	0.25*	(0.13)
EDU	0.09**	(0.04)	0.09**	(0.04)	0.08**	(0.04)
INCOME	0.0003*	(0.00)	0.0003	(0.00)	0.0004**	(0.00)
BIDR14	-0.01	(0.02)	-0.09**	(0.04)	0.00	(0.02)
EXPUB	0.13	(0.11)	-0.60**	(0.30)		
TRAIT	0.53***	(0.09)	-0.41	(0.53)		
BIDR14*EXPUB			0.10**	(0.04)		
BIDR14*TRAIT			0.11	(0.07)		
EXPUB*TRAIT			1.20**	(0.59)	0.67***	(0.25)
INTERACTION			-0.15*	(0.08)	-0.02	(0.03)

Another difference to the results in table 5.12 can be seen in the center column displaying the fully specified interaction model. Unlike the case for the probit regression model including splits 1 to 10, the interaction term in this probit regression is significantly negative. That means that respondents who exhibit all three factors of SDR are significantly less likely to state a positive WTP. Although this interaction effect is hypothesized by the three-factor model, its negative sign is troubling. The indicated higher fraction of zero responses among respondents who display all three factors is contradictive to the trait desirability variable. This is not in line with the predictions of the three-factor model. Furthermore, the signs of several of the constituent terms are counterintuitive, as well. The coefficient of need for approval (*BIDR14*) is significantly negative indicating that for respondents without lack of perceived anonymity and trait desirability, a high need for approval results in a smaller probability of stating a positive WTP. The same holds for *EXPUB*, which means that for the other two factors absent, respondents who perceive a lack of external anonymity as measured by question 40.1 are more likely to state a zero WTP. In addition to that, two of the two-part interaction terms in this model positively affect the number of positive WTP statements. The positive effect of *BIDR14*EXPUB* indicates that for respondents who do not perceive trait desirability but perceive a lack of anonymity, the need for social approval reinforces the inclination to give a positive WTP. Similarly, the positive impact of *EXPUB*TRAIT* indicates that for those respondents with an approval score equal to zero the simultaneous effect of lack of anonymity and trait desirability increases the number of positive WTP responses.

Therefore, when it comes to the decision whether to state a positive WTP hypothesis 1 clearly has to be rejected. The results of the fully specified interaction model including the variable *EXPUB* indicate that instead of a simultaneous effect of all three variables this model rather exhibits different pairs of variables influencing the decision to state a positive WTP. While the regression model of WTP amounts found two of the three factors independently influencing the dependent variable, in this model it is rather the interactions of *EXPUB* with the two remaining factors, respectively. Although there is no interaction effect of all three SDR factors, there are, however, at least effects of certain two-part interactions. This indicates that there is an influence of SDR on the decision whether to state a positive WTP, but that the interaction of the three factors takes some other form as conceptualized in the three factor model.

Influence of SDR on the amount of WTP

The above results are a first indicator that the composition of incentives of SDR according to the three factor model can be rejected. To further test this tentative result, the results of the regression models with the specific WTP amount as dependent variable are discussed. Again, the first step of the analysis will look at treatments 1 to 10 and employ the lack-of-anonymity variable *PUBLIC*, which is followed by a model merely including treatments 1 to 9 and the variable *EXPUB* instead. Table 5.14 gives the results of the regression model of the specific WTP amount based on treatments 1 to 10. Similar to the model to identify the determinants of the likelihood to state a positive WTP above, a set of demographic variables is included here. In this setting, the respondent's age (*AGE*), level of education (*EDU*) and the household income (*INCOME*) turn out to be significantly influencing stated WTP. Unlike the model without any SDR factors as displayed in table 5.11, the coefficient of the fact that the respondent is married (MARRIED) is not significant here. It should be noted that these relationships are constant across all models displayed in table 5.14. The modification of the inclusion of the different factors of SDR into the model does not influence the effect of these basic determinants on WTP.

Following the specification in section 4.3, the SDR variables are included in three different ways. In the first model in the left column, merely the main effects are included in the regression model. Out of the three factors, only trait desirability (*TRAIT*) has a significantly positive effect on WTP statements. Put in another way, respondents who believe that contributing the more the better have a significantly higher WTP than respondents who do not hold this belief. This effect is independent of the values of the other two factors. The coefficient of the need for approval score is positive, too, even though not significant. Irrespective of the level of subjective anonymity and whether or not a respondent perceives trait desirability, this result indicates a weakly positive effect of need for approval. Although these findings appear plausible at first sight, they are contradictive to the three-factor model. According to this model, an effect of one of the three variables independent of the two remaining variables as found in the data is not possible. However, judging merely from this result it seems that both trait desirability and need for social approval have independent distorting effects on the elicitation question. At this point the low but significant correlation between *BIDR14* and *TRAIT* might play a role. The correlation coefficient was found to be only $r=0.111$, which is why both factors can be included in the model without taking the risk of finding insignificant results as a consequence of collinearity. The only problem that might occur is that the significantly positive impact of trait desirability superposes the effect of need for social approval. Therefore, another regression model, which is not reported here, includes the need for approval score (*BIDR14*) as only additional explanatory variable. In this setting, its coefficient is significantly positive, substantiating the above suspicion that the factors independently influence WTP statements. Regardless of the presence of the other two factors, it appears that the higher a respondent's need for social approval the higher her stated WTP amount.

Table 5.14: The three-factor model of desirable responding. Regression model of WTP, including split samples 1-10

	Main effects model		**Full interaction model**		**Short interaction model**	
N=1470	Coeff.	Std. error	Coeff.	Std. error	Coeff.	Std. error
CONSTANT	0.29	(0.37)	-0.11	(0.93)	0.55**	(0.26)
BID	-18.71***	(0.25)	-18.73***	(0.26)	-18.71***	(0.25)
T2	-61.93	(110.58)	-58.77	(110.86)	-59.36	(110.84)
T3	-371.48	(172.89)	-364.86**	(172.43)	-366.35**	(172.40)
T4	58.01	(104.03)	62.68	(103.93)	61.88	(103.96)
T5	-212.01	(134.77)	-208.95	(135.11)	-211.46	(135.12)
T6	-101.50	(112.54)	-103.28	(112.57)	-103.98	(112.66)
T7	-265.32**	(131.90)	-255.28*	(132.17)	-258.01*	(132.29)
T8	-6.93	(108.98)	-8.27	(109.16)	-10.51	(109.20)
T9	-165.83	(114.48)	-156.96	(114.45)	-158.85	(114.52)
T10	-8.47	(116.78)	0.02	(119.37)	-56.50	(114.84)
FEMALE	-62.23	(64.46)	-58.97	(65.79)	-59.60	(65.72)
AGE	-9.40***	(3.56)	-9.18**	(3.59)	-9.22***	(3.58)
MARRIED	-117.33	(72.06)	-116.88	(72.84)	-114.25	(72.66)
WORKER	-40.26	(72.38)	-37.83	(72.98)	-40.06	(72.84)
OFFICIAL	-140.30	(192.39)	-142.35	(191.61)	-142.53	(191.36)
SELF-EMPLOY	-82.77	(81.32)	-72.93	(82.96)	-80.10	(82.68)
HHSIZE	-6.19	(21.60)	-5.80	(21.65)	-7.20	(21.61)
TIMEBN	1.18	(2.41)	1.28	(2.44)	1.24	(2.44)
RUBBER	89.44	(75.99)	84.52	(77.66)	83.98	(77.34)
EDU	114.51***	(26.88)	114.14***	(26.90)	114.12***	(26.85)
INCOME	0.04***	(0.01)	0.04***	(0.01)	0.04***	(0.01)
BIDR14	15.86	(10.85)	87.45	(115.06)	24.54**	(12.04)
PUBLIC	327.28	(278.70)	654.90	(893.44)		
TRAIT	142.31**	(60.98)	227.30	(1983.02)		
BIDR14*PUBLIC			-64.16	(115.46)		
BIDR14*TRAIT			-45.69	(299.62)		
PUBLIC*TRAIT			83.67	(1987.81)	318.45**	(153.15)
INTERACTION			21.60	(300.26)	-24.36	(20.56)

Taken all this evidence together, hypotheses 1 and 2 have to be rejected. For the case of the regression model of WTP amounts (tables 5.14 and 5.15) the factors – especially need for social approval and trait desirability – independently affect the amount of stated WTP. When it comes to the mere decision of stating a positive WTP (tables 5.12 and 5.13), instead of a joint influence of the three factors it appears that each combination of two factors affect this decision. Although this finding calls for the rejection of hypothesis

1 and is therefore in accordance with the rejection of hypothesis 2, it seems premature to dismiss the idea of a multidimensional SDR concept altogether. Of course the hypothesized influence of SDR on the likelihood of stating a positive WTP was expected to stem form the three-part interaction. Yet, the fact that it is not a three-part but merely different types of two-part interactions that affect *posWTP* still indicates the influence of some multi-dimensional form of SDR on WTP responses.

The center column of table 5.14 displays the fully specified interaction model. It can be seen that none of the coefficients is significant. Similar to the probit regression model of positive WTP, the coefficient of the interaction in this model is not significantly different from zero. This implies that in this setting there is no impact of the product of all three factors on the stated WTP amounts. Looking at the regression results in the right-hand column in table 5.14 one can see that the influence of both constituent terms (*BIDR14*) and (*PUBLIC*TRAIT*) is significantly positive, but that the coefficient of the interaction term is not significant. This means that regardless of the other two factors, need for social approval positively affects WTP statements. This is a finding for which weak evidence was already found in the main effects model. Similarly, the fact that a respondent perceives incomplete anonymity and trait desirability at the same time (i.e. *PUBLIC*TRAIT*=1) drives up WTP statements irrespective of need for approval. So, in the short interaction model, too, independent rather than interaction effects of the factors of SDR can be detected.

After using the lack-of-anonymity variable *PUBLIC*, the analysis continues by exchanging it for the variable EXPUB and confining the models on treatments 1 to 9. The results of the three regression models employing the new reduced sample are displayed in table 5.15. In the left column, the main effects show the same pattern of significance as above. The coefficients of all factors are positive, but only the one of trait desirability (*TRAIT*) is significantly different from zero at the 5%-level of confidence.

The same holds for the fully specified interaction model in the center column: again neither the constituent terms nor the interaction are significant. The only difference between the results of the basic approach and this modification can be found in the short interaction model. While in the full sample when *PUBLIC* is employed the interaction is not significant, in this case with only splits 1 to 9 and *EXPUB* as anonymity variable, all three terms are significant. Again the two constituent terms have a positive influence, and this time also the interaction has a significant influence. That means that indeed the interplay of all three variables affects the respondents' decision on the amount of stated WTP like hypothesized above. Yet, surprisingly this influence is negative, which is rather troubling because it contradicts the content of the trait desirability question. Respondents with *TRAIT*=1 think that contributing the more the better, so these respondents should not have a systematically lower WTP. Therefore, despite the significant interaction effect this result should be interpreted as evidence calling for a rejection of hypothesis 2.

Table 5.15: The three-factor model of desirable responding. Regression model of WTP, including split samples 1-9

	Main effects model		**Full interaction model**		**Short interaction model**	
N=1323	Coeff.	Std. error	Coeff.	Std. error	Coeff.	Std. error
CONSTANT	0.56**	(0.26)	0.65**	(0.33)	0.53**	(0.26)
BID	-18.81***	(0.27)	-18.86***	(0.28)	-18.84***	(0.27)
T2	-56.22	(111.29)	-56.76	(111.75)	-55.56	(111.06)
T3	-355.69**	(172.12)	-350.60**	(173.75)	-352.68**	(170.05)
T4	61.12	(104.79)	56.89	(104.61)	55.34	(104.46)
T5	-203.96	(134.93)	-216.16	(135.03)	-210.94	(134.16)
T6	-100.70	(112.27)	-109.14	(115.64)	-105.12	(112.38)
T7	-247.77*	(132.06)	-246.36*	(133.18)	-241.82*	(132.85)
T8	-2.22	(109.04)	-19.58	(109.09)	-11.77	(109.08)
T9	-159.94	(115.59)	-159.52	(115.59)	-151.94	(114.42)
FEMALE	-65.01	(68.59)	-63.15	(69.68)	-61.30	(68.61)
AGE	-9.78***	(3.72)	-9.89***	(3.80)	-9.59***	(3.71)
MARRIED	-111.17	(76.46)	-111.11	(77.00)	-110.92	(75.69)
WORKER	-34.27	(77.57)	-30.61	(79.31)	-27.68	(78.27)
OFFICIAL	-130.18	(199.18)	-131.73	(197.50)	-121.77	(196.80)
SELF-EMPLOY	-54.60	(84.27)	-52.96	(86.08)	-44.31	(85.51)
HHSIZE	-9.26	(22.66)	-8.56	(23.00)	-8.74	(22.62)
TIMEBN	2.09	(2.52)	2.34	(2.56)	2.26	(2.54)
RUBBER	94.86	(78.46)	92.95	(81.28)	95.71	(80.05)
EDU	109.82***	(28.71)	109.64***	(28.81)	109.02***	(28.41)
INCOME	0.05***	(0.01)	0.05***	(0.01)	0.05***	(0.01)
BIDR14	9.44	(11.17)	-2.43	(32.82)	23.45*	(12.14)
EXPUB	98.28	(83.97)	-118.44	(234.38)		
TRAIT	137.88**	(64.68)	-216.92	(490.56)		
BIDR14*EXPUB			29.92	(35.03)		
BIDR14*TRAIT			43.53	(68.55)		
EXPUB*TRAIT			700.91	(509.63)	470.71***	(161.78)
INTERACTION			-91.54	(71.51)	-44.36**	(22.52)

Despite the negative results with respect to hypotheses 1 and 2 the three-factor model will still form the basis for the following analyses, namely of the relationship of enhancement and denial. Although the three-factor model cannot be identified as direct determinant of WTP statements in the above models, all its factors and different constellations of them clearly affect the respondents' decision which amount to select on the payment card. Therefore, it is conceivable that these combinations take a different form when need for social approval is substituted either for the enhancement of the denial component.

The influence of enhancement and denial

One advantage of the BIDR is its ability to separately measure the two dimensions of need for approval, namely enhancement and denial. These two separate scores can be used to test hypothesis 3, which predicts a stronger influence of the denial component than of enhancement. This can be studied by replacing the need for approval score by an enhancement and a denial score, in turn, and calculating the same models as in the previous subsection.[35] Again, after excluding the ballot box treatment only split samples 1 to 9 and the anonymity variable *EXPUB* are employed. The respective regression results are displayed in tables 5.16 and 5.17.

In table 5.16, when the main effects model is calculated with the enhancement component (*ENH*) instead of the overall need for approval score in the left-hand column, only the effect of trait desirability is significantly positive. The coefficient of the enhancement component is highly insignificant. This is different when the main effects with denial are computed as displayed in the left-hand column of table 5.17. In this case, both trait desirability and the denial component of need for social approval (*DEN*) positively affect stated WTP amounts. It becomes clear that when the independent effects of the factors are studied, denial shows the same effects as overall need for approval but in a stronger way, whereas enhancement alone does not have any impact.

In the middle columns of tables 5.16 and 5.17 the full interaction models with enhancement and denial, respectively, are produced. Except for the positive influence of the constituent term of trait desirability in the denial model, none of the estimated coefficients is significantly different from zero. These results are similar to the findings in the model employing the overall need for approval score (cf. table 5.15).

---

35 Due to the similarity of the results, this step of the analysis is only performed with respect to the model with WTP amounts as dependent variable.

Table 5.16: Test of the relative influence of enhancement and denial in the three-factor model: Estimation results of the models including the enhancement component only

	Main effects (ENH)		**Full interaction (ENH)**		**Short interaction (ENH)**	
N=1323	Coeff.	Std. error	Coeff.	Std. error	Coeff.	Std. error
CONSTANT	0.57**	(0.26)	0.62*	(0.34)	0.53**	(0.26)
BID	-18.80***	(0.27)	-18.86***	(0.28)	-18.85***	(0.27)
T2	-53.10	(111.32)	-56.05	(111.71)	-52.37	(110.95)
T3	-345.72**	(171.53)	-341.54*	(174.48)	-340.05**	(170.73)
T4	61.49	(103.27)	52.67	(103.14)	55.20	(102.98)
T5	-193.29	(135.61)	-207.92	(135.26)	-201.62	(134.41)
T6	-98.48	(111.88)	-108.51	(113.70)	-99.22	(111.71)
T7	-234.82*	(132.43)	-236.66*	(132.77)	-227.67*	(132.39)
T8	3.48	(109.23)	-10.45	(109.33)	-0.97	(109.28)
T9	-153.58	(116.00)	-154.68	(115.93)	-144.01	(114.73)
FEMALE	-51.21	(68.11)	-48.13	(68.38)	-46.46	(67.46)
AGE	-8.64**	(3.65)	-8.96**	(3.72)	-8.64**	(3.62)
MARRIED	-104.61	(76.43)	-103.60	(76.86)	-104.28	(75.69)
WORKER	-40.30	(77.62)	-36.55	(78.15)	-32.75	(77.87)
OFFICIAL	-127.43	(199.55)	-115.11	(197.65)	-101.81	(196.97)
SELF-EMPL.	-54.93	(84.27)	-48.12	(86.58)	-39.82	(85.21)
HHSIZE	-9.22	(22.66)	-7.78	(23.02)	-7.82	(22.67)
TIMEBN	1.91	(2.52)	2.08	(2.54)	2.02	(2.53)
RUBBER	96.07	(78.54)	99.68	(80.35)	100.16	(79.67)
EDU	108.86***	(28.74)	107.76***	(28.81)	107.15***	(28.44)
INCOME	0.05***	(0.01)	0.05***	(0.01)	0.05***	(0.01)
ENH	-4.25	(20.86)	-11.37	(64.55)	26.63	(24.39)
EXPUB	104.97	(83.90)	-71.43	(254.26)		
TRAIT	143.62**	(64.76)	-252.13	(519.18)		
ENH*EXPUB			41.65	(69.57)		
ENH*TRAIT			87.01	(130.51)		
EXPUB*TRAIT			759.38	(539.37)	508.33***	(158.17)
INTERACTION			-176.23	(135.85)	-86.46**	(39.27)

It is in the short interaction model in the right-hand columns of the two tables that the impact of enhancement and denial differ once more. While the interaction term of the enhancement model is significantly negative, the sign of the interaction including the denial component is positive even though highly insignificant. Interestingly, the troubling result of a significantly negative interaction effect can only be found in the enhancement model. Therefore, when merely the enhancement component of need for social approval is employed, the results of the overall model calling for a rejection of the three-factor model hypothesis are reproduced. This is somewhat different for the case of denial where neither the constituent terms nor the interaction effect are significant. In other words, the results with respect to the denial component do not support the three-factor model but do not repudiate it as fervently as the enhancement model.

Table 5.17: Test of the relative influence of enhancement and denial in the three-factor model: Estimation results of the models including the denial component only

	Main effects (DEN)		**Full interaction (DEN)**		**Short interaction (DEN)**	
N=1323	Coeff.	Std. error	Coeff.	Std. error	Coeff.	Std. error
CONSTANT	0.56**	(0.26)	0.48	(0.29)	0.70***	(0.25)
BID	-18.83***	(0.27)	-18.86***	(0.28)	-18.79***	(0.27)
T2	-58.58	(111.31)	-52.38	(111.87)	-57.78	(110.27)
T3	-362.78**	(171.33)	-346.01**	(172.45)	-357.59**	(170.49)
T4	58.95	(105.68)	66.63	(105.47)	57.38	(105.59)
T5	-207.93	(134.65)	-198.05	(134.87)	-203.34	(133.46)
T6	-104.08	(112.34)	-103.45	(115.64)	-89.72	(112.39)
T7	-254.34*	(131.88)	-235.49*	(133.46)	-254.44*	(133.53)
T8	-2.58	(109.20)	3.76	(109.18)	11.10	(109.15)
T9	-165.98	(115.43)	-154.65	(115.97)	-164.66	(114.79)
FEMALE	-78.24	(68.08)	-67.96	(69.72)	-81.28	(66.40)
AGE	-10.46***	(3.71)	-9.79***	(3.79)	-10.13***	(3.67)
MARRIED	-111.62	(76.40)	-99.94	(77.32)	-115.12	(75.30)
WORKER	-32.57	(77.41)	-32.37	(80.43)	-38.82	(78.17)
OFFICIAL	-131.54	(198.74)	-120.66	(198.66)	-109.12	(198.51)
SELF-EMPL.	-49.74	(84.24)	-34.65	(85.56)	-50.00	(84.21)
HHSIZE	-9.38	(22.66)	-9.20	(22.85)	-6.77	(22.42)
TIMEBN	2.18	(2.52)	2.13	(2.55)	2.15	(2.53)
RUBBER	96.13	(78.25)	92.13***	(80.35)	104.40***	(79.59)
EDU	111.82***	(28.64)	111.29***	(28.95)	108.18***	(28.48)
INCOME	0.05***	(0.01)	0.05	(0.01)	0.05	(0.01)
DEN	32.54*	(18.46)	34.84	(51.42)	20.36	(19.35)
EXPUB	99.38	(83.87)	85.27	(166.10)		
TRAIT	141.39**	(64.69)	380.59**	(149.25)		
DEN*EXPUB			10.42	(54.10)		
DEN*TRAIT			-67.58	(67.79)		
EXPUB*TRAIT			-56.39	(37.59)	-12.16	(32.54)
INTERACTION			118.05	(98.25)	56.76	(70.41)

So far, the findings with respect to the difference of the impact of enhancement and denial are rather inconclusive. In order to further investigate this difference both components are simultaneously included in one model. The left-hand column of table 5.18 provides results of a main effects model, which includes both the enhancement and denial components along with lack of anonymity and trait desirability. In addition to the significant effect of trait desirability already found in many of the above models, the denial component also influences WTP statements in a significantly positive way. Enhancement on the contrary lacks any effect on WTP. This is an additional indicator supportive of hypothesis 3 that denial exerts the stronger influence on WTP statements compared to enhancement.

Table 5.18: Direct comparison of the relative strength of ENH and DEN components of SDR

	Main effects (ENH and DEN)		**Interaction (ENH and DEN)**	
N=1323	Coefficient	Std. error	Coefficient	Std. error
CONSTANT	0.57**	(0.26)	0.71***	(0.25)
BID	-18.84***	(0.27)	-18.78***	(0.26)
T2	-57.13	(111.55)	-55.19	(109.88)
T3	-358.43**	(170.43)	-348.83**	(170.45)
T4	57.47	(105.76)	57.95	(102.87)
T5	-200.11	(135.47)	-195.98	(133.51)
T6	-104.67	(112.29)	-85.62	(111.76)
T7	-246.24*	(132.10)	-244.48*	(133.71)
T8	3.14	(109.97)	15.58	(108.90)
T9	-164.89	(116.21)	-157.87	(114.61)
FEMALE	-75.32	(68.57)	-67.06	(64.81)
AGE	-9.87***	(3.73)	-9.24***	(3.50)
MARRIED	-104.86	(76.49)	-111.05	(75.13)
WORKER	-37.31	(77.37)	-43.10	(78.02)
OFFICIAL	-129.85	(199.36)	-102.87	(198.22)
SELF-EMPLOY	-45.55	(84.22)	-51.23	(84.03)
HHSIZE	-9.45	(22.66)	-6.62	(22.45)
TIMEBN	2.07	(2.52)	1.96	(2.51)
RUBBER	98.37	(78.19)	105.33	(79.42)
EDU	112.59***	(28.63)	106.80***	(28.43)
INCOME	0.06***	(0.01)	0.05***	(0.01)
ENH	-23.26	(24.79)		
DEN	43.28**	(22.00)		
EXPUB	107.83	(83.79)		
TRAIT	150.74**	(64.84)		
ENH*EXPUB				
ENH*TRAIT				
EXPUB*TRAIT				
INTERACTION_ENH			-20.50	(31.43)
INTERACTION_DEN			59.25	(38.29)

This finding cannot be reproduced when the two interaction terms for enhancement and denial are included in the regression model. The results of this model as displayed in the right-hand column of table 5.18 show that none of the interaction terms is significant. Interestingly, the coefficients of the two have different signs, with denial again showing a positive sign. The reason for both coefficients being insignificant might be a collinearity problem. The correlation between *INTERACTION_ENH* and *INTERACTION_DEN* is $r=0.849$ and highly significant. As a consequence, the regression model is not able to distinguish between the two variables' influences. For the main effects, this problem does not exist because the correlation between the enhancement (*ENH*) and the denial score (*DEN*) is only at $r=0.516$ ($p=0.000$). This is the precondition for the fact that the model can find the strong independent influence of the denial component.

In light of these findings the rejection of hypothesis 3 does not seem to be justified. In fact, the results in table 5.18 indicate that the denial component exerts a stronger influence on WTP statements than enhancement. The test of the three-factor model above showed that instead of a joint influence of all factors rather their independent impact biases WTP statements. When it comes to this independent form of influence, the denial component clearly turns out to be stronger. For the case of a stronger influence of denial in the interaction term, the results merely indicate this, but due to a collinearity problem in the regression model they are not significant. Although it is never significant, the use of the denial component in the interaction models results in a positive sign of the interaction coefficient. This is one of the main startling findings of the test of the three-factor model above. Therefore, the data provide limited evidence for the fact that the three-factor model is more likely to hold when the denial component is used to assess need for approval instead of the enhancement component.

5.5. Discussion of the empirical results

After presenting the results of the measurement instruments and all these models in detail, this section aims at summing up the most important findings and scrutinizing them with respect to the initial research tasks that this study set out to explore. So, stepping away from all these models and looking at them from a broader perspective, what can be said about the influence of socially desirable responding on WTP statements and the appropriateness of the three-factor model?

The first part of the empirical analysis of this study deals with the formulation of question inventories for the assessment of the three factors need for social approval, lack of anonymity, and trait desirability. For the case of need for approval, the impression management subscale of the Balanced Inventory of Desirable Responding (BIDR) is adapted to the socio-cultural background of rural Southwest China. To this end, certain items of the original 20-item inventory are deleted and several of the remaining items are modified. This is done on the basis of in-depth interviews with local citizens regarding the applicability of the behavioral patterns described in those items. Both the applicability of the items with respect to the survey population and the linguistic comprehensibility are scrutinized. The remaining analysis concerning the final 14-item version of the modified BIDR focuses on the inventory's reliability and validity. Employing the data elicited in the main survey, indices for the reliability, namely Cronbach's alpha and split-half correlations, portend the 14-item scale to be a sufficiently reliable question inventtory. Similarly, evidence of the new scale's construct and content validity is accumulated. Construct validity is documented by factor and group analysis and content validity by means of in-depth interviews. In these interviews, it becomes apparent that social norms governing the behavioral patterns in the 14 items in fact exist in the survey population. In addition, extreme statements really represent an exaggeration and are very likely to be a departure from reality. Furthermore, the scale exclusively taps need for social approval manifested by overly claiming desirable characteristics and the complete denial of undesirable traits for the self. It is demonstrated that other conceivable strategies of approval seeking such as moderate and "rebel" responding are either not covered by the concept of need for approval or do not pose a threat to the measurement accuracy of the scale. These findings increase the confidence in the ability of the modified scale to actually tap need for social approval and not any desirable but truthful self-reports of respondents. Merely one item causes concern resulting from a translation error in the Chinese version of the inventory. Subsequently several remaining problems with the new scale are discussed. The more severe shortcomings are interviewer and feedback effects, the inapplicability of strict semantic logic with some items, and the complex nature of the 5-point Likert response scale that might be too sophisticated for some respondents. An artificially high need for approval score especially for older respondents might result from this flaw. The empirical analysis indeed detects such an age effect.

When it comes to assessing lack of perceived anonymity and trait desirability, the questions are simpler and more straightforward. For the case of lack of anonymity two alternative variables are computed. *PUBLIC* assesses perceived anonymity only within the ballot box treatment and assumes respondents to all other treatments to perceive a lack of anonymity. As a consequence of the very low variation of this variable, *EXPUB* is computed. This variable displays the responses to the anonymity question (question

40.1) for the respondents to all treatments. In most of the subsequent analyses, the latter variable is employed. Eventually, trait desirability is assessed by asking whether a respondent believes that contributing the more to the environmental project the better. Like lack of anonymity, this question yields a binary variable. According to the theoretical stipulations of the three-factor model, the product of all three variables, the need for social approval score, lack of anonymity, and trait desirability, results in the main variable of interest – incentives for social desirable responding. By employing an interaction model, the three single factors and the product term as well as all pairwise combinations of the factors are included in a variety of regression models to test the impact of SDR on WTP statements in a contingent valuation survey.

This leads to the main part of the analysis, the test of the impact of SDR on WTP statements in contingent valuation surveys. The analysis of mean WTP statements and their determinants indicates that residents of the city of Jinghong indeed hold positive values for the proposed reforestation program and the associated environmental improvements. Therefore, it is concluded that the data are plausible and can be used to study the effects of SDR. The first step of the previous analyses with respect to this aspect shows that the three factors exert influence of varying intensity both on the amount of stated WTP and the decision whether or not to state a positive amount. While the strongest influence on the amount of WTP statements stems from the variable trait desirability, the variable most closely related to the decision to state a positive WTP is perceived external anonymity. The third factor, need for social approval is also found to impact WTP statements when it is represented by the denial component. The enhancement component on the contrary does not show any significant influence. Neither the denial nor the enhancement components play a role when it comes to the question whether to state a positive WTP. The factor need for social approval does not affect this decision at all. As a result, the present data clearly demonstrate that SDR is a substantial problem in in-person contingent valuation interviews. Unlike previous research that only controlled for the influence of need for social approval (Laughland et al. 1994), this study finds evidence for the impact of all three constituent factors of SDR in the different models. However, the reasons for this discrepancy in results are rather unclear. It might be because of the different measurement scales or because of different survey topics. Laughland et al. (1994) use the Marlowe-Crowne Scale instead of a modified version of the BIDR to assess need for approval. On top of that, the present study does not only employ a prefabricated question inventory but adapts it according to socio-cultural characteristics of the specific survey environment. In the adaption process evidence of the reliability and validity of the new scale is produced, which is not the case in the study of Laughland and colleagues. Regarding the survey topic this study assesses the value of a reforestation project in order to preserve the biodiversity in a certain region, whereas the survey in Laughland et al. deals with food safety and landscape preservation. These are potential causes of the difference in results.

When it comes to the question of the exact form of the relationship of the three factors' influence on WTP the analyses reveal that hypotheses 1 and 2 have to be rejected, i.e. the three factors of SDR do not work simultaneously but influence WTP statements in some other fashion. The classical interaction effect of all three factors, which was hypothesized by the three-factor model derived in the theoretical part of this study, cannot be found to be significant. Instead, both need for social approval and trait desirability seem to affect the amount of WTP responses independently. This is somewhat different when the question whether to state a positive or a zero WTP is studied. Instead of simple independent impacts of certain factors the data reveal that it is rather pairs of variables that jointly affect this decision. The lack of external anonymity is the driving factor in these pairs of factors in particular. It is found that among respondents with need for social approval and respondents who think that contributing the more the better, the fact that they think their answers can be traced back to them increases the likelihood of stating a positive WTP. So, although perceived external anonymity turned out not to play any role for the amount of WTP, it is the main factor influencing the fraction of zero and positive WTP statements, respectively. Although hypothesis 1 has to be rejected, there is a clear impact of the constituent factors of SDR on the fraction of positive WTP statements even though it is not the three-way influence predicted by the behavioral model. Overall, the findings show that all three factors are influencing the statement of WTP responses – either the decision for a positive WTP or the specific amount. It appears therefore justified in a contingent valuation survey to assess and control for all factors of SDR.

Although the direct impact of the three-factor model has to be rejected based on the present data, the result of the different factors independently or as pairs influencing the dependent variable of interest – in this case WTP statements – is not new in the literature as introduced above. Although several studies find an exclusive interaction effect of two or three constituent factors of SDR on dependent variables of different content (Chen et al. 1997, Stocké 2004, 2007), Phillips and Clancy (1972) report evidence indicating that these factors are independent. The interactive effects found by Chen et al. (1997) with respect to affectivity and Stocké (2004) with respect to attitudes towards foreigners cannot be detected in the thematic framework of this contingent valuation survey, either. The specific topic of this survey – the preservation of natural resources – and the social norms associated with it might therefore be a reason for this discrepancy. It has been shown that social norms are at the root of SDR. So, a question going beyond the scope of this study is whether the applicability of the three-factor model is dependent on specific characteristics of social norms determined by the survey topic. In any case, the present study provides some evidence against its applicability in contingent valuation.

The key study investigating the three-factor model of SDR that fundamentally inspired this study's approach can be found in Stocké (2004, 2007). In that study the main effects of the three factors of SDR are found to be either insignificant or significantly negative, which contradicts their hypothesized impact. In a second step, that analysis employs an interaction model and finds the interaction term to positively influence the dependent variable of interest. This leads the author to the conclusion that it would be premature only to consider the main effects of the SDR factors, but instead the interaction would be the driving response bias. This finding is interpreted as the empirical confirmation of the three-factor model of SDR. In the present contingent valuation context, however, the situation is reversed. This study is the first to apply a systematic direct assessment of all three factors of SDR with respect to WTP statements in a contingent valuation survey. While the main effects are mostly significant and affect WTP into the expected direction, the coefficients of the interaction terms lack significance and sometimes even display a counterintuitive sign. Consequently, the result of the direct influence of the three-factor model on WTP statements in contingent valuation surveys is that all factors are potential biases but in an independent and non-conditional way.

A possible methodological reason for the failure to find significant interaction effects might be the fact that the estimation model is a non-linear regression. Several authors have uttered doubts about the applicability of classical interaction models in regression settings different from linear OLS models (Ai and Norton 2003, Greene 2009). These authors argue that the standard meaning of *p*-values does not translate directly from linear into non-linear regression models, such as the probit models applied here.[36] Additionally, it is held that the interaction effect might have different signs for different values of covariates. For the case of the simple probit models of *posWTP* these issues were tested because appropriate procedures already exist (Norton et al. 2004). The results clearly show that both the *p*-values and the signs of the coefficients are stable across different constellations of the binary covariates (i.e. perceived anonymity and trait desirability). For the

36 The models used to analyze the decision to state a positive WTP employing *posWTP* are simple probit models with a binary dependent variable. The regression model of WTP amounts for PC data as specified in 2.24 is a modified maximum likelihood estimation based on a probit model and therefore also belongs to the class of non-linear regression models.

case of the regression model of WTP statements, this procedure could not be applied because to the author's knowledge appropriate computational techniques have not been developed yet.

Hypothesis 3 which stated that the denial component of need for approval has a stronger behavioral influence than enhancement is supported on grounds of the present data. In the main effects models, denial clearly exhibits a much stronger positive impact on the amount of WTP statements than the enhancement component. The influence of the latter is insignificant in this setting and pointing into the counterintuitive direction in the interaction model. Therefore, it is concluded that denial is the component of need for social approval that both displays a stronger effect on WTP responses and performs in line with the theoretical expectations. This finding is confirmed when both main effects are included in the estimation model at the same time. The result that enhancement and denial have a differing influence on the dependent variable in this survey context and must therefore be assessed separately supports the conclusions in Li and Li (2008). These authors find that unlike for Western subjects, the distinction between these two components within the impression management dimension of social desirability matters among Chinese respondents. The present study provides clear evidence in favor of this assertion. In addition to that, the data support the idea that the inclination to deny unfavorable self-descriptions is a stronger motivational factor than the tendency to present oneself more favorably than one actually is among Chinese respondents. This empirical result is in accordance with the notion of loss aversion in prospect theory. The fact that individuals value losses more than gains appears to translate directly into the realm of social approval.

In conclusion it must be stated that incentives for SDR are a source of bias of WTP statements in contingent valuation surveys. A first step to control for this bias is the development of reliable and valid tools of assessment of the three constituting factors. The amount of stated WTP is positively biased by both trait desirability and need for social approval but not by the fact that a respondent perceives a lack of external anonymity. The impact on the fraction of zero and positive WTP statements, however, is driven mainly by that anonymity variable in connection with need for approval and trait desirability, respectively. While the idea of a three-part interaction effect of SDR on WTP statements has to be rejected based on the present data, the idea of different factors of SDR simultaneously affecting WTP statements should not be given up and be investigated further.

Chapter 6

Summary and concluding remarks

The present study set out to investigate the influence of socially desirable responding on WTP statements in contingent valuation surveys. Although many studies utter concern for the biasing effect of SDR in such surveys, the number of approaches that directly assess the role of this response bias in such surveys is extremely limited. Therefore, this study analyzed the impact of SDR on WTP statements both from a theoretical and an empirical point of view. It integrated concepts of psychological and sociological research into the theoretical framework of the CVM. As a result, the perspective on a respondent's task when answering a WTP question is broadened. In addition to the truthful statement of her WTP for a proposed environmental project, the typical respondent might feel other incentives for selecting her response. By means of a sociological model of behavior based on rational choice theory these different incentives and situational factors can be interrelated and their influence can be predicted. Therefore, this study provided a systematic investigation of the impact of different components of the broader phenomenon "socially desirable responding". The conceptualizations of these components mostly originate from psychological research, and so do the question inventories which are employed for their direct measurement. In this respect this study succeeds in combining approaches from three disciplines – economics, sociology, and psychology – to come to a more realistic model of response behavior in contingent valuation surveys.

After the introductory chapter provided rationales for an investigation of SDR in CVM, the second chapter offered a discussion of the theoretical foundations and some practical issues of that method. It became clear that the validity of WTP estimates originating in contingent valuation surveys is threatened by a variety of procedural biases, such as strategic bias, hypothetical biases and the stating of protest responses. Following this, recent advances in psychological and sociological research dealing with the CVM were discussed, from which the present study borrows its basic research design. The chapter closed with the introduction of econometric approaches of both calculating mean WTP estimates and identifying determinants of WTP. Following this introduction of the CVM, chapter 3 provided a detailed exposition of one major methodological problem of CVM: socially desirable responding. The concept and approaches to its measurement were discussed both from the perspective of psychology and sociology. It became evident that SDR consists of a set of factors depending both on the interview situation and topic and the respondent's personality. After elaborating further on the role of social and environmental norms, the multi-factor approach of SDR was modeled as a behavioral model based on the theory of rational choice. On theoretical grounds it was found that the three factors need for social approval, lack of anonymity and trait desirability are connected in a non-compensatory nature so that their product yields incentives to answer to a survey interview in a socially desirable way. In the fourth chapter this behavioral model was connected to the statement of WTP in contingent valuation surveys. The possibility that SDR might work as bias of CVM results stems from the facts that pro-environmental behavior is increasingly governed by social norms and that WTP responses constitute a form of statement of intent. Such statements are especially prone to response bias, since they can be modified by the respondent at little cost in order to increase social approval. The chapter closes with the development of research hypotheses, which are tested in the empirical study reported on in chapter 5. In a survey to assess the social value of a reforestation project in a nature reserve area in rural Southwest China the interacting influence of all three factors of SDR on WTP statements could not be detected. Consequently, regarding the models of SDR influence, the three-factor model has to be refuted. Instead all three factors were found to affect WTP statements either independently or as two-part interactions. The latter finding emphasizes the need to view SDR as a multi-component response bias. It appears insufficient to merely control for one of the factors and omit the others, which could explain why Laughland et al. (1994) do not find any influence of need for approval as measured by the Marlowe-Crowne scale on WTP responses. In addition to that, the socio-cultural background of Southwest China turned out to be an ideal setting to study the effect of SDR. The significant impacts of trait desirability and need for social approval substantiate the apprehension that this response bias might be prevalent in such a collectivistic and post-totalitarian context. Future survey-based environmental valuation studies in China should therefore be aware of this fact and apply measures to control for these influences.

However, this approach also has certain weaknesses and drawbacks that call for further improvement and future research. To begin with, the form of the interaction of these different components of SDR remains rather unclear. Since the data do not support the multiplicative form of the three-factor model but find all factors influencing WTP responses, these factors might as well be linked in any other fashion. The three-factor model as applied in this study treats all factors equally and assigns them the same weights. Yet, it is conceivable that different factors might enter the model with different intensities. These weights in turn might also be contingent on certain characteristics of the respondent, which would make the analytic model even more complicated. Alternatively, it is also conceivable that different factors exert differing influence on responses according to specific WTP amounts. The data provide certain hints to such an idea. While the lack of anonymity does not affect the specific amount of WTP, it very well affects the decision to state a positive WTP. Therefore, future research on this topic should investigate if the three factors independently affect responses for all levels of WTP or if interaction is possible for specific responses, such as very low or very high WTP amounts. So, while the three-factor model as specified in this study can be refuted based on the present data, it would be premature to completely abandon the main idea of an interaction of factors triggering SDR.

In addition to this aspect, several other issues in this study call for further investigation featuring a more rigorous methodological approach as well as theoretical extensions. Firstly, in a contingent valuation survey employing the dichotomous choice or bidding game elicitation formats, the relationship of SDR and compliance bias could be studied empirically. It appears possible that respondents with a strong need for social approval are more likely to exhibit yea-saying. Such an extended analysis could also shed more light on the issue whether SDR is a general source of other procedural biases such as interviewer effects. Related to this alternative question format is the development of alternative questions for the assessment of trait desirability. When the DC format is used, it appears easier to assess the level of desirability associated with stating "yes" than with the PC format in the present study. Secondly, as reported in section 5.2, even with the modified impression management subscale of the BIDR certain impairment of the validity of that measurement scale remains. This includes problems with the use of the 5-point Likert scale, the existence of "rebel" responses and the fact that certain respondents might guess the mode of operation of the BIDR and bias their responses accordingly. The discussion of these critical aspects demonstrates the need for further refinement of the psychological question inventories to assess need for social approval. In addition to that, such a refinement also includes approaches to associate social desirability closer with the specific content of the survey such as environmentally desirable responding. This appears to be a promising approach to identify response bias in all kinds of environmental valuation surveys – not only in CVM. Thirdly, more stringent experimental settings to test the influence of different levels of external and internal anonymity should be devised. The use of the sealed ballot box merely for some questions in the middle of the interview process as implemented in this study obviously did not substantially affect the anonymity perceptions of respondents. Future studies should rather employ entirely self-administered questionnaires to increase objective anonymity. At the same time, perceived anonymity, which is assessed from the perspective of the respondents, should be employed as factor of the behavioral model. So, a future research agenda would have to combine the direct assessment of SDR and its factors on the one hand, and the mode experiments traditionally applied in the CVM literature on the other.

A rather serious theoretical limitation of the three-factor model consists of the fact that it assumes the respondents to be fully rational decision makers that strive for utility maximization by gaining social approval. Further, it is assumed that the respondents have information about the consequences of all response options and also make use of this information. It is clear that this is a rather stylized conceptualization of the interview situation. Instead, it is conceivable that respondents do not rationally calculate the effect of their responses on the interviewer but rather react emotionally or guided by certain habits, customs, or general attitudes. When the need for social approval was discussed it was mentioned that the disutility of social disapproval stems from negative feelings such as embarrassment, shame, and social rejection. In the model, these emotions have motivational importance as arguments of the utility function of the rational respondent. This means that the rationality is merely assumed to apply to the utility maximizing problem of the respondent, whereas the specific form of the utility function is open for emotional, habitual, and customary factors. This allows the analysis of some form of non-rational motivations within the rational choice framework. However, the criticism of the respondent as rational decision maker persists. Tversky and Kahneman (1986) have shown that alternative descriptions of the same problem can lead to different decisions, which they interpret as fundamental criticism of the theory of rational choice. For the case of response bias in in-person surveys, this became apparent in the remarks by Steinert (1984): The respondent might regard the interviewer as a representative of government, as an unwelcome intruder into her privacy, or a poor fellow that should be helped with a burdensome job. Depending on which general attitude is triggered in the respondent, her perspective on the interview might change and the rational choice model might be applicable or not. In response to such criticism, Stocké (2004) considers the so-called model of frame selection. In the tradition of the idea of the framing of decisions (Tversky and Kahneman 1986) this approach contends that a certain fraction of respondents do not maximize expected social approval in a rational way but rather act according to other behavioral patterns that they deem appropriate in that situation. Stocké (2004) argues that under certain circumstances the respondent might assume a completely cooperative and conformist role and answer truthfully throughout the interview. This type of behavior is triggered by a latent positive attitude towards surveys and completely deactivates the rational choice model of the utility maximizing respondent. So, it appears that in this setting the rational choice approach of response behavior merely applies to a certain fraction of respondents, whereas other respondents might be guided by general attitudes. If these two groups can be empirically separated, the rational choice approach could be applied only to one group. However, while this model works fairly well in Stocké's (2004) survey, reliable methods to empirically distinguish between these two groups in a contingent valuation context are still difficult to find. Frör (2008) can show that 60 to 80 percent of respondents of a CVM study in Northern Thailand use the intuitive-experiential rather than the analytical-rational mode of information processing when answering the WTP question. This result questions the applicability of the rational decision framework of analyzing the effect of incentives for SDR. However, the rational choice approach does not assume that respondents have such an exact three-factor model in their minds when confronted with a WTP question. Rather this model tries to interrelate potential factors in a systematic manner to mimic actual behavior. Therefore, this approach serves well as a starting point to model the interaction of all relevant factors in an interview situation, which certainly needs refinement through future research.

In conclusion, this study offers a comprehensive approach to assess directly the influence of SDR on WTP statements in a contingent valuation survey. A behavioral model originating from sociology was developed that allows for a multi-component perspective on socially desirable responding. In addition to that, psychological concepts, such as need for social approval and trait desirability are integrated into the behavioral model as motivational factors. Consequently, in this study the contingent valuation interview is not merely being interpreted as a data recording tool for environmental economists but as a social interaction between the respondent and the interviewer or the surveying institution. When applying this broader perspective on the interview situation, determinants of WTP can be identified, which are not taken into account by conventional economic theory. This procedure is chosen to come to a more realistic and comprehensive analysis of the interview situation and abandon the exclusive focus on the valuation task, expressed by the elicitation question. The aspect of the contingent valuation interview as social interaction has been rather neglected by traditional CVM research, which viewed the interview merely as data generating procedure. By systematically integrating both personal and situational factors into a model of response behavior, it is possible to detect the constellation of factors that produces biased responses. The fact that significant psychological and situational factors such as the independent impacts of need for social approval and trait desirability as well as the interviewer effects can be identified provides a justification of this holistic perspective on the CVM interview. The premise that total economic values of most environmental goods can only be elicited by stated preference techniques does obviously not allow an analogous interpretation of revealed and stated preference data. When analyzing stated preference data, the process of assessment as well as psychological and attitudinal characteristics of the respondent and the interactions of these have to be explicitly taken into account. The behavioral model of incentives for SDR in CVM developed in this study constitutes a first step towards such a broader perspective of the valuation exercise. Although the specific form of the interaction was not supported by the survey data, all factors turned out to be significant determinants of WTP one way or the other. This approach thus puts into practice the calls for a sociological and psychological perspective on contingent valuation by Liebe (2007) and Loomes (2006), respectively. Investigating in a more comprehensive manner the interplay between different factors of SDR could bring some new drive into the discussion regarding the validity of CVM. Equipped with such insights, recommendations for better survey design and implementation could be given and the validity of contingent valuation surveys could be increased.

7. References

Abdalla, C. W., Roach, B. A. and Epp, D. J. (1992): Valuing environmental quality changes using averting expenditures: An application to groundwater contamination, *Land Economics*, 68, pp. 163-69.

Adamowicz, W., Boxall, P., Williams, M. and Louviere, J. (1998): Stated preference approaches for measuring passive use values: Choice experiments and contingent valuation, *American Journal of Agricultural Economics*, 80, pp. 64-75.

Adler, N. J., Campbell, N. and Laurent, A. (1989): In search of appropriate methodology: From outside the People's Republic of China looking in, *Journal of International Business Studies*, 20, pp. 61-74.

Ahlheim, M. (2003): Zur ökonomischen Bewertung von Umweltveränderungen, in: Genser, B. (ed.) *Finanzpolitik und Umwelt*, pp. 9-71, Berlin.

Ahlheim, M., Ekasingh, B., Frör, O., Kitchaicharoen, J., Neef, A., Sangkapitux, C. and Sinphurmsukskul, N. (2010): Better than their reputation: Enhancing the validity of contingent valuation mail survey results through citizen expert groups, *Journal of Environmental Planning and Management*, 53, pp. 163-82.

Ai, C. and Norton, E. C. (2003): Interaction terms in logit and probit models, *Economics Letters*, 80, pp. 123-29.

Ajzen, I. (1991): The theory of planned behavior, *Organizational Behavior and Human Decision Processes*, 50, pp. 179-211.

Akerlof, G. A. (1980): A theory of social custom, of which unemployment may be one consequence, *The Quarterly Journal of Economics*, 94, pp. 749-75.

Alpizar, F., Carlsson, F. and Johannsson-Stenman, O. (2008a): Does context matter more for hypothetical than for actual contributions? Evidence from a natural field experiment, *Experimental Economics*, 11, pp. 299-314.

Alpizar, F., Carlsson, F. and Johansson-Stenman, O. (2008b): Anonymity, reciprocity, and conformity: Evidence from voluntary contributions to a national park in Costa Rica, *Journal of Public Economics*, 92, pp. 1047-60.

Alriksson, S. and Öberg, T. (2008): Conjoint analysis for environmental evaluation: A review of methods and applications, *Environmental Science and Pollution Research*, 15, pp. 244-57.

Alvarez-Farizo, B. and Hanley, N. (2002): Using conjoint analysis to quantify public preferences over the environmental impacts of wind farms. An example from Spain, *Energy Policy*, 30, pp. 107-16.

Alvarez-Farizo, B. and Hanley, N. D. (2006): Improving the process of valuing non-market benefits: Combining citizens' juries with choice modelling, *Land Economics*, 82, pp. 465-78.

Alvarez-Farizo, B., Hanley, N. D., Baberan, R. and Lazaro, A. (2007): Choice modeling at the "market stall": Individual versus collective interest in environmental valuation, *Ecological Economics*, 60, pp. 743-51.

Amemiya, T. (1984): Tobit models: A survey, *Journal of Econometrics*, 24, pp. 3-61.

Andersson, H. and Svensson, M. (2008): Cognitive ability and scale bias in the contingent valuation method, *Environmental and Resource Economics*, 39, pp. 481-95.

Andreoni, J. (1989): Giving with impure altruism: Applications to charity and Ricardian equivalence, *The Journal of Political Economy*, 97, pp. 1447-58.

Andreoni, J. (1990): Impure altruism and donations to public goods: A theory of warm-glow giving, *The Economic Journal*, 100, pp. 464-77.

Andreoni, J. and Petrie, R. (2004): Public goods experiments without confidentiality: A glimpse into fund-raising, *Journal of Public Economics*, 88, pp. 1605-23.

Arana, J. E. and Leon, C. J. (2008): Do emotions matter? Coherent preferences under anchoring and emotional effects, *Ecological Economics*, 66, pp. 700-11.

Arrow, K. J. (1951): Social choice and individual values, New York.

Arrow, K. J. and Fisher, A. C. (1974): Environmental preservation, uncertainty, and irreversibility, *The Quarterly Journal of Economics*, 88, pp. 312-19.

Arrow, K. J., Solow, R. M., Portney, P. R., Leamer, E. E., Radner, R. and Schuman, H. (1993): Report of the NOAA Panel on contingent valuation: Natural resource damage assessment under the oil pollution act, pp. 4601-14. Federal Register 58.

Atteslander, P. and Kneubühler, H.-U. (1975): Verzerrungen im Interview, Opladen.

Bachman, J. G. and O'Malley, P. M. (1984): Yea-saying, nay-saying, and going to extremes: Black-white differences in response styles, *Public Opinion Quarterly*, 48, pp. 491-509.

Bai, X., Li, F. and Cheng, Y. (2004): The measurement equivalence of social desirability (in Chinese), *Psychological Science*, 27, pp. 1083-86.

Bärnighausen, T., Liu, Y., Zhang, X. and Sauerborn, R. (2007): Willingness to pay for social health insurance among informal sector workers in Wuhan, China: A contingent valuation study, *BMC Health Services Research*, 7, pp. 114-29.

Bateman, I. J., Langford, I. H., Jones, A. P. and Kerr, G. N. (2001): Bound and path effects in double and triple bounded dichotomous choice contingent valuation. *Resource and Energy Economics*, 23, pp. 191-213.

Bateman, I. J. and Mawby, J. (2004): First impressions count: Interviewer appearance and information effects in stated preference studies, *Ecological Economics*, 49, pp. 47-55.

Bateman, I. J., Munro, A., Rhodes, B., Starmer, C. and Sugden, R. (1997): Does part-whole bias exist? An experimental investigation, *The Economic Journal*, 107, pp. 322-32.
Baumeister, R. F. (1982): A self-presentational view of social phenomena, *Psychological Bulletin*, 91, pp. 3-26.
Becker, G. and Cherny, S. C. (1994): Gender-controlled measures of socially desirable responding, *Journal of Clinical Psychology*, 50, pp. 746-52.
Becker, G. S. (1974): A theory of social interactions, *Journal of Political Economy*, 82, pp. 1063-93.
Bennett, J. and Blamey, R. (2001): The choice modelling approach to environmental valuation, Cheltenham.
Bennett, M. T. (2008): China's sloping land conversion program: Institutional innovation or business as usual?, *Ecological Economics*, pp. 699-711.
Bernardi, R. A. (2006): Associations between Hofstede's cultural constructs and social desirability response bias, *Journal of Business Ethics*, 65, pp. 43-53.
Bernreuter, R. G. (1933): Validity of the personality inventory, *Personnel Journal*, 11, pp. 383-86.
Berry, C. M., Page, R. C. and Sackett, P. R. (2007): Effects of self-deceptive enhancement on personality-job performance relationships, *International Journal of Selection and Assessment*, 15, pp. 94-109.
Bettman, J. R., Luce, M. F. and Payne, J. W. (1998): Constructive consumer choice processes, *The Journal of Consumer Research*, 25, pp. 187-217.
Bishop, R. C. and Heberlein, T. A. (1979): Measuring values of extramarket goods: Are indirect measures biased?, *American Journal of Agricultural Economics*, 61, pp. 926-30.
Blamey, R. (1998): Contingent valuation and the activation of environmental norms, *Ecological Economics*, 24, pp. 47-72.
Blamey, R. K., Bennett, J. W. and Morrison, M. D. (1999): Yea-saying in contingent valuation surveys, *Land Economics*, 75, pp. 126-41.
Bockstael, N. E. and McConnell, K. E. (2007): Environmental and resource valuation with revealed preferences. A theoretical guide to empirical models, Dordrecht.
Borkenau, P. and Ostendorf, F. (1992): Social desirability scales as moderator and suppressor variables, *European Journal of Personality*, 6, pp. 199-214.
Botelho, A. and Costa Pinto, L. (2002): Hypothetical, real, and predicted real willingness to pay in open-ended surveys: Experimental results, *Applied Economics Letters*, 9, pp. 993-96.
Boyle, K. J. and Özdemir, S. (2009): Convergent validity of attribute-based, choice questions in stated-preference studies, *Environmental and Resource Economics*, 42, pp. 247-64.
Brambor, T., Clark, W. R. and Golder, M. (2006): Understanding interaction models: Improving empirical analyses, *Political Analysis*, 14, pp. 63-82.

Brennan, G. and Pettit, P. (2004): The economy of esteem, New York.
Cameron, T. A. and Huppert, D. D. (1989): OLS versus ML estimation of non-market resource values with payment card interval data, *Journal of Environmental Economics and Management*, 17, pp. 230-46.
Campbell, B. A. (1981): Race-of-interviewer effects among southern adolescents, *Public Opinion Quarterly*, 45, pp. 231-44.
Cao, M. and Zhang, J. (1997): Tree species diversity of tropical forest vegetation in Xishuangbanna, SW China, *Biodiversity and Conservation*, 6, pp. 995-1006.
Carson, R. T., Flores, N. E. and Meade, N. F. (2001): Contingent valuation: Controversies and evidence, *Environmental and Resource Economics*, 19, pp. 173-210.
Carson, R. T. and Groves, T. (2007): Incentive and informational properties of preference questions, *Environmental and Resource Economics*, 37, pp. 181-210.
Carson, R. T. and Hanemann, W. M. (2005): Contingent valuation, in: Mäler, K.-G. and Vincent, J.R. (eds.) *Handbook of environmental economics*, pp. 821-936, Amsterdam.
Carson, R. T., Mitchell, R. C., Hanemann, W. M., Kopp, R. J., Presser, S. and Ruud, P. A. (1992): A contingent valuation study of lost passive use values resulting from the Exxon Valdez oil spill, Anchorage.
Cesario, F. J. and Knetsch, J. L. (1976): A recreation site demand and benefit estimation model, *Regional Studies*, 10, pp. 97-104.
Chen, M. (2008): The relationships between adolescents' social desirability and self-evaluation, and its enlightenment to education (in Chinese), *Journal of Xihua University (Philosophy & Social Sciences)*, 27, pp. 98-100.
Chen, P. Y., Dai, T., Spector, P. E. and Jex, S. M. (1997): Relation between negative affectivity and positive affectivity: Effects of judged desirability of scale items and respondents' social desirability, *Journal of Personality Assessment*, 69, pp. 183-99.
Chen, W. Y. and Jim, C. Y. (2010): Resident motivations and willingness-to-pay for urban biodiversity conservation in Guangzhou (China), *Environmental Management*, 45, pp. 1052-64.
Christie, M. (2007): An examination of the disparity between hypothetical and actual willingness to pay using the contingent valuation method: The case of red kite conservation in the United Kingdom, *Canadian Journal of Agricultural Economics*, 55, pp. 159-69.
Ciriacy-Wantrup, S. v. (1947): Capital returns from soil-conservation practices, *Journal of Farm Economics*, 29, pp. 1181-96.
Clawson, M. (1959): Methods of measuring the demand for and value of outdoor recreation, Washington.
Coleman, J. S. (1990): Foundations of social theory, Cambridge and London.

Cooper, J. C. (1994): A comparison of approaches to calculating confidence intervals for benefit measures from dichotomous choice contingent valuation surveys, *Land Economics*, 70, pp. 111-22.

Couch, A. and Keniston, K. (1960): Yeasayers and naysayers: Agreeing response set as a personality variable, *Journal of Abnormal and Social Psychology*, 60, pp. 151-74.

Cronbach, L. J. (1950): Further evidence on response sets and test design, *Educational and Psychological Measurement*, 10, pp. 3-31.

Crowne, D. P. and Marlowe, D. (1960): A new scale of social desirability independent from psychopathology, *Journal of Consulting Psychology*, 24, pp. 349-54.

Crowne, D. P. and Marlowe, D. (1964): The approval motive, New York.

Cummings, R. G., Brookshire, D. S. and Schulze, W. D. (1986): Valuing environmental goods. An assessment of the contingent valuation method, Savage.

Cummings, R. G. and Taylor, L. O. (1999): Unbiased value estimates for environmental goods: A cheap talk design for the contingent valuation method, *The American Economic Review*, 89, pp. 649-65.

Dai, L. and Zhang, H. (2007): Relationship between social desirability and self-esteem of college students (in Chinese), *Chinese Journal of School Doctors*, 21, pp. 505-07.

Damarin, F. and Messick, S. (1965): Response styles as personality variables: A theoretical integration (ETS RB 65-10), Princeton.

Davis, J. (2004): Assessing community preferences for development projects: Are willingness-to-pay studies robust to mode effects?, *World Development*, 32, pp. 655-72.

Davis, R. K. (1963): The value of outdoor recreation: An economic study of the Maine woods, Ph.D. disseration, Harvard University.

Day, B. and Mourato, S. (2002): Valuing river quality in China, in: Pearce, C. and Palmer, C. (eds.) *Valuing the environment in developing countries*, pp. 25-66, Cheltenham.

DeMaio, T. J. (1984): Social desirability and survey measurement: A review, in: Turner, C.F. and Matrin, E. (eds.) *Surveying subjective phenomena 2*, pp. 257-80, New York.

Desvousges, W. H., Johnson, F. R., Dunford, R. W., Hudson, S. P., Wilson, K. N. and Boyle, K. J. (1993): Measuring natural resource damages with contingent valuation: Tests of validity and reliability, in: Hausman, J.A. (ed.) *Contingent valuation: A critical assessment*, pp. 91-164, Amsterdam.

Dickie, M. (2003): Defensive behavior and damage cost methods, in: Champ, P.A., Boyle, K.J. and Brown, T.C. (eds.) *A primer on nonmarket valuation*, pp. 395-444, Dordrecht.

Diefenbach, H. (2009): Die Theorie der rationalen Wahl oder „Rational Choice"-Theorie (RCT) in: Brock, D., Junge, M., Diefenbach, H., Keller, R. and

Villányi, D. (eds.) *Soziologische Paradigmen nach Talcott Parsons*, pp. 239-90, Wiesbaden.
Diekmann, A. and Preisendorfer, P. (2003): Green and greenback: The behavioral effects of environmental attitudes in low-cost and high-cost situations, *Rationality and Society*, 15, pp. 441-72.
Dohrenwend, B. P. (1966): Social status and psychological disorder: An issue of substance and an issue of method, *American Sociological Review*, 31, pp. 14-34.
Dohrenwend, B. P. and Dohrenwend, B. S. (1969): Social status and psychological disorder: A causal inquiry, New York.
Du, Y. (1998): The value of improved water quality for recreation in East Lake, Wuhan, China: An application of contingent valuation and travel cost methods, Discussion Paper, Institute of Economics at the Hubei Academy of Social Sciences.
Dunlap, R. E. and Van Liere, K. D. (1978): The "New environmental paradigm". A proposed measuring instrument and preliminary results, *Journal of Environmental Education*, 9, pp. 10-19.
Dunlap, R. E., Van Liere, K. D., Mertig, A. G. and Jones, R. E. (2000): Measuring endorsement of the new ecological paradigm: A revised nep scale, *Journal of Social Issues*, 56, pp. 425-42.
Dziegielewska, D. A. and Mendelsohn, R. (2007): Does "no" mean "no"? A protest methodology, *Environmental and Resource Economics*, 38, pp. 71-87.
Economy, E. (2006): Environmental governance: The emerging economic dimension, *Environmental Politics*, 15, pp. 171-89.
Edwards, A. L. (1953): The relationship between the judged desirability of a trait and the probability that the trait will be endorsed, *Journal of Applied Psychology*, 37, pp. 90-93.
Edwards, A. L. (1957): The social desirability variable in personality assessment and research, New York.
Elster, J. (1989): Social norms and economic theory, *Journal of Economic Perspectives*, 3, pp. 99-117.
Eng, I. (1998): Historical contingency and commercialisation in Xishuangbanna, China, *Tijdschrift voor Economische en Sociale Geografie*, 89, pp. 446-58.
Esser, H. (1986): Können Befragte lügen? Zum Konzept des "wahren Wertes" im Rahmen der handlungstheoretischen Erklärung von Situationseinflüssen bei der Befragung, *Kölner Zeitschrift für Soziologie und Sozialpsychologie*, 38, pp. 314-36.
Esser, H. (1991): Die Erklärung systematischer Fehler in Interviews: Befragtenverhalten als "Rational Choice", in: Wittenberg, R. (ed.) *Person - Situation - Institution - Kultur. Günter Büschges zum 65. Geburtstag*, pp. 59-78, Berlin.
Esser, H. (1999): Die Wert-Erwartungstheorie, in: Esser, H. (ed.) *Soziologie - spezielle Grundlagen*, pp. 247-93, Frankfurt a.M.

Ethier, R. G., Poe, G. L., Schulze, W. D. and Clark, J. (2000): A comparison of hypothetical phone and mail contingent valuation responses for green-pricing electricity programs, *Land Economics*, 76, pp. 54-67.

Ewert, A. and Galloway, G. (2009): Socially desirable responding in an environmental context: Development of a domain specific scale, *Environmental Education Research*, 15, pp. 55-70.

Fischer, A. (2003): Decision behaviour and information processing in contingent valuation surveys, Berlin.

Fischer, A. and Hanley, N. D. (2007): Analysing decision behaviour in stated preference surveys: A consumer psychological approach, *Ecological Economics*, 61, pp. 303-14.

Fisher, R. J. (2000): The future in social-desirability bias research in marketing, *Psychology and Marketing*, 17, pp. 73-77.

Fix, P. and Loomis, J. (1997): The economic benefits of mountain biking at one of its Meccas: An application of the travel cost method to mountain biking in Moab, Utah, *Journal of Leisure Research*, 29, pp. 342-52.

Foster, V., Bateman, I. J. and Harley, D. (1997): Real and hypothetical willingness to pay for environmental preservation: A non-experimental comparison, *Journal of Agricultural Economics*, 48, pp. 123-37.

Foster, V. and Mourato, S. (2000): Valuing the multiple impacts of pesticide use in the UK: A contingent ranking approach, *Journal of Agricultural Economics*, 51, pp. 1-21.

Fox, J. A., Shogren, J. F., Hayes, D. J. and Kliebenstein, J. B. (1998): CVM-X: Calibrating contingent values with experimental auction markets, *American Journal of Agricultural Economics*, 80, pp. 455-65.

Freeman, M. A. (2003): The measurement of environmental and resource values, 2nd edn., Washington.

Frew, E. J., Whynes, D. K. and Wolstenholme, J. L. (2003): Eliciting willingness to pay: Comparing closed-ended with open-ended and payment scale formats, *Medical Decision Making*, 23, pp. 150-59.

Frew, E. J., Wolstenholme, J. L. and Whynes, D. K. (2004): Comparing willingness-to-pay: Bidding game format versus open-ended and payment scale formats, *Health Policy*, 68, pp. 289-98.

Frör, O. (2008): Bounded rationality in contingent valuation: Empirical evidence using cognitive psychology, *Ecological Economics*, 68, pp. 570-81.

Gove, W. R. and Geerken, M. R. (1977): Response bias in surveys of mental health: An empirical investigation, *The American Journal of Sociology*, 82, pp. 1289-317.

Greene, W. H. (2007): Limdep^{tm} version 9.0 reference guide, Plainview.

Greene, W. H. (2009): Testing hypotheses about interaction terms in nonlinear models, Leonard N. Stern School of Business, Department of Economics, New York.

Greenleaf, E. A. (1992): Measuring extreme response style, *Public Opinion Quarterly*, 56, pp. 328-51.

Griffin, C. C., Briscoe, J., Singh, B., Ramasubban, R. and Bhatia, R. (1995): Contingent valuation and actual behavior: Predicting connections to new water systems in the state of Kerala, India, *The World Bank Economic Review*, 9, pp. 373-95.

Guo, Q., Wang, H. and Han, D. (2006): Social desirability responding and its relationship with personality tests (in Chinese), *Education Science*, 22, pp. 92-94.

Haab, T. C. and McConnell, K. E. (2002): Valuing environmental resources, Cheltenham.

Hackl, F. and Pruckner, G. J. (2003): Warm-glow, free-riding and vehicle neutrality in a health-related contingent valuation study, Department of Economics, Johannes Kepler University of Linz.

Halstead, J. M., Lindsay, B. E. and Brown, C. M. (1991): Use of the tobit model in contingent valuation: Experimental evidence from the Pemigewasset wilderness area, *Journal of Environmental Management*, 33, pp. 79-89.

Halstead, J. M., Luloff, A. E. and Stevens, T. H. (1992): Protest bidders in contingent valuation, *Northeastern Journal of Agricultural and Resource Economics*, 21, pp. 160-69.

Hammitt, J. K. and Zhou, Y. (2006): The economic value of air-pollution-related health risks in China: A contingent valuation study, *Environmental and Resource Economics*, 33, pp. 399-423.

Hanemann, W. M. (1994): Valuing the environment through contingent valuation *The Journal of Economic Perspectives*, 8, pp. 19-43.

Hanemann, W. M. and Kanninen, B. (1999): The statistical analysis of discrete-response CV data, in: Bateman, I. J. and Willis, K. G. (eds.) *Valuing environmental preferences. Theory and practice of the contingent valuation method in the US, EU, and developing countries*, pp. 302-441, Oxford.

Hanemann, W. M. (1984): Welfare evaluations in contingent valuation experiments with discrete responses, *American Journal of Agricultural Economics*, 66, pp. 332-41.

Hanemann, W. M. (1985): Some issues in continuous- and discrete-response contingent valuation studies, *Northeastern Journal of Agricultural and Resource Economics*, 14, pp. 5-13.

Hanemann, W. M., Loomis, J. B. and Kanninen, B. J. (1991): Statistical efficiency of double-bounded dichotomous choice contingent valuation, *American Journal of Agricultural Economics*, 73, pp. 1255-63.

Hanley, N., Wright, R. E. and Vic, A. (1998): Using choice experiments to value the environment, *Environmental and Resource Economics*, 11, pp. 413-28.

Hanley, N. D. (1989): Valuing rural recreation benefits: An empirical comparison of two approaches, *Journal of Agricultural Economics*, 40, pp. 361-74.

Hanley, N. D., Mourato, S. and Wright, R. E. (2001): Choice modelling approaches: A superior alternative for environmental valuation?, *Journal of Economic Surveys*, 15, pp. 435-62.
Harris, P. G. (2006): Environmental perspectives and behavior in China *Environment and Behavior*, 38, pp. 5-21.
Harrison, G. W. and Rutström, E. E. (2008): Experimental evidence on the existence of hypothetical bias in value elicitation methods, in: Plott, C.R. and Smith, V.L. (eds.) *Handbook of experimental economics results*, pp. 752-67, Amsterdam.
Hartmann, P. (1991): Wunsch und Wirklichkeit. Theorie und Empirie sozialer Erwünschtheit, Wiesbaden.
Hatchett, S. and Schuman, H. (1975): White respondents and race-of-interviewer effects, *Public Opinion Quarterly*, 39, pp. 523-28.
Hausman, J. A. (1993): Contingent valuation: A critical assessment, Amsterdam.
Heberlein, T. A., Wilson, M. A., Bishop, R. C. and Schaeffer, N. C. (2005): Rethinking the scope test as a criterion for validity in contingent valuation, *Journal of Environmental Economics and Management*, 50, pp. 1-22.
Hebert, J. R., Ma, Y., Clemow, L., Ockene, I. S., Saperia, G., Stanek, E. J. I., Merriam, P. A. and Ockene, J. K. (1997): Gender differences in social desirability and social approval bias in dietary self-report, *American Journal of Epidemiology*, 146, pp. 1046-55.
Heine, S. J. and Hamamura, T. (2007): In search of East Asian self-enhancement, *Personality and Social Psychology Review*, 11, pp. 4-27.
Heine, S. J., Lehman, D. R., Markus, H. R. and Kitayama, S. (1999): Is there a universal need for positive self-regard?, *Psychological Review*, 106, pp. 766-94.
Heine, S. J. and Renshaw, K. (2002): Interjudge agreement, self-enhancement, and liking: Cross-cultural divergences, *Personality and Social Psychology Bulletin*, 28, pp. 578-87.
Helmes, E. (2000): The role of social desirability in the assessment of personality constructs, in: Jackson, D.N., Goffin, R.D. and Helmes, E. (eds.) *Problems and solutions in human assessment*, pp. 357, Berlin.
Hicks, J. R. (1939): The foundations of welfare economics, *Economic Journal*, 49, pp. 696-712.
Hicks, J. R. (1942): Consumers' surplus and index-numbers, *Review of Economic Studies*, 9, pp. 126-37.
Hofstede, G. H. (1984a): Cultural dimensions in management and planning, *Asia Pacific Journal of Management*, 1, pp. 81-99.
Hofstede, G. H. (1984b): Culture's consequences: International differences in work-related values, 2nd edn., Newbury Park.
Holländer, H. (1990): A social exchange approach to voluntary cooperation, *The American Economic Review*, 80, pp. 1157-67.

Hyman, H. A. (1954): Interviewing in social research, Chicago.
Jim, C. Y. and Chen, W. (2006a): Impacts of urban environmental elements on residential housing prices in Guangzhou (China), *Landscape and Urban Planning*, 78, pp. 422-34.
Jim, C. Y. and Chen, W. Y. (2006b): Recreation–amenity use and contingent valuation of urban greenspaces in Guangzhou, China, *Landscape and Urban Planning*, 75, pp. 81-96.
Jinghong, Statistical Bureau of Jinghong Municipality (2008): Jinghong statistical yearbook 2007.
Johansson, P.-O. (1993): Cost-benefit analysis of environmental change, Cambridge.
Jorgensen, B. S. and Syme, G. J. (2000): Protest responses and willingness to pay: Attitude toward paying for stormwater pollution abatement, *Ecological Economics*, 33, pp. 251-65.
Jorgensen, B. S., Syme, G. J., Bishop, B. J. and Nancarrow, B. E. (1999): Protest responses in contingent valuation, *Environmental and Resource Economics*, 14, pp. 131-50.
Jorgensen, B. S., Wilson, M. A. and Heberlein, T. A. (2001): Fairness in the contingent valuation of environmental goods: Attitude toward paying for environmental improvements at two levels of scope, *Ecological Economics*, 36, pp. 133-48.
Kahneman, D. and Knetsch, J. L. (1992): Valuing public goods: The purchase of moral satisfaction, *Journal of Environmental Economics and Management*, 22, pp. 57.
Kahneman, D. and Tversky, A. (1979): Prospect theory: An analysis of decision under risk, *Econometrica*, 47, pp. 263-92.
Kaiser, F. G. (1998): A general measure of ecological behavior, *Journal of Applied Psychology*, 28, pp. 395-422.
Kaiser, F. G. and Wilson, M. (2000): Assessing people's general ecological behavior: A cross-cultural measure, *Journal of Applied Social Psychology*, 20, pp. 952-78.
Kam, C. D. and Franzese, R. J. (2007): Modelling and interpreting interactive hypotheses in regression analysis, Ann Arbor.
Kanninen, B. J. (1995): Bias in discrete contingent valuation, *Journal of Environmental Economics and Management*, 28, pp. 114-25.
Kanninen, B. J. (1993): Optimal experimental design for double-bounded dichotomous choice contingent valuation, *Land Economics*, 69, pp. 138-46.
Kealy, M. J. and Turner, R. W. (1993): A test of the equality of closed-ended and open-ended contingent valuations, *American Journal of Agricultural Economics*, 75, pp. 321-31.

Keillor, B., Owens, D. and Pettijohn, C. (2001): A cross-cultural/cross-national study of influencing factors and socially desirable response bias, *International Journal of Marketing Research*, 43, pp. 63-84.
King, M. F. and Bruner, G. C. (2000): Social desirability bias: A neglected aspect of validity testing, *Psychology and Marketing*, 17, pp. 79-103.
Kotchen, M. J. and Reiling, S. D. (2000): Environmental attitudes motivations and contingent valuation of nonuse values: A case study involving endangered species, *Ecological Economics*, 32, pp. 93-127.
Krenz, C. and Sax, G. (1987): Acquiescence as a function of test type and subject uncertainty, *Educational and Psychological Measurement*, 47, pp. 575-82.
Krosnick, J. A. (1999): Maximizing questionnaire quality, in: Robinson, J.P., Shaver, P.R. and Wrightsman, L.S. (eds.) *Measures of political attitudes*, pp. 37-57, San Diego.
Krutilla, J. V. (1967): Conservation reconsidered, *The American Economic Review*, 57, pp. 777-86.
Lalwani, A. K., Shavitt, S. and Johnson, T. (2006): What is the relation between cultural orientation and socially desirable responding?, *Journal of Personality and Social Psychology*, 90, pp. 165-78.
Lalwani, A. K., Shrum, L. J. and Chiu, C.-Y. (2009): Motivated response styles: The role of cultural values, regulatory focus, and self-consciousness in socially desirable responding, *Journal of Personality and Social Psychology*, 96, pp. 870-82.
Lancaster, K. J. (1966): A new approach to consumer theory, *The Journal of Political Economy*, 74, pp. 132-57.
Laughland, A. S., Musser, W. N. and Musser, L. M. (1994): An experiment in contingent valuation and social desirability, *Agricultural and Resource Economics Review*, 23, pp. 29-36.
Le Goffe, P. (2000): Hedonic pricing of agriculture and forestry externalities, *Environmental and Resource Economics*, 15, pp. 397-401.
Leggett, C. G., Kleckner, N. S., Boyle, K. J., Duffield, J. W. and Mitchell, R. C. (2003): Social desirability bias in contingent valuation surveys administered through in-person interviews, *Land Economics*, 79, pp. 561-75.
Li, A. and Bagger, J. (2007): The balanced inventory of desirable responding (BIDR): A reliability generalization study, *Educational and Psychological Measurement*, 67, pp. 525-44.
Li, F. and Li, Y. (2008): The balanced incentory of desirable responding (BIDR): A factor analysis, *Psychological Reports*, 103, pp.727-31.
Li, H., Mitchell Aide, T., Youxin, M., Wenjun, L. and Min, C. (2007): Demand for rubber is causing the loss of high diversity rain forest in SW China, *Biodiversity Conservation*, 16, pp. 1731-45.
Liebe, U. (2007): Zahlungsbereitschaft für kollektive Umweltgüter. Soziologische und ökonomische Analysen, Wiesbaden.

Lienhoop, N. and Macmillan, D. C. (2007): Contingent valuation: Comparing participant performance in group-based approaches and personal interviews, *Environmental Values*, 16, pp. 209-32.
LILAC (2007): Vorhabenbeschreibung: Ländliche Entwicklung durch Kandnutzungsdiversifizierung: Akteursbasierte Strategien und integrative Technologien für Agrarlandschaften im südwestchinesischen Bergland, (eds. Sauerborn, J. and Chen, J.), pp. 105. University of Hohenheim, Stuttgart.
Lin, F. and Chen, J. (2005): Contingent valuation method in social benefit valuation of urban mass transit (in Chinese), *Donghua Shifan Daxue Xuebao (Journal of East China Normal University)*, 37, pp. 48-53.
Lindbeck, A. (1997): Incentives and social norms in household behavior, *The American Economic Review*, 87, pp. 370-77.
Lindhjem, H. and Navrud, S. (2008): Internet CV surveys – a cheap, fast way to get large samples of biased values?, unpublished paper.
List, J. A., Berrens, R. P., Bohara, A. K. and Kerkvliet, J. (2004): Examining the role of social isolation on stated preferences, *The American Economic Review*, 94, pp. 741-52.
Liu, C., Xiao, J. and Yang, Z. (2003): A compromise between self-enhancement and honesty: Chinese self-evaluations on social desirable scales, *Psychological Reports*, 92, pp. 291-98.
Lockwood, M. (1998): Integrated value assessment using paired comparisons, *Ecological Economics*, 25, pp. 73-87.
Loomes, G. (2006): (How) can we value health, safety and the environment?, *Journal of Economic Psychology*, 27, pp. 713-36.
Loomis, J. and King, M. (1994): Comparison of mail and telephone-mail contingent valuation surveys, *Journal of Environmental Management*, 41, pp. 309-24.
Loomis, J., Yorizane, S. and Larson, D. (2000): Testing significance of multi-destination and multi-purpose trip effects in a travel cost method demand model for whale watching trips, *Agricultural and Resource Economics Review*, 29, pp. 183-91.
Loomis, J. B. (1990): Comparative reliability of the dichotomous choice and open-ended contingent valuation techniques, *Journal of Environmental Economics and Management*, 18, pp. 78-85.
Loureiro, M. L. and Lotade, J. (2005): Interviewer effects on the valuation of goods with ethical and environmental attributes, *Environmental and Resource Economics*, 30, pp. 49-72.
Luttik, J. (2000): The value of trees, water and open space as reflected by house prices in the Netherlands, *Landscape and Urban Planning*, 48, pp. 161-67.

Macmillan, D. C., Philip, L., Hanley, N. D. and Alvarez-Farizo, B. (2002): Valuing the non-market benefits of wild goose conservation: A comparison of interview and group based approaches, *Ecological Economics*, 43, pp. 49-59.
Mäler, K.-G. (1974): Environmental economics: A theoretical inquiry, Baltimore.
Mannesto, G. and Loomis, J. B. (1991): Evaluation of mail and in-person contingent value surveys: Results of a study of recreational boaters, *Journal of Environmental Management*, 32, pp. 177-90.
Manning, P. K. (1966): Problems in interpreting interview data, *Sociology and Social Research*, 50, pp. 302-16.
Mansfield, C., Johnson, F. R. and Van Houtven, G. (2006): The missing piece: Valuing averting behavior for children's ozone exposures, *Resource and Energy Economics*, 28, pp. 215-28.
Marta-Pedroso, C., Freitas, H. and Domingos, T. (2007): Testing for the survey mode effect on contingent valuation data quality: A case study of web based versus in-person interviews, *Ecological Economics*, 62, pp. 388-98.
Martens, S. (2006): Public participation with Chinese characteristics: Citizen consumers in China's environmental management, *Environmental Politics*, 15, pp. 211-30.
McCrae, R. R. and Costa, P. T. J. (1983): Social desirability scales: More substance than style, *Journal of Consulting and Clinical Psychology*, 51, pp. 882-88.
McFadden, D. (1974): Conditional logit analysis of qualitative choice behavior, in: Zarembka, P. (ed.) *Frontiers in econometrics, economic theory and mathematical economics*, pp. 105-42, New York.
McKinley, J. C., Hathaway, S. R. and Meehl, P. E. (1948): The Minnesota multiphasic personality inventory iv. The K scale, *Journal of Consulting Psychology*, 12, pp. 26-31.
Messonnier, M. L., Bergstrom, J. C., Cornwell, C. M., Teasley, R. J. and Cordell, H. K. (2000): Survey response-related biases in contingent valuation: Concepts, remedies, and empirical application to valuing aquatic plant management, *American Journal of Agricultural Economics*, 82, pp. 438-50.
Meston, C. M., Heiman, J. R., Trapnell, P. D. and Paulhus, D. L. (1998): Socially desirable responding and sexuality self-reports, *The Journal of Sex Research*, 35, pp. 148-57.
Meyerhoff, J. and Liebe, U. (2006): Protest beliefs in contingent valuation: Explaining their motivation, *Ecological Economics*, 57, pp. 583-94.
Mick, D. G. (1996): Are studies of dark side variables confounded with social desirable responding? The case of materialism, *Journal of Consumer Research*, 23, pp. 106-19.
Middleton, K. L. and Jones, J. L. (2000): Social desirability response sets: The impact of country culture, *Psychology and Marketing*, 17, pp. 149-63.

Millham, J. (1974): Two components of need for approval score and their relationship to cheating following success and failure, *Journal of Research in Personality*, 8, pp. 378-92.

Millham, J. and Jacobson, L. I. (1978): The need for approval, in: London, H. and Exner, J.E. (eds.) *Dimensions of personality*, pp. 365-90, New York.

Mitchell, R. C. and Carson, R. T. (1981): An experiment in determining willingness to pay for national water quality improvements, in: *Report to the United States Environmental Protection Agency*. United States Environmental Protection Agency, Washington.

Mitchell, R. C. and Carson, R. T. (1989): Using surveys to value public goods: The contingent valuation method, Washington.

Mohr, E. (1994): Environmental norms, society, and economics, *Ecological Economics*, 9, pp. 229-39.

Mol, A. J. and Carter, N. T. (2006): China's environmental governance in transition, *Environmental Politics*, 15, pp. 149-70.

Morrison, M. and Brown, T. C. (2009): Testing the effectiveness of certainty scales, cheap talk, and dissonance-minimization in reducing hypothetical bias in contingent valuation studies, *Environmental and Resource Economics*, 44, pp. 307-26.

Moum, T. (1988): Yea-saying and mood-of-the-day effects in self-reported quality of life, *Social Indicators Research*, 20, pp. 117-39.

Murphy, J. J., Allen, P. G., Stevens, T. H. and Weatherhead, D. (2005): A meta-analysis of hypothetical bias in stated preference valuation, *Environmental and Resource Economics*, 30, pp. 313-25.

Nederhof, A. J. (1985): Methods of coping with social desirability bias, *European Journal of Social Psychology*, 15, pp. 263-80.

Neill, H. R., Cummings, R. G., Glanderton, P. T., Harrison, G. W. and McGuckin, T. (1994): Hypothetical surveys and real economic commitments, *Land Economics*, 70, pp. 145-54.

Nielsen, J. S. (2011): Use of the internet for willingness-to-pay surveys: A comparison of face-to-face and web-based interviews, *Resource and Energy Economics*, 33, pp. 119-29.

Niu, J., Liu, C. and Hou, J. (2005): Evaluating the value of urban agricultural leisure landscape by contingent valuation method (in Chinese), *Zhongguo Nongye Keji Daobao (Review of China Agricultural Science and Technology)*, 7, pp. 72-76.

Norton, E. C., Wang, H. and Ai, C. (2004): Computing interaction effects and standard errors in logit and probit models, *The Stata Journal*, 4, pp. 154-67.

Nunes, P. A. L. D. (2002): The contingent valuation of natural parks, Cheltenham.

Nunes, P. A. L. D. and Schokkaert, E. (2003): Identifying the warm glow effect in contingent valuation, *Journal of Environmental Economics and Management*, 45, pp. 231-45.

Olson, M. (1965): The logic of collective action: Public goods and the theory of groups, Cambridge.
Orne, M. T. (1962): On the social psychology of the psychological experiment, *American Psychologist*, 17, pp. 776-89.
Palmquist, R. B. (1991): Hedonic methods, in: Braden, J. B. and Kolstad, C. D. (eds.) *Measuring the demand for environmental quality*, pp. 77-120, Amsterdam.
Park, T., Loomis, J. B. and Creel, M. (1991): Confidence intervals for evaluating benefits estimates from dichotomous choice contingent valuation studies, *Land Economics*, 67, pp. 64-73.
Paulhus, D. L. (1984): Two-component models of social desirable responding, *Journal of Personality and Social Psychology*, 46, pp. 598-608.
Paulhus, D. L. (1991): Measurement and control of response bias, in: Robinson, J. P., Shaver, P. R. and Wrightsman, L. S. (eds.) *Measures of personality and social psychological attitudes*, pp. 17-59, San Diego.
Paulhus, D. L. (1998): BIDR-7 user's manual, North Tonawanda.
Paulhus, D. L. (2002): Socially desirable responding: The evolution of a construct, in: Braun, H. I., Jackson, D. N. and Wiley, D. E. (eds.) *The role of constructs in psychological and educational measurement*, pp. 49-69, Mahwah.
Paulhus, D. L. and Reid, D. B. (1991): Enhancement and denial in socially desirable responding, *Journal of Personality and Social Psychology*, 60, pp. 307-17.
Pauls, C. A. and Stemmler, G. (2003): Substance and bias in social desirability responding, *Personality and Individual Differences*, 35, pp. 263-75.
Payne, J. W., Bettman, J. R. and Schkade, D. A. (1999): Measuring constructed preferences: Towards a building code, *Journal of Risk and Uncertainty*, 19, pp. 243-70.
Philip, L. J. and Macmillan, D. C. (2005): Exploring values, context and perceptions in contingent valuation studies: The CV market stall technique and willingness to pay for wildlife conservation, *Journal of Environmental Planning and Management*, 48, pp. 257-74.
Phillips, D. L. (1971): Knowledge from what?, Chicago.
Phillips, D. L. (1973): Abandoning method, San Francisco.
Phillips, D. L. and Clancy, K. J. (1970): Response biases in field studies of mental illness, *American Sociological Review*, 35, pp. 503-15.
Phillips, D. L. and Clancy, K. J. (1972): Some effects of "Social desirability" in survey studies, *The American Journal of Sociology*, 77, pp. 921-40.
Podsakoff, P. M., MacKenzie, S. B., Lee, J.-Y. and Podsakoff, N. B. (2003): Common method biases in behavioral research: A critical review of the literature and recommended remedies, *Journal of Applied Psychology*, 88, pp. 879-903.

Polome, P., van der Veen, A. and Geurts, P. (2006): Is referendum the same as dichotomous choice contingent valuation?, *Land Economics*, 82, pp. 174-88.
Powe, N. A., Garrod, G. D. and McMahon, P. L. (2005): Mixing methods within stated preference environmental valuation: Choice experiments and post-questionnaire qualitative analysis, *Ecological Economics*, 52, pp. 513-26.
Randall, A. (1991): Total and nonuse values, in: Braden, J. B. and Kolstad, C. D. (eds.) *Measuring the demand for environmental quality*, pp. 303-21, Amsterdam.
Randall, A., Ives, B. and Eastman, C. (1974): Bidding games for valuation of aesthetic environmental improvements, *Journal of Environmental Economics and Management*, 1, pp. 132-49.
Randall, D. M. and Fernandes, M. F. (1991): The social desirability response bias in ethics research, *Journal of Business Ethics*, 10, pp. 805-17.
Ready, R. C., Buzby, J. C. and Hu, D. (1996): Differences between continuous and discrete contingent value estimates, *Land Economics*, 72, pp. 397-411.
Rege, M. and Telle, K. (2004): The impact of social approval and framing on cooperation in public good situations, *Journal of Public Economics*, 88, pp. 1625-44.
Ren, L. (2009): Surveying public opinion in transitional China: An examination of survey response, Doctoral Thesis, University of Pittsburgh.
Ridker, R. G. (1967): Economic costs of air pollution: Studies in measurement, New York.
Riker, W. H. and Ordeshook, P. C. (1973): An introduction to positive political theory, Englewood Cliffs.
Robinson, J., Clouston, B., Suh, J. and Chaloupka, M. (2009): Are citizens' juries a useful tool for assessing environmental value?, *Environmental Conservation*, 35, pp. 351-60.
Rosen, S. (1974): Hedonic prices and implicit markets: Product differentiation in pure competition, *The Journal of Political Economy*, 82, pp. 34-55.
Roy, A., Walters, P. G. P. and Luk, S. T. K. (2001): Chinese puzzles and paradoxes: Conducting business research in China, *Journal of Business Research*, 52, pp. 303-10.
Ryan, M., Scott, D. and Donaldson, A. C. (2004): Valuing health care using willingness to pay: A comparison of the payment card and dichotomous choice methods, *Journal of Health Economics*, 23, pp. 237-58.
Samuelson, P. A. (1954): The pure theory of public expenditure, *The Review of Economics and Statistics*, 36, pp. 387-89.
Sauer, U. and Fischer, A. (2010): Willingness to pay, attitudes and fundamental values – on the cognitive context of public preferences for diversity in agricultural landscapes, *Ecological Economics*, 70, pp. 1-9.

Schläpfer, F. and Bräuer, I. (2007): Theoretical incentive properties of contingent valuation questions: Do they matter in the field?, *Ecological Economics*, 62, pp. 451-60.
Schulze, W. D., d'Arge, R. C. and Brookshire, D. S. (1981): Valuing environmental commodities: Some recent experiments, *Land Economics*, 57, pp. 151-72.
Schwartz, S. H. (1977): Normative influences on altruism, in: Berkowitz, L. (ed.) *Advances in experimental social psychology*, pp. 221-80, New York.
Scott, D. and Willits, F. K. (1994): Environmental attitudes and behavior, *Environment and Behavior*, 26, pp. 239-60.
Shapiro, J. (2001): Mao's war against nature: Politics and the environment in revolutionary China, Cambridge.
Shlapentokh, V. E. (1985): Two levels of public opinion: The Soviet case, *Public Opinion Quarterly*, 49, pp. 443-59.
Smith, D. B. and Ellingson, J. E. (2002): Substance versus style: A new look at social desirability in motivating contexts, *Journal of Applied Psychology*, 87, pp. 211-19.
Smith, P. B., Bond, M. H. and Kagitcibasi, C. (2006): Understanding social psychology across cultures. Living and working in a changing world, London.
Smith, R. D. (2006): It's not just what you do, it's the way that you do it: The effect of different payment card formats and survey administration on willingness to pay for health gain, *Health Economics*, 15, pp. 281-93.
Steinert, H. (1984): Das Interview als soziale Interaktion, in: Meulemann, H. and Reuband, K.-H. (eds.) *Soziale Realität im Interview. Empirische Analysen methodischer Probleme*, pp. 17-59, Frankfurt/New York.
Stephan, G. and Ahlheim, M. (1996): Ökonomische Ökologie, Berlin.
Stöber, J., Dette, D. E. and Musch, J. (2002): Comparing continuous and dichotomous scoring of the balanced inventory of desirable responding, *Journal of Personality Assessment*, 78, pp. 370-89.
Stocké, V. (2004): Entstehungsbedingungen von Antwortverzerrungen durch soziale Erwünschtheit: Ein Vergleich der Prognosen der Rational-Choice Theorie und des Modells der Frame-Selektion, *Zeitschrift für Soziologie*, 33, pp. 303-20.
Stocké, V. (2007): The interdependence of determinants for the strength and direction of social desirability bias in racial attitude surveys, *Journal of Official Statistics*, 23, pp. 493-514.
Stocké, V. and Hunkler, C. (2007): Measures of desirability beliefs and their validity as indicators for socially desirable responding, *Field Methods*, 19, pp. 313-36.
Strazzera, E., Genius, M., Scarpa, R. and Hutchinson, G. (2003): The effect of protest votes on the estimates of WTP for use values of recreational sites, *Environmental and Resource Economics*, 25, pp. 461-76.

Stricker, L. S. (1963): Acquiescence and social desirability response styles, item characteristics, and conformity, *Psychological Reports*, 12, pp. 319-42.
Sturgeon, J. C. (2010): Governing minorities and development in Xishuangbanna, China: Akha and Dai rubber farmers as entrepreneurs, *Geoforum*, 41, pp. 318-28.
Sunstein, C. R. (1996): Social norms and social roles, *Columbia Law Review*, 96, pp. 902-68.
Switzer, G. E., Wisniewski, S. R., Belle, S. H., Dew, M. A. and Schultz, R. (1999): Selecting, developing, and evaluating research instruments, *Social Psychiatry and Psychiatric Epidemiology*, 34, pp. 399-409.
Tan, L. and Grace, R. C. (2008): Social desirability and sexual offenders, *Sexual Abuse: A Journal of Research and Treatment*, 20, pp. 61-87.
Tobin, J. (1958): Estimation of relationships for limited dependent variables, *Econometrica*, 26, pp. 24-36.
Tourangeau, R., Rips, J. and Rasinski, K. A. (2000): The psychology of survey response, Cambridge.
Tourangeau, R. and Smith, T. W. (1996): Asking sensitive questions: The impact of data collection mode, question format, and question context, *Public Opinion Quarterly*, 60, pp. 275-304.
Tversky, A. and Kahneman, D. (1986): Rational choice and the framing of decisions, *Journal of Business*, 59, pp. 251-78.
Vartia, Y. O. (1983): Efficient methods of measuring welfare change and compensated income in terms of ordinary demand functions, *Econometrica*, 51, pp. 79-98.
Venkatachalam, L. (2004): The contingent valuation method: A review, *Environmental Impact Assessment Review*, 24, pp. 89-124.
von Neumann, J. and Morgenstern, O. (1947): Theory of games and economic behavior, 2nd edn., Princeton.
Walsh, R. G., Loomis, J. B. and Gillman, R. A. (1984): Valuing option, existence, and bequest demands for wilderness, *Land Economics*, 60, pp. 14-29.
Wang, H. and Mullahy, J. (2006): Willingness to pay for reducing fatal risk by improving air quality: A contingent valuation study in Chongqing, China, *Science of the Total Environment*, 367, pp. 50-57.
Wang, X., Wang, X. and Ma, H. (1999): Rating scales for mental health (in Chinese), Beijing.
Wang, X. J., Zhang, W., Li, Y., Yang, K. Z. and Bai, M. (2006): Air quality improvement estimation and assessment using contingent valuation method, a case study in Beijing, *Environmental Monitoring and Assessment*, 120, pp. 153-68.
Wang, Y., Zhang, Y., Wang, Q. and Wang, W. (2007): Residents' willingness to pay for improving air quality in Jinan, China, *Chinese Journal of Population, Resources and Environment*, 5, pp. 12-19.

Wei, Y., Davidson, B., Chen, D., White, R., Li, B. and Zhang, J. (2007): Can contingent valuation be used to measure the in situ value of groundwater on the North China Plain?, *Water Resource Management*, 21.

Weisbrod, B. A. (1964): Collective-consumption services of individual-consumption goods, *The Quarterly Journal of Economics*, 78, pp. 471-77.

Whitehead, J. C., Groothius, P. A. and Blomquist, G. C. (1993): Testing for non-response and sample selection bias in contingent valuation, *Economics Letters*, 41, pp. 215-20.

Whittaker, D., Vaske, J. J., Donnelly, M. P. and DeRuiter, D. S. (1998): Mail versus telephone surveys: Potential biases in expenditure and willingness to pay data, *Journal of Park and Recreation Administration*, 16, pp. 15-30.

Whynes, D. K., Wolstenholme, J. L. and Frew, E. (2004): Evidence of range bias in contingent valuation payment scales, *Health Economics*, 13, pp. 183-90.

Wiggins, J. S. (1964): Convergences among stylistic response measures from objective personality tests, *Educational and Psychological Measurement*, 24, pp. 551-62.

Winkler, N., Kroh, M. and Spiess, M. (2006): Entwicklung einer deutschen Kurzskala zur zweidimensionalen Messung von sozialer Erwünschtheit, *DIW Discussion Papers*, 579, Berlin.

Xu, J. (2006): The political, social, and ecological transformation of a landscape, *Mountain Research and Development*, 26, pp. 254-62.

Xu, Z., Cheng, G., Zhang, Z., Su, Z. and Loomis, J. (2003): Applying contingent valuation in China to measure the total economic value of restoring ecosystem services in Ejina region, *Ecological Economics*, 44, pp. 345-58.

Xu, Z., Loomis, J., Zhiqiang, Z. and Hamamura, K. (2006): Evaluating the performance of different willingness to pay question formats for valuing environmental restoration in rural China, *Environment and Development Economics*, 11, pp. 585-601.

Yang, G. and Calhoun, C. (2007): Media, civil society, and the rise of a green public sphere in China, *China Information*, 21, pp. 211-31.

Yang, W., Chang, J., Xu, B., Peng, C. and Ge, Y. (2008): Ecosystem service value assessment for constructed wetlands: A case study in Hangzhou, China, *Ecological Economics*, 68, pp. 116-25.

Zerbe, W. J. and Paulhus, D. L. (1987): Socially desirable responding in organizational behavior: A reconception, *Academy of Management Review*, 12, pp. 250-64.

Zhai, G. and Suzuki, T. (2008): Public willingness to pay for environmental management, risk reduction and economic development: Evidence from Tianjin, China, *China Economic Review*, 19, pp. 551-66.

Zhang, J., Zhang, Y., Chen, J. and Tianzhu, Z. (2003): Urban residents' willingness to pay for reclaimed water and its affecting factors (in Chinese), *Zhongguo Geishui Paishui (China Water and Waste Water)*, 19, pp. 96-98.

Zhao, J., Yang, K., Tai, J. and E-Nuo, W. (2005): Willingness to pay for ecosystem services of urban river in Shanghai (in Chinese), *Huanjing Kexue (Environmental Science)*, 26, pp. 5-10.

Ziegler, A. D., Fox, J. M. and Xu, J. (2009): The rubber juggernaut, *Science*, 324, pp. 1024-25.

8. Appendix: The full questionnaire

Environmental impacts of rubber cultivation in Nabanhe Watershed National Nature Reserve

Recently scientists have been more and more concerned about the land-use changes in Xishuangbanna and the Nabanhe Watershed National Nature Reserve (NNNR). This nature reserve is located north-west of Jinghong, partly in Jinghong Municipality and partly in Menghai County.

(INT: Show the map on the first page of the booklet to the respondent)

The conversion of natural forest into rubber plantations has led to a severe loss of biodiversity in this area. Therefore, researchers from China and Germany initiated a survey project to find out about the perception and opinion of residents in Jinghong regarding these land-use changes. Your household has been randomly selected for this survey among all households in Jinghong.

Therefore, now we would like to ask you some questions regarding land-use changes. Your answers to this questionnaire might have great influence on the further land-use policy in this region since we will forward the overall results of this study to the relevant government departments. Therefore, it is very important that you answer the questions carefully and truthfully.

Of course, your answers will be treated confidentially!

The questionnaire consists of five parts:

1. Your personal knowledge about rubber cultivation in Xishuangbanna
2. A rubber conversion program for the NNNR
3. Some questions regarding the environment in general and related issues
4. Your individual household data which are needed for statistical reasons
5. Your opinion on surveys in general, which are needed for scientific research

Thank you very much for your cooperation!

1. Your personal knowledge about rubber cultivation in Xishuangbanna

1 Have you noticed the rapid expansion of rubber cultivation in Xishuangbanna?

- ○ Yes
- ○ No *(INT: go to question 8)*

2 How serious do you think are the following consequences of rubber cultivation in Xishuangbanna?

(INT: If the respondent holds that a problem does not exist at all, tick "not serious at all" (1))

		Not serious at all (1)	Not so serious (2)	Serious (3)	Quite serious (4)	Very serious (5)	Not a consequence of rubber (6)
2.1	Loss of water resources, some streams and rivers may dry up	○	○	○	○	○	○
2.2	Longer dry season / drier climate	○	○	○	○	○	○
2.3	More dust in Jinghong	○	○	○	○	○	○
2.4	Loss of soil / soil erosion	○	○	○	○	○	○
2.5	Destruction of forest	○	○	○	○	○	○
2.6	Massive reduction of plant species	○	○	○	○	○	○
2.7	Massive reduction of animal species	○	○	○	○	○	○
2.8	Food safety endangered by polluted ground water	○	○	○	○	○	○
2.9	Air and water pollution by rubber processing	○	○	○	○	○	○
2.10	Less foggy days	○	○	○	○	○	○

3 Do you think that these consequences of rubber cultivation in Xishuangbanna will affect the living conditions of the residents of Jinghong?

- ○ Yes
- ○ No
- ○ Don't know

4 Do you think that other people living in Jinghong are aware of these consequences?

- ○ Yes, most of them
- ○ Yes, but only very few of them
- ○ No
- ○ Don't know

5a How do you think the economic situation of people in Jinghong has been affected by rubber cultivation in Xishuangbanna?	○ Economic situation has improved ○ Economic situation is worse than in the past ○ Economic situation has not been affected by rubber cultivation ○ Don't know
5b How do you think the environmental situation in Jinghong has been affected by rubber cultivation in Xishuangbanna?	○ Environmental situation has improved ○ Environmental situation is worse than in the past ○ Environmental situation has not been affected by rubber cultivation ○ Don't know
5c Taking into account both the economic and environmental situation, how do you think life of people in Jinghong in general has been affected by rubber cultivation in Xishuangbanna?	○ Life has improved ○ Life is worse than in the past ○ Life has not been affected by rubber cultivation ○ Don't know
6 Now please think about the consequences for you personally. Again taking both the economic and environmental situation into account, how has your personal life in general been affected by rubber cultivation in Xishuangbanna?	○ My life has improved ○ My life is worse than in the past ○ My life has not been affected by rubber cultivation in Xishuangbanna
7 Did you recently visit a rubber plantation?	○ Yes ○ No
8 Have you heard about the nature reserve area around Mandian also known as Nabanhe Watershed National Nature Reserve (NNNR)?	○ Yes ○ No *(INT: go to part 2)*
9 Have you ever gone there?	○ Yes ○ No
10 Have you noticed an expansion of rubber cultivation in the NNNR in the last 15 years?	○ Yes ○ No
11 Again taking both the economic and environmental situation into account, how has your personal life been affected by rubber cultivation in the NNNR?	○ My life has improved. ○ My life is worse than in the past ○ My life has not been affected by rubber cultivation in the NNNR

2. A rubber conversion program for the NNNR

The NNNR has always been a so-called biodiversity hotspot where many endangered plants and animals exist which are already completely extinct in many other places. This variety of plants and animals is jeopardized by the fast spreading plantation of rubber trees. As a consequence of the ecological damages that might result from rubber cultivation in the NNNR, government authorities as well as scientists are thinking about a program to convert rubber plantations in the NNNR back into forest. This program will be called "Return Rubber Into Forest". This program will partly restore the original forest area in the NNNR and thereby create habitats for rare plants and animals so that the NNNR can resume its original function as an important biodiversity preservation area for whole China.

- hand over booklet to interviewees, one minute break -

Preserving biodiversity in NNNR means an important contribution to the survival of these rare species which might be useful for medicine and as inputs in many production processes in the future. If these plants and animals will be extinct, our children and grandchildren will never have the chance to see them and to benefit from their existence, i.e. as important ingredients for medicine.

The "Return Rubber Into Forest" program would further lead to an increase in the overall forest area as compared to today and to a better water quality in the Naban, Mandian and Mekong rivers. For example, there would be less pesticide contamination in the water, since less pesticides would be brought out to the fields. As a consequence less pesticide residues would be in the whole ecosystem and, therefore, fruits and vegetables would be less contaminated. The danger ensuing from agricultural products to human health would be reduced.

All in all, the "Return Rubber Into Forest" program would be an important contribution for the conservation of the environmental heritage of Xishuangbanna.

12 How important do you think are the following characteristics of the Return Rubber into Forest program?

The implementation of the Return Rubber into Forest will lead to:	Not important at all (1)	Little important (2)	Quite important (3)	Very important (4)	No opinion (5)
12.1 Partial restoration of the original forest area	○	○	○	○	○
12.2 Partial restoration of plant species in the afforested area	○	○	○	○	○
12.3 Partial restoration of animal species in the afforested area	○	○	○	○	○
12.4 Securing the water supply for the future	○	○	○	○	○
12.5 Better water quality, esp. less pesticide contamination in groundwater and rivers	○	○	○	○	○
12.6 Less pesticide residues in the agricultural food products	○	○	○	○	○

12.7	Less pesticide residues in the whole natural environment	○	○	○	○	○
12.8	Conservation of the environmental heritage of Xishuangbanna for future generations	○	○	○	○	○

13 How much do you appreciate the Return Rubber Into Forest program as a whole on a scale from 1 (not at all) to 10 (very much)?

1	2	3	4	5	6	7	8	9	
○	○	○	○	○	○	○	○	○	

14 **The "Rubber into Forest" program will be organized by the NNNR under the guidance of higher levels of government. In order to finance this environmental protection program a fund will be founded to which all citizens of Jinghong will have to contribute. This fund will be organized by the relevant government departments. The money in this fund will be used exclusively for the "Rubber into Forest" program.**

Considering the benefits of this program for all people in this region and for you personally, we would like to ask you to mark in the following list how much at most your household would be willing to contribute every three months to this fund for the next five years in order to get the "Rubber into Forest" program realized:

○	0 RMB
○	1 - 5 RMB
○	6 - 15 RMB
○	16 – 25 RMB
○	26 – 35 RMB
○	36 – 45 RMB
○	46 - 55 RMB
○	56 - 80 RMB
○	81 - 110 RMB
○	111 - 140 RMB
○	141 - 170 RMB
○	171 - 210 RMB
○	211 - 260 RMB
○	261 – 320 RMB
○	More than 320 RMB

		Not difficult at all (1)	not so difficult (2)	Quite difficult (3)	Very difficult (4)
15	How difficult was it for you to come to a decision regarding the amount of money you would be willing to contribute to the Return Rubber Into Forest program?	○	○	○	○

		Agree (1)	Don't agree (2)	Don't know (3)
16	Regarding the proposed Return Rubber Into Forest program, I would like to know your opinion on the following general statements?			
16.1	I think it is not acceptable to express the value of nature in terms of money.	○	○	○
16.2	I know too little about the characteristics of this project to make an exact statement of how much I am willing to pay to support it.	○	○	○
16.3	(*INT: Only ask if the interviewer selected a zero WTP*) I would be willing to contribute only if everybody else contributes as well.	○	○	○
16.4	I don't believe that the money collected for that fund would really be spent on the "Return Rubber into Forest" program only.	○	○	○
16.5	The individual contributions should depend on people's incomes.	○	○	○
16.6	I would personally be willing to pay even more than I just stated on the payment card, but I am concerned that other, poorer households will not be able to afford the contribution.	○	○	○
16.7	I have the right to live in a sound environment and should not have to pay extra for it.	○	○	○
16.8	I would contribute more to that fund than I just stated on the payment card if I could be sure that the rubber farmers will not benefit from that program.	○	○	○
16.9	(*INT: Only ask if the interviewer selected a zero WTP*) The Return Rubber Into Forest Program is not worth any money to me.	○	○	○
16.10	I don't think that the Return Rubber Into Forest Program will have the expected effects.	○	○	○
16.11	Taxes and fees of residents of Jinghong are already so high that there should be no additional financial burden.	○	○	○

3. Questions regarding the environment in general and related issues

Since we cannot interview every household in Jinghong, we would like to know a bit more about some of your general opinions. This is very important for a proper evaluation of your answers.

17 Now I would like to ask you some general questions regarding environmental problems. Please tell me how you judge the following statements?

		Wrong (1)	Partly right, partly wrong (2)	Right (3)
17.1	I like to be in nature because I love the natural environment.	○	○	○
17.2	Environmental threats arising from deforestation are not as serious as it is often said; this problem has been exaggerated.	○	○	○
17.3	In my opinion, ecological conservationists are pessimistic and somewhat not normal.	○	○	○
17.4	The problem of natural resource depletion is not as bad as some people say.	○	○	○
17.5	We don't need to worry about environmental problems because science will solve them in the future.	○	○	○
17.6	The most worrying about deforestation is that our children's generation will not have enough wood.	○	○	○
17.7	Humans need an intact nature to survive.	○	○	○
17.8	Nature has a value all its own.	○	○	○
17.9	Most environmental problems will solve themselves given enough time. So we don't need to take an effort to protect the environment.	○	○	○
17.10	I don't care about environmental problems.	○	○	○
17.11	It makes me sad to see natural environments destroyed.	○	○	○
17.12	The only reason for environmental protection is to maintain a high quality of life for humans.	○	○	○
17.13	Nature is only important because it can contribute to the well-being of humans.	○	○	○
17.14	Environmental conservation has been neglected in the past.	○	○	○

18 And now we would like to ask you some questions regarding your personal life situation. How satisfied are you all in all with the following areas of your life?	Complete-ly unsatis-fied (1)	Rather unsatis-fied (2)	Neither satisfied, nor un-satisfied (3)	Rather satisfied (4)	Complete-ly satis-fied (5)	Does not apply (6)
18.1 Your health	○	○	○	○	○	○
18.2 Your job	○	○	○	○	○	○
18.3 Your housework	○	○	○	○	○	○
18.4 Your household income	○	○	○	○	○	○
18.5 Your place of dwelling	○	○	○	○	○	○
18.6 Your free time	○	○	○	○	○	○
18.7 Your family life	○	○	○	○	○	○
18.8 Your household's security resulting from the social security net	○	○	○	○	○	○

19 How satisfied are you with your life, all things considered?	Completely unsatisfied (1)	Rather unsatisfied (2)	Neither satisfied, nor unsatisfied (3)	Rather satisfied (4)	Completely satisfied (5)
	○	○	○	○	○

20 How often do you get news from the following sources?	Daily (1)	Weekly (2)	Monthly (3)	Less frequently (4)	Not at all (5)	Not available (6)
20.1 Newspapers and Magazines	○	○	○	○	○	○
20.2 Broadcasts on radio or TV, and internet	○	○	○	○	○	○
20.3 Talk with friends or colleagues	○	○	○	○	○	○
20.4 Announcements by local government/authority	○	○	○	○	○	○

4. Your individual household data which are needed for statistical reasons		
21	Where do you live?	Community: ____________
22	Which ethnic group do you belong to?	____________
23	How do you judge the economic situation of your household in comparison with the average households in Jinghong?	much worse (1) ○ · worse (2) ○ · better (3) ○ · much better (4) ○
24	Are you…	1 ○ Male? 2 ○ Female?
25	How old are you?	____________ years
26	What marital status do you have? What applies to you from this list?	1 ○ I am married and live together with my spouse 2 ○ I am married and live separated from my spouse 3 ○ I am not married 4 ○ I am divorced 5 ○ I am widowed
27	How many children are living in your household?	____________ child(ren)
28	How many persons are actually living in your household, including yourself?	____________ person(s)
29	How many persons actually living in your household are 14 years or older?	____________ person(s)
30	How many years have you been living in Xishuangbanna now?	____________ year(s)
31	How many years have you been living in Jinghong now?	____________ year(s)
32	Are you the household head?	1 ○ Yes (INT: Go to question 34) 2 ○ No

33	What is your relationship to the household head?	________________________
34	Which is your highest level of education? Please give your answers according to the list.	1 ○ I didn't graduate from Primary School 2 ○ Primary School 3 ○ Junior High 4 ○ Senior High 5 ○ College Graduate 6 ○ Bachelor Degree 7 ○ Master Degree (or higher)
35	What is your main occupation?	1 ○ Worker / employee 2 ○ Employee of state unit 3 ○ Official 4 ○ Owner or renter of a farm / rubber tapping 5 ○ Self-employed 6 ○ Trainee, student, pupil 7 ○ Housewife, househusband 8 ○ Retiree, early retirement 9 ○ Unemployed 10 ○ Rental income from letting houses or apartments 11 ○ Owner of rubber trees
36	How many *mu* of rubber trees does your household own?	________________________mu **Are your rubber trees located in the NNNR?** 1 ○ Yes 2 ○ No
37	What is the monthly income of your household altogether? *(Please state the sum of wages, incomes from self-employment and pensions minus tax payments and social security insurance.* *If you are responsible for the support of a part of your family not living in your household, please deduct this amount.)* Your statement will be treated confidentially!	1 ○ less than 500 RMB 2 ○ 500 up to less than 1.000 RMB 3 ○ 1.000 up to less than 1.500 RMB 4 ○ 1.500 up to less than 2.000 RMB 5 ○ 2.000 up to less than 3.000 RMB 6 ○ 3.000 up to less than 4.000 RMB 7 ○ 4.000 up to less than 5.000 RMB 8 ○ 5.000 up to less than 10.000 RMB 9 ○ 10.000 up to less than 15.000 RMB 10 ○ 15.000 up to less than 20.000 RMB 11 ○ more than 20.000 RMB

5. Your opinion on surveys in general – needed for scientific research

The interview on rubber cultivation in Xishuangbanna is now finished. If you have another five minutes, I would like you to answer a set of questions on general topics, not necessarily linked to rubber cultivation. In a Harmonious Society it is important that those who make political and social decisions know the wishes, attitudes and ideas of the people for whom they make these decisions. Therefore, assessing the attitudes and suggestions of the general public about many problems of our country today becomes more and more important. So, by answering this set of questions you can help to make surveys and interviews better and more beneficial for the development of the society. If you agree to spend another couple of minutes for this survey, I will now go on with the following questions.

38.1	Do you think it is acceptable to make no contribution at all to the Return Rubber into Forest program if one really does not like this project at all?	1 ○ Yes, it is acceptable 2 ○ No, it is not acceptable 3 ○ There is no need to worry
38.2	When it comes to contributing to the Return Rubber into Forest program, do you think the more the better?	1 ○ Yes 2 ○ No

39.1	When asked to rate the Return Rubber into Forest program on a scale from 1 to 10 do you think it is acceptable to grant only one point if one does not like the project at all?	1 ○ Yes, it is acceptable 2 ○ No, it is not acceptable 3 ○ There is no need to worry
39.2	When it comes to rating the Return Rubber into Forest program on a scale from 1 to 10, do you think giving the more points the better?	1 ○ Yes 2 ○ No

40.1	How likely do you believe it is that your responses can be traced back to you when all questionnaires will be evaluated?	1 ○ Impossible 2 ○ It is possible 3 ○ I am certain
40.2	Would you mind if your willingness to pay were known by your neighbors of friends?	1 ○ Yes 2 ○ No

41	Now we would like you to answer some general questions regarding yourself. How true are the following statements regarding yourself?					
		Completely wrong (1)	Predominantly wrong (2)	Partly wrong, partly true (3)	Predominantly true (4)	Completely true (5)
41.1	I am a person that doesn't cover up mistakes.	○	○	○	○	○
41.2	There have been occasions when I have taken advantage of someone.	○	○	○	○	○
41.3	I am a person that doesn't swear.	○	○	○	○	○
41.4	I obey laws, even if I'm unlikely to get caught.	○	○	○	○	○
41.5	I would never say something bad about a friend behind his or her back.	○	○	○	○	○
41.6	When I hear people talking privately, I cannot help listening.	○	○	○	○	○
41.7	It may happen that I receive too much change from a salesperson without telling him or her.	○	○	○	○	○
41.8	When I was young, I tended to steal things.	○	○	○	○	○
41.9	I am a person that never drops litter on the street.	○	○	○	○	○
41.10	I take pleasure in reading sexy books or magazines.	○	○	○	○	○
41.11	I would never take things that don't belong to me.	○	○	○	○	○
41.12	I have taken sick-leave from work or school even though I wasn't really sick.	○	○	○	○	○
41.13	If I damage merchandise in the supermarket I definitely report it to the staff.	○	○	○	○	○
41.14	I am a person that doesn't gossip about other people's business.	○	○	○	○	○

Questions for the interviewer		
42	Interviewer number	
43	Time of the interview	**Weekday:** **Time:**
44	Interview language	○ **Mandarin Chinese** ○ **local dialect**

HOHENHEIMER VOLKSWIRTSCHAFTLICHE SCHRIFTEN

Band 1 Walter Deffaa: Anonymisierte Befragungen mit zufallsverschlüsselten Antworten. Die Randomized-Response-Technik (RRT). Methodische Grundlagen, Modelle und Anwendungen. 1982.

Band 2 Thomas Michael Baum: Staatsverschuldung und Stabilisierungspolitik in der Demokratie. Zur neoinstitutionalistischen Kritik der keynesianischen Fiskalpolitik. 1982.

Band 3 Klaus Schröter: Die wettbewerbspolitische Behandlung der leitungsgebundenen Energiewirtschaft. Dargestellt am Beispiel der Fernwärmewirtschaft der Bundesrepublik Deutschland. 1986.

Band 4 Hugo Mann: Theorie und Politik der Steuerreform in der Demokratie. 1987.

Band 5 Max Christoph Wewel: Intervallarithmetische Dependenzanalyse in der Ökonometrie. Ein konjekturaler Ansatz. 1987.

Band 6 Heinrich Pascher: Die U.S.-amerikanische Deregulation Policy im Luftverkehrs- und Bankenbereich. 1987.

Band 7 Harald Lob: Die Entwicklung der französischen Wettbewerbspolitik bis zur Verordnung Nr. 86-1243 vom 01. Dezember 1986. Eine exemplarische Untersuchung der Erfassung der Behinderungsstrategie auf der Grundlage des Konzepts eines wirksamen Wettbewerbs. 1988.

Band 8 Ulrich Kirschner: Die Erfassung der Nachfragemacht von Handelsunternehmen. Eine Analyse der ökonomischen Beurteilungskriterien und der wettbewerbsrechtlichen Instrumente im Bereich der Verhaltenskontrolle.1988.

Band 9 Friedhelm Herb: Marktwirtschaftliche Innovationspolitik. 1988.

Band 10 Claus Schnabel: Zur ökonomischen Analyse der Gewerkschaften in der Bundesrepublik Deutschland. Theoretische und empirische Untersuchungen von Mitgliederentwicklung, Verhalten und Einfluß auf wirtschaftliche Größen. 1989.

Band 11 Jan B. Rittaler: Industrial Concentration and the Chicago School of Antitrust Analysis. A Critical Evaluation on the Basis of Effective Competition. 1989.

Band 12 Thomas Märtz: Interessengruppen und Gruppeninteressen in der Demokratie. Zur Theorie des Rent-Seeking. 1990.

Band 13 Andreas Maurer: Statistische Verfahren zur Ermittlung von oligopolistischen Strukturen. 1990.

Band 14 Peter Mendler: Zur ökonomischen und politisch-institutionellen Analyse öffentlicher Kredithilfen. 1992.

Band 15 Heinrich J. Engelke: Die Interpretation der Rundfunkfreiheit des Grundgesetzes: Eine Analyse aus ökonomischer Sicht. 1992.

Band 16 Thomas Fischer: Staat, Recht und Verfassung im Denken von Walter Eucken. Zu den staats- und rechtstheoretischen Grundlagen einer wirtschaftsordnungspolitischen Konzeption. 1993.

Band 17 Stefan Elßer: Innovationswettbewerb. Determinanten und Unternehmensverhalten. 1993.

Band 18 Reinhard Scharff: Regionalpolitik und regionale Entwicklungspotentiale. Eine kritische Analyse. 1993.

Band 19 Karin Beckmann: Probleme der Regionalpolitik im Zuge der Vollendung des Europäischen Binnenmarktes. Eine ökonomische Analyse. 1995.

Band 20 Bernd Nolte: Engpaßfaktoren der Innovation und Innovationsinfrastruktur. Eine theoretische und empirische Analyse für ländliche Wirtschaftsräume in Baden-Württemberg. 1996.

Band 21 Klaus-Rainer Brintzinger: Die Nationalökonomie an den Universitäten Freiburg, Heidelberg und Tübingen 1918 - 1945. Eine institutionenhistorische, vergleichende Studie der wirtschaftswissenschaftlichen Fakultäten und Abteilungen südwestdeutscher Universitäten. 1996.

Band 22 Steffen Binder: Die Idee der Konsumentensouveränität in der Wettbewerbstheorie. Teleokratische vs. nomokratische Auffassung. 1996.

Band 23 Alexander Burger: Deregulierungspotentiale in der Gesetzlichen Rentenversicherung. Reformnotwendigkeiten versus Reformmöglichkeiten. 1996.

Band 24 Burkhard Scherer: Regionale Entwicklungspolitik. Konzeption einer dezentralisierten und integrierten Regionalpolitik. 1997.

Band 25 Frauke Wolf: Lorenzkurvendisparität. Neuere Entwicklungen, Erweiterungen und Anwendungen. 1997.

Band 26 Hans Pitlik: Politische Ökonomie des Föderalismus. Föderative Kompetenzverteilung im Lichte der konstitutionellen Ökonomik. 1997.

Band 27 Stephan Seiter: Der Beitrag Nicholas Kaldors zur Neuen Wachstumstheorie. Eine vergleichende Studie vor dem Hintergrund der Debatte über den Verdoorn-Zusammenhang. 1997.

Band 28 André Schmidt: Ordnungspolitische Perspektiven der europäischen Integration im Spannungsfeld von Wettbewerbs- und Industriepolitik. 1998.

Band 29 Bernd Blessin: Innovations- und Umweltmanagement in kleinen und mittleren Unternehmen. Eine theoretische und empirische Analyse. 1998.

Band 30 Oliver Letzgus: Die Ökonomie internationalen Umweltschutzes. 1999.

Band 31 Claudia Hafner: Systemwettbewerb versus Harmonisierung in Europa. Am Beispiel des Arbeitsmarktes. 1999.

Band 32 Jürgen Kulle: Ökonomie der Musikindustrie. Eine Analyse der körperlichen und unkörperlichen Musikverwertung mit Hilfe von Tonträgern und Netzen. 1998.

Band 33 Michael Ganske: Intertemporale Aspekte von Staatsverschuldung und Außenhandel. 1999.

Band 34 Margit Ströbele: Die Deregulierungswirkungen der europäischen Integration. Das Beispiel der Sondermärkte. 1999.

Band 35 Marion Benesch: Devisenmarktinterventionen in Theorie und Praxis. Eine umfassende Analyse ihrer Zielsetzungen, Wirkungsweisen und wirtschaftspolitischen Bedeutung. 1999.

Band 36 Torsten Gruber: Unterschiedliche geldpolitische Transmissionsmechanismen und Stabilitätskulturen als mögliche Ursachen geldpolitischer Spannungen in der Europäischen Währungsunion. 2000.

Band 37 Bertram Melzig-Thiel: Arbeit in der Informationsgesellschaft. Chancen und Risiken neuer Informations- und Kommunikationstechnologien für die Beschäftigung. 2000.

Band 38 Annette Fritz: Die Entsorgungswirtschaft im Spannungsfeld zwischen Abfallpolitik und Kartellrecht. Eine industrieökonomische Branchenstudie. 2001.

Band 39 Harald Strotmann: Arbeitsplatzdynamik in der baden-württembergischen Industrie. Eine Analyse mit amtlichen Betriebspaneldaten. 2002.

Band 40 Dietrich Benner: Qualitätsungewißheit bei Gütern mit Vertrauenseigenschaften. Entwicklung und Anwendung eines entscheidungstheoretisch fundierten Analyserahmens. 2002.

Band 41 Jürgen M. Schechler: Sozialkapital und Netzwerkökonomik. 2002.

Band 42 Kay-Uwe May: Haushaltskonsolidierung durch Ausgabekürzungen. Restriktionen und Strategien. 2002.

Band 43 Peter Kühnl: Der Wechselkurs als Zwischenziel der Geldpolitik im Aufholprozess. Die monetärkeynesianische Entwicklungsstrategie der Berliner Schule vor dem Hintergrund der makroökonomischen Entwicklung ausgewählter Länder Mittel- und Osteuropas. 2003.

Band 44 Steffen Wirth: Nichtparametrische Analyse von Bildungsertragsraten. Neuere Entwicklungen und Anwendungen. 2003.

Band 45 Bernhard Holwegler: Innovation, Diffusion und Beschäftigung. Die ökonomische Theorie der Technologiediffusion und ihr Beitrag zur Erklärung technologischer Arbeitslosigkeit. 2003.

Band 46 Guntram R. M. Hepperle: Zukunftsorientierte Industriepolitik. Möglichkeiten und Grenzen. 2004.

Band 47 Udo Vullhorst: Stabilisierungspolitik bei supranationaler Geldpolitik und nationaler Fiskalpolitik. Eine spieltheoretische Betrachung. 2004.

Band 48 Matthias Rösch: Die Bedeutung von Investivlöhnen und Gewinnbeteiligungen für Einkommensverteilung und Beschäftigung. 2004.

Band 49 Michael Bubik: Erfolgskriterien für Unternehmenszusammenschlüsse. Eine theoretische und exemplarische Analyse. 2005.

Band 50 Jörg Weltin: Internationale Unternehmensbesteuerung. Allokation der Besteuerungsrechte unter veränderten Rahmenbedingungen. 2005.

Band 51 Susanne Reichart: Zum Konvergenzprozess der mittel- und osteuropäischen EU-Beitrittsländer. 2005.

Band 52 Daniel Hartmann: Geldpolitik und Beschäftigung. Die geldpolitische Strategie der Federal Reserve: Vorbild oder Auslaufmodell? 2005.

Band 53 Marc Peter Radke: Explaining Financial Crises. A Cyclical Approach. 2005.

Band 54 Katja Hölsch: Umverteilungseffekte in Europa. Eine Analyse für ausgewählte Länder. 2006.

Band 55 Ulrike Lehr: Contingent Valuation Daten und Bayes'sche Verfahren. Ein Vorschlag zur Verbesserung von Umweltbewertung und Nutzentransfer. 2006.

Band 56 Jutta Maute: Hyperinflation, Currency Board, and Bust. The Case of Argentina. 2006.

Band 57 Michael Knittel: Geldpolitik und Stabilität des Bankensystems. Das Liquiditätsproblem aus Sicht der Theoriegeschichte und der gegenwärtigen Finanzmarktentwicklung. 2007.

Band 58 Oliver Frör: Rationality Concepts in Environmental Valuation. 2007.

Band 59 Jochen Gert Arend Wiegmann: Produktivitätsentwicklung in Deutschland. 2008.

Band 60 Nicola Meier: China – The New Developmental State? An Empirical Analysis of the Automotive Industry. 2009.

Band 61 Carsten H. Wander: Logistik und Wettbewerb. Zur Rolle logistischer (Re-)Organisation in einer wettbewerbsbasierten Marktwirtschaft. 2009.

Band 62 Sven Wydra: Produktions- und Beschäftigungseffekte neuer Technologien. Am Beispiel der Biotechnologie. 2010.

Band 63 Andreas Schaal: Die Relevanz von Venture Capital für Innovation und Beschäftigung. Theoretische Klärung und empirische Analyse. 2010

Band 64 Sybille Sobczak: Geldpolitik und Vermögensmärkte. Volkswirtschaftliche Bedeutung von und geldpolitische Reaktion auf Asset Price Bubbles. 2010

Band 65 Constanze Dobler: The Impact of Formal and Informal Institutions on Economic Growth. A Case Study on the MENA Region. 2011.

Band 66 Tobias Börger: Social Desirability and Environmental Valuation. 2012.

www.ingramcontent.com/pod-product-compliance
Ingram Content Group UK Ltd.
Pitfield, Milton Keynes, MK11 3LW, UK
UKHW021831100926
8556IPUK00004B/282